THE OLD HOUSE

HEALTHY HOME COOKING
UNDERSTANDING COMPUTERS
THE ENCHANTED WORLD
LIBRARY OF NATIONS
HOME REPAIR AND IMPROVEMENT
CLASSICS OF EXPLORATION
PLANET EARTH
PEOPLES OF THE WILD
THE EPIC OF FLIGHT
THE SEAFARERS
WORLD WAR II
THE GOOD COOK
THE TIME-LIFE ENCYCLOPAEDIA OF GARDENING
THE GREAT CITIES
THE OLD WEST
THE WORLD'S WILD PLACES
THE EMERGENCE OF MAN
LIFE LIBRARY OF PHOTOGRAPHY
TIME-LIFE LIBRARY OF ART
GREAT AGES OF MAN
LIFE SCIENCE LIBRARY
LIFE NATURE LIBRARY
THE TIME-LIFE BOOK OF BOATING
TECHNIQUES OF PHOTOGRAPHY
LIFE AT WAR
LIFE GOES TO THE MOVIES
BEST OF LIFE
LIFE IN SPACE

This volume is part of a series offering home owners detailed instructions on repairs, construction and improvements which they can undertake themselves.

HOME REPAIR
AND IMPROVEMENT

THE OLD HOUSE

BY THE EDITORS OF
TIME-LIFE BOOKS

TIME-LIFE BOOKS
AMSTERDAM

TIME-LIFE BOOKS
EUROPEAN EDITOR: Kit van Tulleken
Assistant European Editor: Gillian Moore
Design Director: Ed Skyner
Chief of Research: Vanessa Kramer
Chief Sub-Editor: Ilse Gray

HOME REPAIR AND IMPROVEMENT
EDITORIAL STAFF FOR THE OLD HOUSE
Editor: Robert M. Jones
Assistant Editor: Mark M. Steele
Designer: Kenneth E. Hancock
Chief Researchers: Oobie Gleysteen, Phyllis Wise
Picture Editor: Neil Kagan
Text Editors: Leslie Marshall, Lydia Preston,
Brooke Stoddard, David Thiemann
Staff Writers: Lynn R. Addison, William C. Banks,
Megan Barnett, Robert A. Doyle, Malachy Duffy,
Steven J. Forbis, Peter Pocock, William Worsley
Copy Co-ordinators: Margery duMond, Brian Miller
Art Associates: George Bell, Lorraine D. Rivard,
Richard Whiting
Picture Coordinator: Renée DeSandies
Editorial Assistant: Susan Larson

EUROPEAN EDITION
Series Director: Jackie Matthews
Text Editor: Charles Boyle
Writers: Neil Fairbairn, Chris Farman, Stephen Jones,
Martin Leighton
Designer: Paul Reeves
Assistant Designer: Mike Snell
Sub-Editors: Wendy Gibbons, Hilary Hockman

EDITORIAL PRODUCTION
Co-ordinator: Maureen Kelly
Assistant: Deborah Fulham
Editorial Department: Theresa John, Debra Lelliott

THE CONSULTANTS: Leslie Stokes was a self-employed carpenter and joiner
for seven years, specializing in purpose-made joinery and internal
fittings. Since 1976 he has taught in the building department at the
Hammersmith and West London College.

Richard Pilling, the plumbing consultant for the book, is a lecturer in
Plumbing and Mechanical Services at Erith College of Technology, in
Belvedere, Kent. He has also worked as a heating engineer in industry.

Charles Miller has supervised heavy construction projects for more than
40 years. He is a former member of the Architectural Board of Review of
Mamaroneck, New York.

Claxton Walker, a former builder and industrial-arts teacher in the U.S.,
now lectures on topics including house structure and construction.

Roswell W. Ard is a consulting structural engineer in northern
Michigan. He has written professional papers on wood-frame
construction techniques.

Contents

1 Getting to Know Your House   **7**
Appraising an Old House Before You Buy   8
Inspecting the Living Spaces   14
How to Find Professional Help   20

2 Saving the Best of Yesteryear   **23**
Restoring Fine Details: Locks and Ironwork   24
The Fragile Beauty of Marble and Stained Glass   28
Rescuing the Elegance of Old Wood Trim   32
Sharp Profiles for Plaster Cornices   40
The Enduring Beauty of Handsome Old Floors   48
Doors: Repairs and Renovation   54
Getting Windows to Work Right   58

3 Making Do with Ageing Utilities   **65**
Keeping Fireplaces Safe, Clean and Efficient   66
Coaxing More Heat from the System   70
Renovating the Plumbing, a Little at a Time   74
Safe Circuits for the Household Wiring   80

4 First Aid for Structural Faults   **87**
Making the Roof Watertight   88
Bandaging Surface Cracks with Fibreglass   96
Maintaining Exterior Masonry   98
Plaster Repairs for Walls and Ceilings   108
Floor Sags: Their Causes and Their Cures   112
Preserving Timber from Rot and Woodworm   118

Credits and Acknowledgements   **124**

Index/Glossary   **124**

1 Getting to Know Your House

A tool kit for inspections. Only a few lightweight tools are needed for a thorough house inspection. Binoculars allow you to view the roof safely from the ground and a torch provides light in shadowy areas where flaws are often found. An awl is ideal for probing suspected rot in wood, and a plumb bob can be used to check that walls are vertical. Other useful accessories include a tape measure or folding rule, a socket tester to check electric socket outlets—and a pen and paper to note down your findings.

The appeal of a period house often lies as much in its atmosphere and character as in the details of its construction. Large rooms, high ceilings and decorative mouldings and cornices evoke nostalgia for a more expansive and generous age than our own. In practice, however, romantic ideals may all too often give way to the realization that not all builders of earlier generations were in fact master craftsmen, and that the follies of previous owners or the passage of time itself have imposed some quite unexpected difficulties.

Living in an old house often becomes a compromise between preservation and practicality. However tempting fast cosmetic repairs might be, more serious flaws such as deteriorated masonry or structural timbers may have to be given top priority. A thorough inspection of an old house will allow you to estimate the gravity of major problems before you buy, and will help you to establish practical work priorities afterwards. A leaking roof, for example, should be remedied as soon as possible, not only for comfort but to prevent further water damage inside the house. For safety, frayed or inadequate electrical wiring should be replaced immediately. Since fixing faulty plumbing often requires that you open walls and ceilings, worn-out pipes should be replaced in the earliest stages of a renovation. Heating also must be given high priority. Make sure your boiler is operating well long before the cold weather arrives; if you do not yet own the house, verify during your inspection—which forms the subject of this chapter—that the heating system is in good condition.

In addition to inspecting the house itself, evaluate the general locality. Find out if other nearby homes are already being repaired or entirely renovated—usually an indication that property values will rise. Visit the area at different times of the day to check that traffic is not excessive and that parking is available. You will also have to find out about local rates, the quality of schools and the convenience of public transport and shopping facilities.

Whether you want to repair most of the house yourself or intend to hire professionals for much of the work, plan carefully. Commit your plans to paper long before work begins, taking into account the extent of the work needed at each phase of the job, what you can realistically afford and when each task should be completed. When you are setting up a timetable for work you plan to do yourself, allow for unforeseen delays—an object or material that must be specially ordered, for example, or just bad weather on a day you planned to work outdoors. Have a list of alternative indoor projects if outdoor work is not possible. To avoid delays, assemble all the materials and tools needed before you begin working on a project.

Appraising an Old House Before You Buy

Evaluating an old house is always a process of compromise. The need for minor repairs, such as painting, patching plasterwork and freeing any stuck windows, may disqualify a house if its overall appeal to you is only marginal, while major work, such as foundation and roofing repairs, may seem quite acceptable if you have found a truly exceptional old house.

Fortunately for impulsive buyers, many old houses are remarkably sound; in bygone eras, the cost of top-grade materials and labour was low and pride in craftsmanship was usually high. However, making a thorough and objective inspection of any house that you are considering buying is a wise approach for two reasons: to make sure there are no fatal flaws that preclude buying at all, and to arrive at a realistic estimate of the cost of any renovations that may be necessary. If you then decide that you wish to make an offer for the house, have your findings checked over by a professional surveyor.

Be firm in your request for at least two hours to make a detailed inspection, even if the vendor seems cool to the idea. The vendor will want to display the best features of the house; your responsibility as the buyer is to discover the worst. The inspection is primarily visual, but assemble these few simple tools as aids: binoculars for examining details on the roof; an awl to probe rotting wood; a torch; a tape measure or folding rule; a plug-in socket tester for checking electrical outlets; a plumb bob for checking that walls are vertical; a 4 metre length of string and some drawing pins for checking any sag in timbers; and a pencil and paper to take notes.

As you approach the house, notice its general surroundings and its orientation to the sun. A house that is much grander or much more modest than others in the neighbourhood may not be a good financial risk. As for the sun, year-round energy savings are greatest when large windows face the equator.

Strategically placed trees will act as buffers against both the heat of a summer afternoon and prevailing winds. On the other hand, a house that is nestled in thick woods may always be slightly damp. It is also important to consider the overall security of the house, noting the visibility and accessibility of the doors and windows and the type of fences round the property.

Your evaluation of the exterior of the house should pivot primarily on how well it repels water, and the first area to scrutinize is the roof. Most of the problem areas shown opposite can be viewed from ground level, but you should take advantage of any skylights or dormer windows to make a closer inspection.

Examine the condition of the roofing materials and note the pitch of the roof: a steeply pitched roof is less likely to leak but is more difficult to repair than one with a gentle pitch. Focus your binoculars on roof areas that are particularly vulnerable to leaks, such as joints between converging slopes and around chimneys, and any exposed flashing. Even when a roof does not leak, water channelled off it improperly can cause damage, so inspect all gutters and downpipes, especially any sections under tree branches where the acidity of wet fallen leaves may have eaten through. Gutter runs that are longer than 12 metres should have two downpipes.

Check next for damage to exterior walls. In masonry walls look for crumbling mortar that will require repointing. A section of rotten weatherboarding can be replaced if there is enough good wood left to secure it to the wall. In a traditional timber-frame house, rotten structural timber may have to be completely replaced, though in some instances beam ends can be restored by specialist treatment.

Houses built more than 50 or 60 years ago are not likely to have damp-proof courses, so check that there are no serious problems of rising damp by looking for damp patches and powdery white efflorescence near the bottom of walls. If you suspect that there may be a damp problem, check the wall inside in the same place with the moisture meter.

Carefully probe the wood framing of timber-framed houses in any areas where there may be present or past infestation by woodworm. In hot regions, such as Australia and New Zealand, look for termite tubes, signs of boring or small piles of sawdust along foundation walls and wherever timber is close to the ground.

Evidence of previous termite treatment— 20 mm holes refilled with mortar in masonry walls or in a cellar or basement concrete floor—is not necessarily a bad sign, as it may have been done to forestall termites and may include a long-term guarantee against further infestations.

Throughout every phase of the inspection, evaluate your findings in two ways: note the extent of any immediately visible damage, then trace the long-term, less obvious effects of the damage on other parts of the house. Badly damaged chimney flashing, for example, is unsightly and may be a source of leaks, but it may indicate even more serious trouble: past leaking may have damaged the roof timbers, and any insulation, wiring and interior finish of the house. In the same way, correlate symptoms to pinpoint seemingly mysterious problems. The most obvious source of water damage on a plaster ceiling is a leaky roof, but leaky pipes and missing sealants in a bathroom overhead could also be the source of the problem.

Use the same techniques to evaluate any secondary structures on the property as well as the house itself. Inspect porches for leaks in their roofs, or for rot at ground level. Make certain garage doors work well. Next examine the ground level. If it is level or slopes down towards the foundation, look for signs of a wet cellar or basement and foundation damage.

Check for dead or dying trees that will require the services of a professional tree surgeon. If limbs have been pruned back at least 2 metres from the house, potential damage from falling branches is reduced, as is the likelihood of gutters clogging with leaves. Examine all garden paths and drives for cracks and sinking; generally, displacements greater than 25 mm are hazardous and require repair or repaving. Low points in a driveway should have a functioning drain, particularly if the driveway slopes towards the house. Check that any retaining walls in the garden do not bulge or lean noticeably, and that they have drainage holes—referred to as weep holes—that allow water to flow through. A wall that leans more than 25 mm laterally for every 300 mm it rises vertically may have to be rebuilt.

Starting at the Top

Critical areas on the roof. Using binoculars, inspect the entire roof and analyse the condition of the roof surface itself according to type *(below)*. Check for any dips in the roof and along the ridge. Inspect all exposed flashing around the chimney, in roof valleys and around any protruding pipes. Bent, rusted or cracked flashing or separations along gutters require immediate attention and should alert you to look for corresponding water damage inside.

Mortar failure in a chimney is a common source of leaks. In both interior and exterior chimneys, look for loose or damaged bricks, gaps in mortar joints, or a cracked and chipped flaunching. These defects should be remedied as soon as possible.

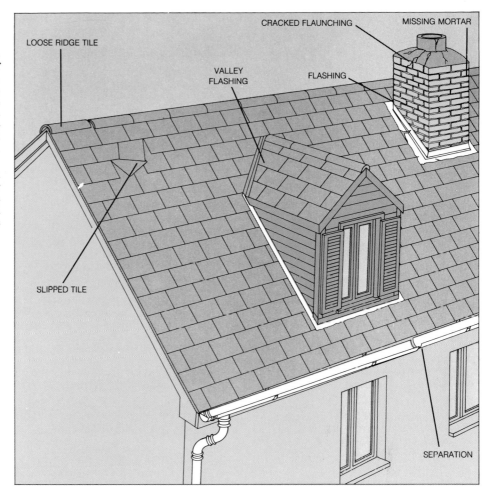

Roof Coverings: a Variety of Materials

Climatic conditions as well as the quality of the roofing material may affect how long a roof can last, so the information below is necessarily general.

Thatch
This ancient roofing material is having something of a revival in popularity, but skilled thatchers are in short supply and may have to be booked well in advance. Straw thatch lasts little longer than 30 years, while the more expensive reed thatch can last for 80 years.

Stone tiles
Also known as flags, this material is common in some regions. Its lifespan will vary according to the type of stone used and its thickness, but some stone roofs are more than 200 years old.

Slate
This regional roofing material became widely popular. Depending on its thickness and quality, slate can last between 100 and 200 years. Modern imitation slate tiles, made of concrete and fibres, are much cheaper than real slate, but last only 30 to 40 years.

Shingles
Wood shingles are becoming increasingly rare and expensive. They can last 35 to 50 years, but deteriorating shingles must be replaced at once.

Clay tiles
There are many different shapes of this widely used roofing material. Good quality plain tiles can last over 100 years, and in some cases more than 200 years.

Concrete tiles
This increasingly popular modern roofing medium imitates clay and stone tiles and is usually cheaper. Some manufacturers guarantee concrete tiles for 100 years, but they are heavier than clay tiles and the pigment that is used to colour them can fade in time.

Felt
Bituminized felt is often found on flat-roofed extensions to old houses and on outhouses. Many old roofing felts have a lifespan of only seven to 10 years, but some modern felts can last much longer.

Metal
A metal roof, of lead, zinc or aluminium, may last 50 years. Metal is often found on old flat roofs, dormers and flashings.

Evaluating the Walls

Checking for signs of structural weakness. Cracks in masonry, lintels and sills, distorted door or window frames, and leaning or twisted walls—either independently or in combination—indicate movement or weakness in the foundations. Hairline cracks in mortar are usually unimportant, but cracks which are more than a millimetre wide suggest more serious structural damage; look inside the house to ascertain the extent of such cracks. Check also for leaning and twisting of walls by sighting up corners and along walls. If you suspect a lean, drop a plumb bob from a window or ladder to establish the extent, holding or affixing the top of the plumb bob at least 50 mm from the wall.

Settlement can be caused by a number of conditions including inadequate foundations, poorly tied-in extensions, broken drains, underground streams, changes in the moisture content of clay soil, trees with extensive root systems growing nearby, mining subsidence and vibration from traffic. If the evidence you note leads you to doubt the wall's stability, bring in a surveyor or a structural engineer who will advise you as to the cause and nature of the damage as well as indicate the extent of remedial work necessary.

Faulty gutters and downpipes. Examine gutters for rust spots and breaks. Check also for separation along the back seam of the downpipe—generally caused by clogging and freezing. Step away from the house and examine the position of each gutter in relation to the fascia board behind it—gutters should slope slightly towards the downpipes. Check that the gulleys below downpipes are in good condition and that any drains below the downpipes are not clogged.

Wherever you spot a fault in a gutter system, examine the nearby soffit and fascia board, or exposed rafter ends, the wall below, and any timbers at ground level. At the same time, also look out for peeling paint, dark rot spots or any other signs of water damage.

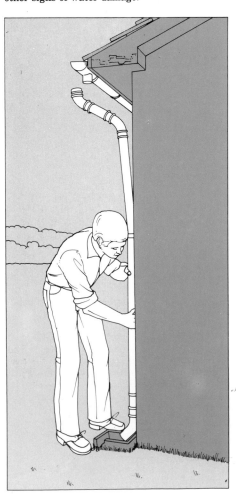

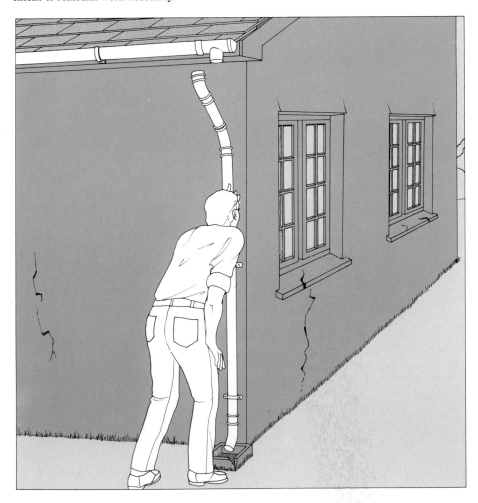

Inspecting masonry walls. Check the condition of brick or stonework on all exterior walls. Probe mortar joints with a key. If the mortar seems soft and sandy and falls out easily, you must undertake the time-consuming job of repointing—scraping and refilling the mortar joints in order to maintain the wall.

Isolated bricks or stones that have cracked or flaked due to frost damage will have to be replaced or sealed. A large area of spalling indicates a serious damp problem.

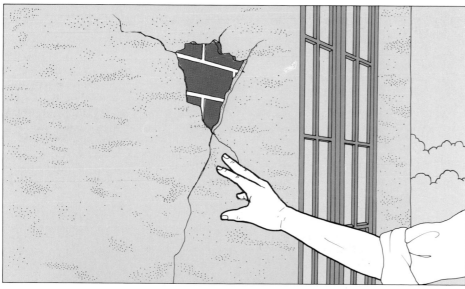

Evaluating bulges in rendering. Examine rendered walls at an oblique angle in order to spot bulges. Press lightly to test the springiness of small bulges—generally caused by localized separation between the rendering and the wall—and listen for a hollow sound when you tap them. All bulges and major cracks in rendering should be repaired as soon as possible, to prevent water damage inside the wall.

Detecting rising damp. At the foot of the walls, look for signs of rising damp, detectable as a "tide mark" of efflorescence that can be situated a metre or more above ground level. If the house has a physical damp-proof course (DPC)—usually visible as a course of different brick or as a thin line of slate, lead or bituminous felt running through a mortar course about 150 mm above the ground—inspect this carefully to see if it has been broken by subsidence or is otherwise faulty.

Bridging, caused by earth, rubble or even a concrete path or patio placed above the DPC and allowing moisture to bypass the DPC, is remedied by removing the offending material; in the case of a path or patio, this task will involve a great deal of physical labour.

Is the Cellar Snug and Dry?

A cellar inspection provides an excellent opportunity for checking the basic structural soundness of a house, as both the foundations and the ground floor timbers are usually visible. For the best evaluation, correlate the defects you see; small foundation cracks in an old house, for instance, are probably not significant if the timbers—joists, wall plates and beams—appear straight and solid. This type of crack typically occurs early on as foundations settle, or it may develop gradually over many years.

Large cracks with no old paint or dust inside them—or filled with different shades of mortar, a sign of recurrent patching—indicate newer, more serious structural damage, and joist ends may be out of alignment. To evaluate these cracks, it is best to consult a structural engineer.

If the drainage around a house is poor, even small foundation cracks will allow ground water to seep in. If a cellar is obviously wet or shows evidence of flooding, it may be necessary to correct gutter faults, improve outside drainage, tank the inside of a foundation wall, seal the wall on the outside or even, in extreme cases, install a sump pump.

Make sure that the cellar is adequately ventilated, and that airbricks or windows are not blocked. Look for signs of damp—often indicated by mould on the walls—and dry rot, which has a mushroom-like odour and spreads on slender tendrils, forming into a fluffy white sheet with a fungal growth that will devour timber, plaster and masonry.

Examining timbers. Measure any noticeable sag in a joist or beam by tacking a string taut between opposite bottom corners of the member; a sag greater than 10 mm in 1500 mm may call for additional support beneath that joist or beam. Examine all exposed timbers—joists, beams, wall plates, and the underside of the floorboards above—for damp, rot or insect damage. Also check for solid bridging or herringbone strutting between joists, indicating sturdy construction.

Detecting signs of damp or flooding. While examining cellar floors and walls for water stains, use a torch to check for rust stains around metal fixings, and for rust and mud under a boiler, if there is one—a telltale clue frequently overlooked by owners who have repainted to disguise evidence of flooding. Examine the walls for efflorescence (rough white deposits caused by water reacting with the minerals in mortar); look at any low-lying woodwork for dark spots of rot; check tile floors for white powdery deposits—efflorescence from the underlying concrete. Note how things are stored; unused furniture and storage boxes on shelves or raised platforms often imply persistent dampness or even flooding.

Analysing cracks. Horizontal cracks in the middle of a cellar wall, accompanied by noticeable bulging inwards or slipped brickwork, indicate excessive pressure exerted by the ground outside the wall, caused by water pressure in the soil or compaction due to recent nearby construction. Vertical cracks in a corner of the cellar that widen to 6 mm or more at the top are typically caused by a sinking footing beneath the foundations. Since either type of crack can threaten the integrity of an entire wall, you should consult a structural engineer for a precise diagnosis. Smaller cracks—common in old houses—may pose no threat to the structure of the building but can be a source of leaks.

Is the Attic Weathertight?

Looking at the attic can be a very informative part of a house inspection because the underside of the roof and its frame, as well as wiring, ducts and insulation, are exposed to view. When checking for roof leaks in the attic, remember that water flows unpredictably down framing members; look for dark, discoloured wood and rust streaks around nailheads to trace this flow. Correlate any water paths in the attic with your findings during your inspection of the finished interior (page 14).

Proper ventilation is essential in an attic. Otherwise, condensation that forms in winter when the warm house air meets the cool attic air may cause moisture damage to roof timbers, insulation and wiring; and in summer, hot air from an unvented attic will radiate down into the house. Check that existing vents—in the gable ends and at the eaves—are unobstructed. If there are no vents, look for moisture damage.

If the attic has been insulated, check that ventilation at the eaves is adequate. For energy efficiency, temperate climates require at least a 150 mm thickness of insulation—insert a ruler between the exposed joists to check the thickness of any existing insulation material.

In an attic without floorboards, stand on a plywood or chipboard sheet laid across the joists to prevent damage, during your inspection, to the ceiling of rooms below.

Throughout the attic inspection, note the available storage space and the feasibility of a later conversion to living space. In a terraced house, where masonry walls between houses are shared, the masonry should rise to the roof to serve as fire walls separating your attic from those of the houses adjacent to it.

Checking the roof timbers. Examine structural members for sagging and signs of rot, insects or water damage, probing suspect areas with an awl (right). Pay particular attention to the joints between rafters and the ends of joists—rot at these points can threaten the structural integrity of the roof. If more than four consecutive rafters are rotted, rebuilding of the roof may be in order; consult a professional.

Inspecting the roof space. If there is no roofing felt, examine the soundness of the roof covering and look for broken, slipped or missing tiles or slates; pay particular attention to the joints between different materials or sections—around the chimney, along a roof valley or at gable ends—which are the areas most vulnerable to damage. Check the condition of the battens and the nails or hooks used to secure the tiles or slates. Trace any water runs inside the roof, which show as discoloration of the roof timbers and as rust streaks from nails. Note any damage caused by these leaks—rotting at the ends of rafters, or staining or sagging of the plaster ceilings of rooms below.

Examine the masonry at gable ends or party walls for cracks and damp that may be due to damaged coping stones on top of the walls.

Inspecting the Living Spaces

By correlating visible damage in the finished interior with flaws noted earlier in your inspection—a water-stained ceiling beneath a suspected leak in the attic, for example, or a squeaky floor above sagging joists noted in the cellar or basement—you can form a clear idea of what must be done to fix up an old house. During your inspection of the interior you can also estimate the potential expenses of painting and other redecoration, but these are likely to be of far less consequence than the cost of essential repairs.

As a rule, if your attic and cellar inspections give you a favourable impression, the problems with the interior will be minor. Various simple structural and cosmetic repairs, for instance, can restore damaged and squeaky floorboards that might have seemed hopeless at first glance *(pages 48–53)*, and even substantially damaged plaster on ceilings and walls can be inexpensively patched or replaced with plasterboard *(pages 108–111)*.

During your inspection of the living quarters, note the type of windows; as a rule, timber-framed windows are more energy-efficient and easier to repair than metal-framed windows. Make sure all window catches are secure. Check that staircases are structurally sound and that their handrails and balusters are secure. Take time to measure rooms to make sure they will hold your possessions comfortably.

In the kitchen and bathroom, examine exposed pipes for mould, rust stains or other signs of dampness and leaks. Turn on the taps full force to see if water pressure is adequate and the hot water is hot. If you are considering remodelling the kitchen, make sure that there is adequate space for new appliances and room for a convenient layout without any extensive structural changes. Measure the space around a recessed refrigerator, for instance, to make sure it is large enough for a newer model. To install a dishwasher or washing machine linked to existing plumbing, you need at least 650 mm of space next to the sink. It is most practical to put a new sink in the same location as the old one, since the plumbing is already there. Inspect the flooring for damaged tiles or linoleum that will require replacement.

Cracked walls and ceiling. Inspect plaster walls and ceilings for areas of heavy patching and any cracks wider than 3 or 4 mm. Wide vertical cracks in a corner, horizontal cracks which widen towards the centre along the intersection of the ceiling and a partition wall, or large cracks which radiate from doorframes and window frames, usually indicate movement in the structure. If you detect a crack wider than 6 mm which crosses the centre of a ceiling, look for a visible sag which will indicate that the plaster is pulling away from its lath. This is a serious condition that requires immediate replastering, or alternatively patching with plasterboard.

Check plasterboard for loosening popped-up nails—an easy-to-fix cosmetic problem.

Testing the windows. Check the operation of all windows and look for broken sash cords, rot in wood framing, missing putty and peeling paint. Windows sealed shut by paint are not difficult to free *(page 58)*, but if windows are stubborn when there does not seem to be a paint seal, the frames may have settled. Solving this problem is more difficult; you will have to remove and trim the windows.

Also check all doors to see that they operate smoothly and fit precisely in their jambs; note the quality of the door furniture.

Inspecting stairs. Grasp the newel post firmly in both hands near its base and try to wobble it backwards, forwards and sideways. If it is not rock-solid, examine the joint between the base of the post and the string. Any serious deterioration here can threaten the integrity of the whole balustrade. Check that balusters are intact.

If the stairs squeak when you walk up them, check underneath whether the joints between the risers and treads have become loosened with wear. Strings separated from the wall or a newel post out of vertical may reflect more serious problems such as settlement of the house foundations, failure of supporting joists, or differential shrinkage in the timbers. Look underneath the stairs for signs of rot and woodworm, particularly in the string bearers and treads.

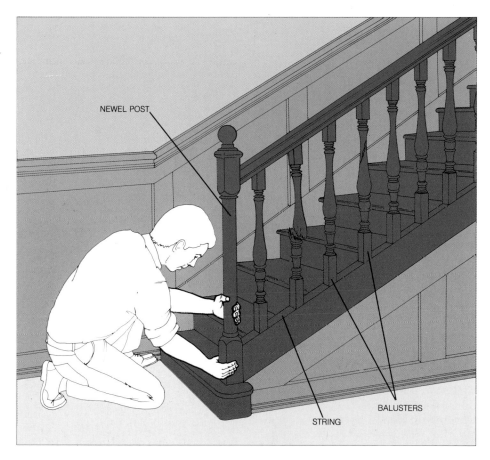

NEWEL POST

BALUSTERS

STRING

A Checklist for an Interior Survey

From small gaps between the ends of skirting boards to significant cracks down load-bearing walls, the number of problems you may inherit with an old house is potentially very large. This checklist summarizes the more common faults.

Floors. A sound timber floor should not squeak as you walk over it, nor should it be over-springy, which can indicate poor or rotted joists. Check for splintering, gaps between boards and sprung nails, and that any replacement boards are the right thickness. You can see if a floor has sagged from gaps under the skirting boards. If there is a loose floor board, lift it in order to inspect for dry or wet rot and wood-boring insects.

Walls. Rising damp in walls may be indicated by peeling or sodden wallpaper, or by flaking or discoloured paintwork. Decide whether cracks are superficial or relate to structural damage you have noted

outside. In kitchens and bathrooms, look for the dark mould characteristic of condensation, most often evident in corners. Check the skirting boards, and sight along walls or feel them for smoothness: layers of paint, wallpaper or patching may make walls uneven and reduce your redecorating options. Note the general state of decoration: this will give you a good indication of how well the house has been looked after.

Windows and Doors. In addition to the structural problems mentioned on the opposite page, check that curtain pelmets and architraves round windows and doors are sound. Large gaps in the mitre joints of architraves and above closed doors or tapered top rails may be due to subsidence. On internal doors these are usually due only to normal settlement.

Ceilings. Look for damp patches, cracks in plaster, and missing or damaged de-

tails such as ceiling roses and cornices. A sagging ceiling could quite possibly mean trouble in the roof, leaky plumbing or rotten floor joists above.

Fireplaces. Check the soundness of the fireplaces and the hearths. Check the supports of fire surrounds for rot. Check the chimney's up-draught by lighting a piece of paper below the fire throat.

Alterations and Additions. Look for any evidence of walls that may have been removed to open out rooms. Such alterations may explain structural damage you have come across elsewhere, and you should try to find out if the work has been properly carried out in accordance with the local building regulations. Ensure that any additions, such as partitions or blocked doorways, are properly aligned with other walls, and that there is no sign of any cracks at their junctions with the original structure.

The Wiring:
Is It Safe?

Since most electrical wiring is hidden inside walls, a complete inspection of all the parts of an electrical system is never possible, but you can still determine whether the wiring is safe and adequate to your needs or whether complete rewiring of the house will be necessary.

Note the number and positions of socket outlets in each room. If one or two walls in a room have no socket at all, you may want to install additional ones *(pages 84–85)*. Sockets for round-pin plugs instead of the modern square-pin type do not necessarily indicate that the wiring is dangerous—round-pin plugs can be added safely to a new system—but give cause for suspicion.

Look next at the fuses. Separate fuse boxes for lighting and power circuits *(right, above)* generally indicate old-fashioned (pre-1947) wiring, and an array of dissimilar fuse boxes suggests that periodic attempts have been made to upgrade an inadequate system. In either case, complete rewiring will probably be necessary. If fuses in a consumer unit are of the rewirable type, check that they are fitted with fuse wire of the correct rating *(page 81)*.

Check the wiring wherever it is exposed to view—usually only between joists in an attic. If you find old-fashioned cable sheathed in black, rough-textured rubber, the whole system must be rewired. Do not touch the cable as it will almost certainly be brittle. Old installations with single-core cable run through thin-walled steel conduit will most probably also need rewiring. Modern cable will be sheathed in grey or white PVC.

A recently wired house must be adequately earthed and bonded according to the wiring regulations. Look for green or green-and-yellow sheathed wires attached to mains water or gas pipes, and also to any metal baths, sinks and towel rails.

Modern wiring has a life expectancy of at least 30 years, but modifications by previous owners may have reduced the safety of the system. If you are in any doubt as to the safety or adequacy of your wiring, employ a qualified electrician to conduct tests and prepare a report.

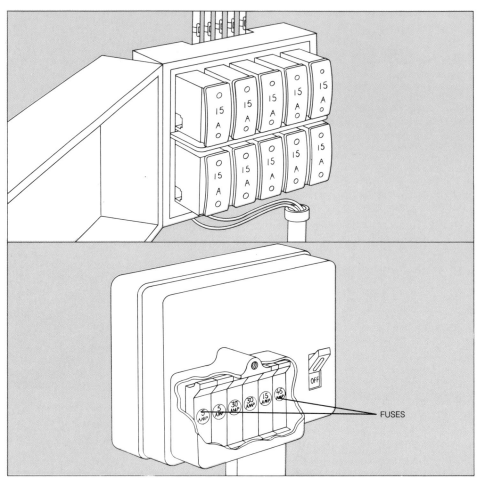

Assessing your system's age. At the point from which the mains electricity supply is distributed to the separate circuits, a typical old-fashioned installation includes a separate two-tiered wooden fuse box *(top)* for lighting and power circuits. Two fuses protect each circuit; the box shown contains fuses for five 15 amp power circuits. Such an installation is probably at least 35 years old and in urgent need of replacing. Separate fuse boxes for lighting and power circuits were superseded in the 1950s by the metal-cased consumer unit *(above)*, which houses fuses of different current ratings in the same unit as the mains on/off switch. In this six-way consumer unit, two 5 amp fuses protect the lighting circuits, two 30 amp fuses protect the power circuits (generally one on each floor), and 15 amp and 45 amp fuses protect individual circuits for an immersion heater and a cooker. In modern consumer units, a row of switches or buttons indicates that the circuits are protected by miniature circuit breakers (MCBs) instead of fuses.

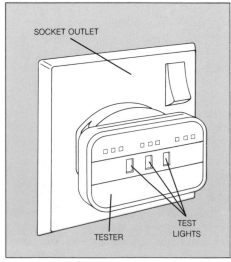

Testing the sockets. Check all the sockets in the house with a plug-in socket outlet tester. Shaped like an ordinary 13 amp plug, this device has a number of test lights which glow in differing combinations to indicate disconnected wires, wires attached to the wrong terminals and other faults. It is no substitute for a professional wiring report, but is a useful tool for a preliminary inspection. Consult the manufacturer's instructions for a proper reading of your instrument.

Plumbing: Is It Free of Clogs?

The original plumbing in an old house usually includes cast-iron drainpipes and lead or galvanized-steel supply pipes. Cast-iron drainpipes are generally trouble-free for at least 30 years and even then, if painted regularly, rarely present problems. Lead pipes, however, may have become brittle and need replacing with copper, and galvanized-steel pipes almost always begin to clog with rust after 30 years. The copper pipes used widely since about 1960, though they may leak at weak joints, have a life span yet to be determined.

In areas of hard water, all pipes can clog—or "fur"—with calcium or limescale, easily identified by the hard white deposit that forms round tap spouts. Clogged pipes often lead to leaks as well as low water pressure at the taps, and sections of pipe that are seriously affected—generally only hot water pipes—should be replaced. If rust on pipes is confined to threaded joints, the pipes should last a few more years, but rust on smooth outside surfaces means they must be replaced within a year.

Cold water cisterns of galvanized steel, often situated in the attic, can also rust. On the inside, rust indicates that the cistern will need replacing within two or three years; on the outside, it signals the imminent danger of a leak, and in this case the cistern should be replaced with a uPVC model of the same size.

If there is a septic tank for sewage, check the maintenance records for evidence that the tank has been emptied at regular intervals. Long, irregular gaps between servicing suggest the tank has been allowed to develop leaks.

Listening for leaks. Locate the main stoptap near the point of entry of the mains water supply, and make sure it works properly. (Some houses have two taps, one on each side of a meter; if this is the case, check both.) If a stoptap is seized open, try to ease it with penetrating fluid; if this fails, it will have to be replaced. With the stoptap open and all the fixtures in the house closed, including the float valves in cisterns, listen for a gurgling or murmuring sound in the supply pipe—a sign that a leak somewhere in the house is letting the water move. Touching the blade of a screwdriver against the pipe and putting your ear to the handle will amplify any sound within the pipe and allow you more space in cramped conditions.

Examining the drains. Look outside the house for a steel or cast-iron inspection chamber lid and raise it to look underneath; if necessary, scrape out mud and debris from between the lid and frame, then lever up the lid with two flat-bladed screwdrivers. Inside the chamber, check for damage to the sloping concrete surfaces—known as benching—and the vertical walls, which must be repaired with sand and cement. If possible, get a helper to run taps and flush toilets to check for blockages. Observe whether or not water flows freely out of the chamber.

Look round the property for other inspection chambers. A builder's drawing, or advice from neighbours living in similar properties, will help to speed up the search.

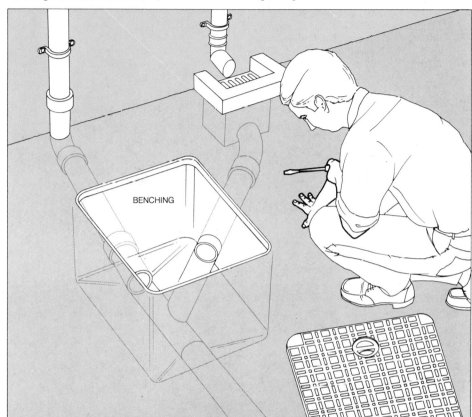

BENCHING

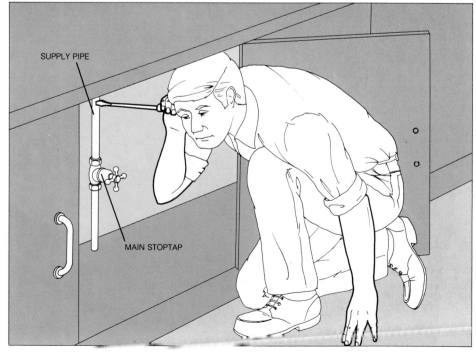

SUPPLY PIPE

MAIN STOPTAP

Keeping yourself in hot water. Remove the quilted jacket that insulates the hot water cylinder; a jacket that is torn or less than 50 mm thick should be replaced. Inspect the welded seams on the cylinder itself. If there are any signs of leakage, the cylinder is unsound and will have to be replaced immediately. Look for moisture around all pipe connections and around electric immersion heaters, which may be fitted to either the top or the side of the cylinder. Wet patches or stains on the floor around the cylinder's base will help confirm that the system is leaking.

Testing the water pressure. In the highest bathroom of the house, turn on the cold water tap in the basin full force, then do the same with the cold water tap in the bath. If the flow at the basin loses a quarter or more of its original force, rust corrosion or limescale may be starting to clog pipes in supply lines. Turn off the cold water and repeat the test with the hot water taps; if the water pressure drops again, the hot water pipes are also becoming clogged. Such partially clogged pipes will probably need to be replaced within three to five years.

Inspect the caulking, especially around the edge of the bath, and both wall and floor tiles in the bathroom, for deterioration that may permit water damage in rooms below. To prevent such damage, cracked or missing caulking and loose tiles should be replaced as soon as possible.

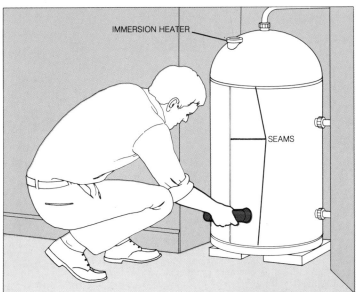

Checking the toilet. Flush the toilet and look for water leaking from the junction between the pan outlet and the soil pipe, an indication that the seal must be replaced. Check also for leakage between the cistern and the pan; this may mean that the seal is worn out, or merely that the cistern bolts need tightening. If the flushing lever has to be operated more than once in quick succession, either the diaphragm or the whole siphon will require replacing. Check that the water level in the pan returns to a depth of 100 to 150 mm after flushing. A deeper level than this may indicate a blockage; a very low level of water can allow foul air to enter the house and will require the services of a plumber.

Remove the cistern top and check that the water level is in line with the W.L. mark on the inside of the cistern. Check also that the float valve stops passing water when the cistern is full.

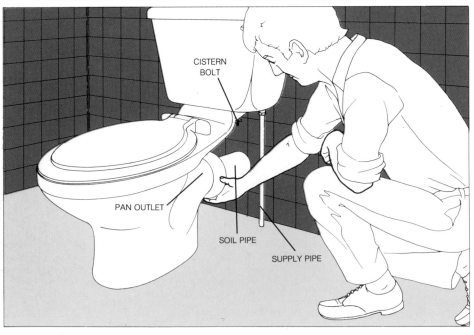

Evaluating the Heating System

Central heating is a development of the past 40 years, and has a relatively short life expectancy. Your challenge in an initial survey is to determine whether an old system is still reliable, and you should always conduct a test by lighting the boiler and letting it run for at least 30 minutes—whatever the time of year.

Heating systems are defined by the fuel they burn and the way they distribute heat. In most old systems, solid fuel or oil provides the heat, and the hot water from the boiler is circulated to room radiators, either by a pump or by convection. Made of cast iron or steel, radiators and boilers have a life span that varies between 10 and 40 years, depending upon operating conditions. Check all parts of the system for water leakage, which is caused by internal corrosion; rust on the outside of radiators indicates that corrosion is seriously advanced. If the system has convector units—aluminium-finned tubes housed in metal cabinets—in place of radiators, dust between the fins must be removed every three to six months to permit the efficient transfer of heat.

Where central heating has been installed within the last 25 years, the boiler may be gas fired. First check for leaks by turning off the main gas valve and observing the small test dial located near the meter. If the red pointer has not moved after 15 minutes, relight the boiler pilot flame—and pilots on any other appliances in the house—and turn on the boiler. The flames should be sharply defined blue cones that do not leap away from the main burner. If you are in any doubt about a gas appliance, turn off the main gas valve and ask the gas company, or a registered gas installer, to check it for you.

For any boiler, a clear flue is essential to safe and efficient operation. Conduct a test by holding a lighted twist of paper near the flue opening; the smoke should be drawn in without delay.

A solid-fuel boiler. In this heating unit, coal stored in a hopper at the front of the unit automatically feeds into a combustion chamber. To inspect the boiler, remove the casing and top cover plates and look for rusting and pitting of the waterways that surround the fire; corrosion will have to be treated with thorough cleaning and a heat-resistant metal primer. Open the fire door at the bottom and check the condition of the grate. Test the declinkering mechanism, which clears spent fuel from the grate, by pulling the lever in and out *(below)*. Ensure also that the combustion fan switches on and off when the thermostat is turned up and down respectively.

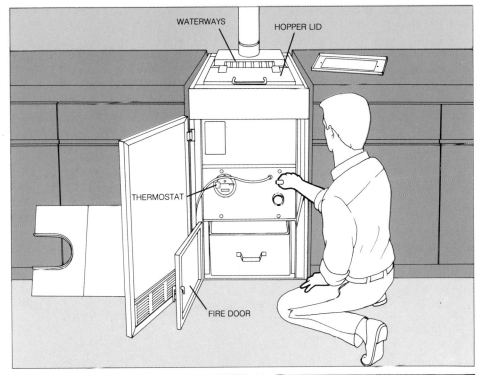

WATERWAYS | HOPPER LID

THERMOSTAT

FIRE DOOR

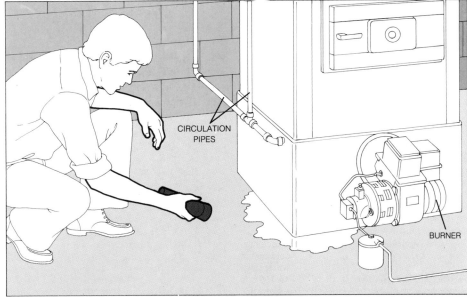

CIRCULATION PIPES

BURNER

An oil-fired boiler. Obvious signs of leaking, such as puddles on the floor and rust stains, suggest a worn-out system. Check inside the burner for a heavy deposit of soot—evidence of inefficient combustion—and examine the flue for rust. To find the installation date, look for an old service tag attached to the boiler or a nearby wall; a unit which is 40 years old will probably need replacement. Check also that the oil storage tank is sound and free of rust inside and out; traces of oil along its welded seams are an indication that the tank is seriously corroded

How to Find Professional Help

There are few improvements that a home handyman cannot successfully accomplish with patience and careful planning. Although a professional generally can work faster, a home owner has the greatest of all incentives to do a job well—he has to live with the results.

However, if you are like the majority of home owners, you have neither the time nor the tools to do every job yourself. Choose which jobs to undertake according to your likes and dislikes. If you are afraid of heights but enjoy painting, hire a roofer and buy some paintbrushes; someone who hates painting but loves swinging a hammer on high might do just the opposite. If you take on work you do not enjoy, you will resent the time spent on it; furthermore, you are likely to take shortcuts and will probably do a sloppy job.

For reasons of safety and, in some cases, legal requirements, jobs such as changing a consumer unit or connecting gas pipes must be carried out by an expert. And for certain other jobs—for example, excavating a basement or cellar, or pumping out drains—only a professional will have the necessary equipment. When you do call for help, you will be able to maintain maximum control and save the most money if you deal directly with the special crafts-men you need—acting, in effect, as your own general contractor.

A handy source for finding craftsmen is the classified section of the telephone book. The directory below, based on the *Yellow Pages*, tells you what these craftsmen will or will not do, and what to look for in a contract with them. In the case of craftsmen who advertise their membership of a trade association such as the Federation of Master Builders, check what services the association provides: some—but not all—run warranty schemes that protect clients in the event of a tradesman going bankrupt, and will act as arbitrators in any dispute between a tradesman and his client.

Successful subcontracting depends on careful planning and thorough research, and it is equally important that you should obtain some assurance as to the quality of a subcontractor's work and his ability to finish work on time. Ask for references from previous clients and, if possible, inspect his past workmanship. In many cases you can get sound recommendations in your own area. It is a sign of good performance when a builder can rely on word of mouth to keep him busy in one location.

Whenever possible, secure more than one estimate, but make sure you are comparing like with like. If materials are included, for instance, make sure your bidders are quoting on materials of comparable quality. Often the precision of a builder's tender for a job is itself a guide to the quality of his work.

Once you have settled on a subcontractor, draw up a contract. Make rough sketches and spell out, in writing, exactly what work is to be done, specifying the quantities, brand names, grades and model numbers for any materials that are involved. Include a timetable for work and payments and stipulate that the workmen will clean up after the job. Finally, make certain that your subcontractor carries general liability and third party insurance.

Architect

A traditional contract with an architect gives him full responsibility for a project and pays him a percentage of the total cost, but for renovation projects it is often possible and preferable to find an architect who will agree to a more flexible arrangement. On such a basis, the architect can serve largely as an adviser: he can help you decide what to do, provide drawings and recommend specialists to help. But make sure the architect's tastes and ideas are compatible with your own.

Bricklayer

Often listed under "Builders" in classified directories, these craftsmen will repoint mortar joints, clean brickwork and repair rendering, and will perform the heavier jobs of building or rebuilding masonry walls, fireplaces and chimneys. Be sure to plan well in advance, since bricklayers may be hard to find during times when the weather is good.

Building Contractor

Generally, you will save time and money dealing directly with subcontractors. But if you have a large number of complicated or interrelated jobs, this middleman may be essential. He will digest the plans, assemble a team of specialists, schedule the work and see that it is executed properly. Some contractors, particularly those who operate small companies, will allow you to do some of the work yourself to save money. If you take on an intermediate part of a long job, you should of course plan to conform to the contractor's schedule. Listings are found under "Builders".

Carpenter and Joiner

The versatility of carpenters makes their skills essential for any renovation work. Some specialize in rough carpentry: building timber-framed internal walls, laying floors, and making forms for concrete. Others, sometimes called "joiners", do finish carpentry: hanging doors and installing built-in cupboards and decorative trim. Experienced carpenters, however, are often competent at both types of work. Carpenters work closely with the other trades; they can often recommend other specialists and give you advice on scheduling. While most will use the materials you supply, many get discounts at timber merchants and they may be willing to pass all or part of the savings on to you.

Concrete Contractor

Use a concrete contractor when you want a professional to pour cement—for a slab floor, walls or piers—or to repair a drive or path. You may have to make several telephone calls. Many companies are reluctant to do small jobs or give estimates.

Damp and Rot Specialists

In a highly competitive field, many specialists deal exclusively with specific damp-proofing, woodworm or dry rot problems. Shop around to obtain the best price and guarantee. Listings in the classified directory will be under "Damp-Proofing".

Drain and Sewer Cleaner

These specialists pump out and clean drains, sewers and septic tanks. Many firms are also able to offer an ordinary plumbing service. This is a highly competitive specialist field, and most firms, which you will find listed under "Drain, Sewer and Pipe Cleaning", offer customers a 24-hour emergency service.

Electrician

Whenever you call in an electrician, you can reasonably expect that any job will be done to professional standards provided that the electrician is an approved contractor for the national inspection council for electrical installation contracting. Most electricians will be happy to take on small jobs or, on the other hand, to completely rewire an old house. The relocation of wiring is a job which usually involves quite substantial work on walls and under floors, so such work should be made an early priority in your planning.

Excavation Contractor

This subcontractor has the heavy equipment which is necessary for doing grading, trenching or back-filling around a house, or even for excavating a basement or cellar, or swimming pool. It may be difficult for you to find one who will be prepared to take on a small grading job, so also try listings under "Paving Services" and "Landscape Gardeners". The latter prefer jobs in which they are able to sell you some trees, plants or earth, but they are equipped to do grading round houses.

Floor Layer

Professional floor layers work with carpeting, linoleum, wood mosaics and tile floor coverings, and may specialize in one of these. Many also undertake floor stripping and sanding. Usually, floor layers supply materials and labour; check the quality and price of materials that are to be used as well as the workmanship. A floor-laying service is sometimes available through department stores, but the place to look in the directory is under "Flooring Services" and "Carpet Planners and Fitters".

Glazier

Contract with a glazier—often listed under the heading "Double-Glazing Installers" in the directory—to cut, fit and install insulating glass or plate-glass windows, mirrors and glass doors. Glaziers generally will provide both materials and labour.

Heating Contractor

Look for listings under "Central Heating—Domestic" for work on either boilers or heating systems. Most companies feature a specific brand of appliance, so first determine the most appropriate unit for your needs. Generally, the contractor provides all the equipment and oversees his own crew of specialist plumbers and electricians. For repair jobs, make sure that you ascertain the minimum charge for a service call as well as the hourly rate.

Insulation Installer

Insulation materials come in a variety of forms—rolls, sheets, pellets, blocks and pastes—and some contractors specialize in only one or two. In many areas, the home insulation business has become a very competitive market. Get several estimates and familiarize yourself with the type, insulating value and fire rating of the material each salesman is promoting.

Painter and Decorator

Some professionals do both, but painting and wallpapering are often considered separate trades. Most of the cost of either goes for labour, so shop for the best rate you can get for quality work. A local subcontractor recommended by your neighbours is often the best bet unless you need exterior painting that requires scaffolding. In that case you will probably want to contract with a larger firm.

Plasterer

Plasterers capable of repairing or making ornamental mouldings are among the cream of the building craftsmen. But even skimming plasterboard or plastering exterior walls calls for experience. Check listings in the directory under "Plastering or Screeding", but it will also repay you to ask local carpenters, general contractors or neighbours for any recommendations. Be

sure to get in touch with a plasterer as far in advance as possible.

Plumber

Plumbing work, like electrical work, is regulated by code. The plumber assembles and maintains any piping that carries water, steam or gas. He can also install and connect household appliances, such as a water heater or dishwasher.

Roofer

A roofer resurfaces or repairs the outer layer of a roof to ensure that it is watertight; some will work on the underlying structure, others employ carpenters to replace sheathing or rafters. Select a recommended roofer specializing in your type of surface—slate, tile or stone. Insist on a guarantee for a new roof; try to get one for any repair work as well. Many roofers repair gutters and will waterproof walls, basements and cellars. Listings will be found under "Roofing Services".

Stonemason

This craftsman works with stone as a structural material in walls and chimneys and as a decorative surface for floors, patios and stairs. You may have to make several calls to find a stonemason willing to do a small repair job.

Surveyor

Because all houses develop faults as they age, a survey of an old house is essential. But a surveyor can also offer useful advice if you are contemplating altering the house by, for example, removing walls or adding another storey. Fees vary according to the amount of detail you require in a surveyor's report, so discuss these matters with your surveyor in advance. You will find these professionals listed under the heading "Surveyors—Building".

Wrought-Ironsmith

Telephone listings for ornamental ironsmiths are listed under "Blacksmiths and Forgemasters", "Metal Workers" and "Wrought Ironwork". These craftsmen can fabricate and install, or repair, metal balconies, gates, fences, stairways, window grilles and the like.

Restoring a plaster moulding. Stiff plaster is pressed on to the chipped section of a decorative ceiling cornice with a special plasterer's tool. To match the original design, the new plaster will be carefully sculpted with the sharp blade at the opposite end of the tool.

One aspect of renovating an old property brings a special and lasting fulfilment that few other home-improvement tasks can rival. The satisfaction begins after essential repairs have been taken care of—when the roof no longer leaks and the stairs have been made safe. Then you can start bringing to light the house's elegant details and decorations and restoring them to their original prominence and splendour.

This is a quest that can bring rich rewards: whether your old house is a mansion or a modest suburban terrace, its neglected treasures may include well-proportioned original doors and windows, hand-crafted wooden mouldings and plaster cornices, fine floors and staircases, elegant fire surrounds and stained-glass panels. These features deserve to be retained, not merely for their own beauty and character but because they are integral to the style of the house and the sense of harmony and proportion its builders sought to achieve.

Unfortunately, the ornaments that delighted the home owners of yesteryear are today often damaged or hidden. Handsome panel doors may have sagged or loosened at the joints, or may even have been concealed behind sheets of hardboard; a fine-grained timber balustrade or an intricate plaster moulding may have been buried under layers of paint or distemper. The challenge to a new owner is to peel away the generations of paint, linoleum or other disfiguring disguise to reveal the hidden gems, then to get them looking and working like new.

Some features may be buried in a fairly permanent fashion: fine beams, originally exposed, may have been covered by a later ceiling. Other decorative details need only modest attention to be transformed from eyesores to conversation pieces. Old locks, knobs and knockers—cleaned, oiled, stripped of paint and polished—will both function as well as any modern replacement and complement the design of the door. Stained-glass windows—a feature of many Victorian and Edwardian houses—can be braced and restored with replacement panes, then scrubbed to sparkle like new.

Fixing up old treasures can require as much ingenuity as finding them. You cannot glue shattered bits of marble back to the edge of a mantel shelf, but you can fill the chip with a mixture that looks pretty much like the real thing. If a section of elaborate old wooden moulding needs to be replaced, you can duplicate its profile using special blades fitted to an electric router. When nothing else will work, you can resort to creative cannibalizing. To replace a cracked floorboard in the middle of the dining room, pilfer a matching board from inside a cupboard. To duplicate the ornate detail of a cast-plaster moulding, steal its design from a good section, then cast a new piece.

Restoring Fine Details: Locks and Ironwork

Stained-glass windows, antique brass escutcheons and old-fashioned surface-mounted door locks are only a few of the charming accoutrements that adorn old houses and set them apart from their modern neighbours. These fixtures, and others such as iron railings and marble mantelpieces, often need only small repairs and cleaning to restore them to their full glory. Such small fixes not only embellish the house, but in some cases—stiffening a loose railing, for example—are imperative for safety reasons.

Traditionally, iron railings were made of cast iron and set into blocks of Portland stone with lead caulking. In older houses the ironwork is often badly corroded, especially at the base of uprights, and rivets used to join posts to handrails may have broken. Frequently the stone is worn or chipped away. Restoring stonework and

large areas of railing is a job for a specialist, but the handyman can make a loose stair-railing safe either by replacing or simply resetting a corroded or loose upright (pages 26–27).

To secure the post in the step, use quick-setting cement, which will not crack and is available in small quantities from D.I.Y. stores, rather than undertake the dangerous job of pouring molten lead. A broken joint between handrail and post is repaired by cutting a thread in the top of the post and driving a screw through the handrail. A tap wrench and tap to cut the thread can be hired from a tool-hire shop; alternatively, a local ironworker can do the job for you. He can also supply and cut a length of mild-steel bar to replace a corroded post.

Even a sturdy railing is likely to need refinishing, not for looks alone but to stop the ravages of rust. Scrape off old paint and all

rust (opposite page, below), then brush on a rust-resistant primer coat of red oxide or zinc chromate and one or two coats of enamel formulated for exterior metal.

Interior metalwork contributes much to the character of an old house. Old locks are often made of cast iron, and thus susceptible to corrosion. Sometimes they are of brass, and may require thorough cleaning (page 27, box). Old locks on exterior doors should be replaced or supplemented by newer models for the sake of security, but sluggish interior locks, once cleaned and lubricated, should work like new if all the parts are intact. Some specialist companies can supply spare parts for old locks, while others make reproduction period locks or even exact copies of your original. Although innumerable different designs were produced, the basic mechanism of old locks is similar to those illustrated below.

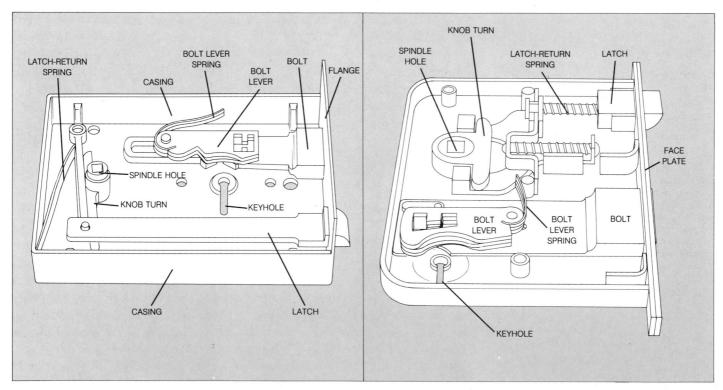

Two types of interior lock. A rim lock (above, left) is mounted on the face of the door, while a mortise lock (above, right)—a later development—is concealed within the closing edge of the door. To clean or repair, first take the lock off the door. For a rim lock, remove the knobs and spindle, then unscrew the mounting screws; for a mortise lock, follow the instructions at the top of the page opposite. Set the lock on a flat surface, and, with a cloth covering your hand and the lock to catch springs that may pop out, unscrew the screws holding the cover in place. Use tweezers to lift out fluff and large particles of dirt, then check for broken, misaligned or missing parts. Such locks usually have one or two bolt levers and two or three springs, flat or coiled. Turning the door key pushes up the bolt levers and then moves the bolt in or out. Springs return the bolt levers to place; another spring keeps the latch extended. Get a locksmith to replace any broken or missing springs. A bent bolt can sometimes be straightened in a vice, but the force necessary to achieve this may break the bolt.

Before cleaning the parts, sketch or photograph the lock. If you have two the same, leave one assembled as a model. Then remove all the parts. Bathe them in paraffin, clean them with an old toothbrush and dry them thoroughly; then grease them with a lock-lubricating solution available from a locksmith and replace them in the lock.

Removing a Mortise Lock

Easing out the lock. Wedge the door in an open position. Remove one knob from the spindle by unscrewing the grub screw that secures it, then withdraw the other knob with spindle attached. Remove the backing plates round the spindle hole and the escutcheons round the keyhole. (If the door has handles that are attached to the handle plates on the door faces, take off the handle plates and withdraw the spindle.) Break the paint seal round the face plate on the closing edge of the door by tapping with a hammer and nail punch. Remove face plate by unscrewing the fixing screws, then remove from the fore-end the two screws holding the lock in place. To pull the lock out of its recess, insert the blade of a thick screwdriver through the spindle hole and, with one hand on each side of the door, pull towards you *(right)*. If this does not dislodge the lock, insert a metal rod through the keyhole and knock it forwards gently with a hammer. Work alternately with the spindle hole and the keyhole until you can insert the screwdriver blade behind the fore-end and prise out the lock.

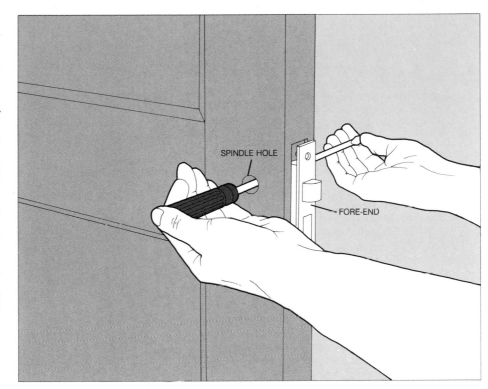

Stripping a Flaking Iron Railing

Burning off old paint. Using a butane torch with a flame-spreader nozzle, direct the flame against a section of rail until the paint begins to blister. Always hold the torch upright and direct the flame away from you. Point the flame away from the rail and remove the softened paint with a scraper. Heat and scrape the rest of the paint. For areas where the scraper cannot reach, use an electric drill with a wire brush attachment, a hand-held wire brush or a water-rinsing paint stripper. Caution: never use the torch after applying paint stripper.

Remove any rust you find under the paint with a wire brush; apply a liquid rust inhibitor, then paint with red oxide or zinc chromate primer and one or two coats of paint.

Securing a Loose Stair-Railing Post

1 Removing the loose post. If the top of the loose post is still joined to the original handrail, use a hacksaw to cut through the shank of the rivet or screw *(right)*. Now grasp the top of the post firmly with both hands and move it backwards and forwards and from side to side, gradually loosening the bond between the lead caulking, the post and the stone step, until you can lift the post out of the stone. Knock the plug of lead caulking from the bottom of the post with a hammer or prise it out from the step, using a cold chisel and hammer to dislodge it if necessary. If the bottom of the post is badly corroded, get a new post cut to length to replace it.

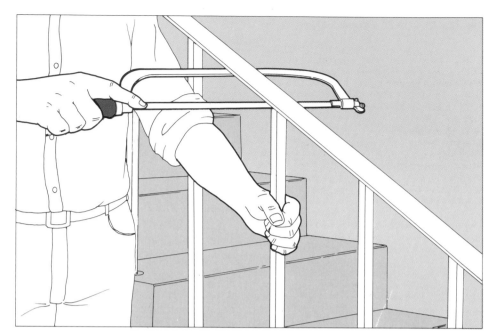

2 Drilling a pilot hole for the tap. Clamp the post firmly in a vice so that its top face—the angled edge that meets the underside of the handrail—is horizontal. Mark the centre of the top face—or of the embedded shank of the original rivet or screw—with a nail punch and hammer *(right)*. Fit a 5 mm (No. 9 BSI) high-speed steel bit into an electric drill and dip the end of the bit in cutting compound (penetrating oil or grease will do). Place the bit in the punch mark and, holding the drill vertically, bore a hole into the post. Continue drilling until the bit penetrates the side of the bar *(inset)*.

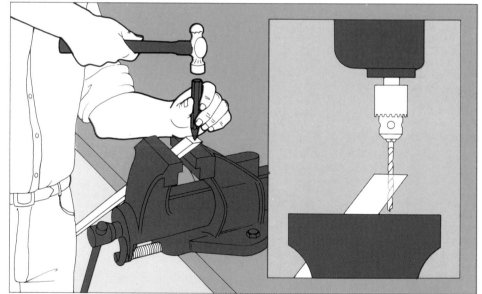

3 Cutting a screw thread with a tap. Fit a 6 mm coarse-thread taper tap into a tap wrench and secure it by turning one of the handles between finger and thumb to tighten the jaws of the wrench. Insert the tap into the pilot hole and turn it clockwise to start cutting the thread *(right)*. Initially, turn the wrench two full revolutions clockwise and half a revolution anticlockwise. Then turn half a revolution anticlockwise after every full revolution clockwise. This clears the threads of accumulated swarf—slivers of metal cut by the tap—which could otherwise cause the tap to break. Continue cutting until the tap has penetrated the side of the post, then withdraw the tap by turning it anticlockwise. Test the thread you have cut by screwing in a 6 mm coarse-thread machine screw with a slotted head.

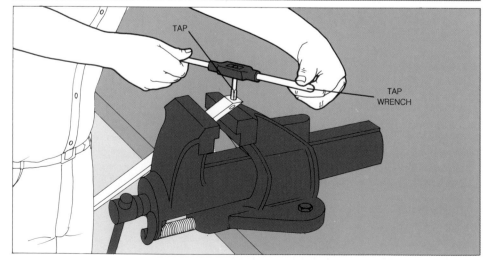

4 **Screwing the post to the handrail.** Knock the head of the original screw or rivet out of the handrail from below with a hammer and nail punch. If necessary, enlarge the countersinking of the hole in the handrail to accept the head of the machine screw, using a countersink bit and holding the drill at 90 degrees to the handrail. Insert the bottom of the post into the hole in the step and offer the top face up to the handrail. Drive the machine screw through the handrail into the post until firmly tightened *(right)*. File off any projecting sharp edges of the screw head. If desired, use a fibreglass resin filler compound to cover the screw head; allow to dry, sand flush, and repaint to match the rest of the handrail.

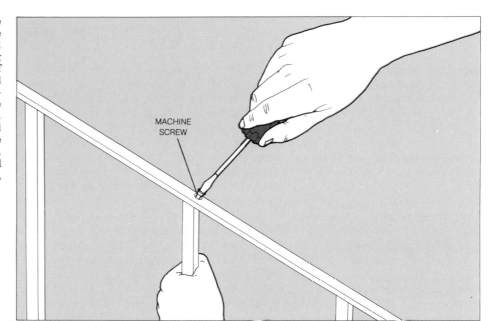

MACHINE
SCREW

5 **Resetting the post in the step.** Wedge spacer bars of scrap timber between the post and its neighbours on either side to keep it central in the hole in the step. Mix a small quantity of quick-setting cement. Moisten the inside of the hole in the step, then fill with cement, packing it down carefully with a garden dibber or tapered piece of wood, and trowel the surface flush with the step. Do not remove the spacer bars until the cement is completely hard—about 24 hours. If fibreglass resin filler is used in place of cement, there is no need to moisten the hole first.

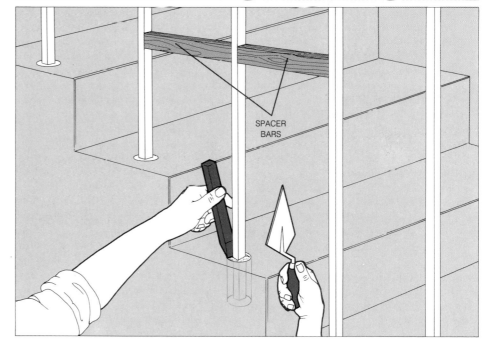

SPACER
BARS

Cleaning and Polishing Brass

Unlike iron, brass does not rust, but without regular polishing it will tarnish. Light tarnish can be removed with any proprietary brass cleaner, but for heavy tarnish, follow these steps.

☐ Dissolve the tarnish by soaking the brass in a plastic container holding a mixture of 250 ml of vinegar, 4 tablespoons of salt and 1 litre of water. Wear rubber gloves; these ingredients make dilute hydrochloric acid. Let the brass soak in the solution overnight.

☐ With the tarnish removed, use a proprietary brass polish and a soft cloth, or an electric drill with a buffing attachment, to shine the brass.

☐ To slow further tarnishing, use a clear, spray-on acrylic coating. Apply three coats, letting each one dry for two hours. This should prevent tarnish for several years. When tarnish reappears, strip off the acrylic with a commercial paint remover, and then repolish the brass and reapply the acrylic.

The Fragile Beauty of Marble and Stained Glass

Marble mantelpieces and leaded stained-glass windows lend an air of elegance to an old house. But marble and glass are fragile, and the passing years take their toll in cracks, chips, stains and sags. Often only minor repairs are necessary. Cracked or broken pieces of stained glass can be replaced with coloured glass available at craft shops. Stains in marble can be removed by washing or by applying a poultice *(box, opposite page)*. Cracks or chips in marble can be filled with an epoxy mixture coloured to match the marble.

Before beginning any marble repair, however, be sure you are really working with marble. In the 19th century, many mantelpieces made of slate, and sometimes wood, were marbleized—painted to look like the real thing. Check for this, examine the back of a piece or, if this is not possible, scratch the surface. For marble-ized mantelpieces, do not use any of the repair or cleaning techniques discussed here—only a professional can touch up and restore these mantelpieces.

The reverse is also quite possible—that you have a real marble mantelpiece disguised by ordinary paint, maybe dozens of layers thick and many decades old. Removing the encrusted paint and cleaning the original surface is a painstaking and messy job, which you may wish to leave to a specialist. However, if you prefer to do it yourself, then apply a water-based methylene-dichloride paint stripper *(page 32)*, and use a plastic or wooden scraper to avoid scratching the marble. Underlying stains can be treated using the methods described in the box opposite.

Repairing severe cracks or breaks in a real marble mantelpiece calls for the skill of an expert stoneworker who can disassemble the mantelpiece, glue the pieces together, then reinforce the stone with steel bars. But a small chip on any horizontal marble surface can be filled almost invisibly with an epoxy mixture. Supplies are found in hardware shops: a two-part epoxy glue (one part resin, one part hardener), painter's whiting (also called Paris white), and dry powdered mineral pigments.

To make the epoxy filler, pour enough whiting into the epoxy resin to make a thick paste. Add pigment, then hardener according to directions, and use the filler immediately. (Before mixing a large quantity, mix a small amount, keeping track of the proportions, and test the filler on a scrap of wood to be sure the colour is right.) After the patch in the marble has hardened and has been sanded smooth, polish it with a wax polish or a marble-polishing liquid available at specialist stores.

A cracked piece of stained glass can also be repaired with glue—a clear epoxy spread over a crack may be sufficient to prevent further damage. When it is not, replace the glass.

To work with glass, you need several tools, all readily available. For scoring the glass before breaking it, use a glass cutter with a ball on the end of the handle; choose one with a single wheel which has a tungsten cutting edge. For final shaping and fitting, the craftsman's tool is a pair of grozing pliers, although, if used with care, ordinary pliers can do the job quite effectively. To cut the lead channels—called "came"—holding the glass in place, use a trimming knife or a special lead knife with a curved blade. And for soldering, use an 80 watt soldering iron and wire solder that is 50 per cent tin and 50 per cent lead.

Wear goggles when cutting glass and work in a well-ventilated area when you are soldering—fumes are given off by the liquid flux, either oleic acid or zinc chloride. Gloves are optional—experts never use them because they are awkward and slippery. If you choose not to wear gloves, work slowly and carefully—some of the glass edges will be razor-sharp. Clear the table frequently of all glass fragments.

If you can easily remove the window, and especially if the lead came has become hard and brittle or if several panes need to be replaced, place the window flat on a worktable and use the repair technique shown on pages 30–31. But if the window cannot be removed without the danger of causing further damage, you can renew the broken pane with the window in place, often without cutting the lead came. You will need a special "oyster knife" or an im-provised substitute made by cutting down the blade of a kitchen knife or putty knife to about 50 mm in length, then sharpening the cut end. Working from outside, use this to prise up the came on all sides of the broken pane, taking care not to break neighbouring panes. (It may be necessary to cut the came at the corner joints, and re-solder them once the new pane is in place.) Remove the broken pane, replace with a new one cut to shape *(page 31)*, then press the came back down and smooth it with a piece of wood. Seal the new pane by forcing some glazing putty (stained to match the came with vegetable black, fireblack or any black oil-based paint) under the came with your knife. Alternatively, you can obtain leaded-light cement for this purpose from specialist shops.

Fortunately, the easiest and most common stained-glass repairs require neither glass-cutting nor soldering. Leaded windows have a tendency to bow in time, often as a result of repeated cleaning from one side. If a window is bowed by more than 25 mm, take it to an expert for restructuring, but if it is less severely bowed, try weighting it on a worktable with books—add one average-sized book every hour—to flatten it out. When it is flat, solder thin strips of steel to the came across the less important side (usually this is the outside) to prevent future bowing.

If the sections of glass rattle because the lead channels are no longer snug round them, use stained putty or leaded-light cement to fill the gaps as described above. If your window is already on the worktable you can try an alternative method using glazing putty mixed with linseed oil to make a slack dough. Stain the mixture with vegetable black, fireblack or black oil-based paint, and scrub it into the channels with a nailbrush. Remove the excess by sprinkling whiting over it and wiping it up with a soft cloth. This is rather a messy job, but it does clean both glass and lead at the same time.

Once your window is repaired, keep it bright and sparkling by giving it an occasional scrub with powdered household cleanser and a nailbrush.

Epoxy Filler for an Invisible Patch

1 Filling in the chip. Use a hot-air gun *(page 35)* or hair dryer to dry the damaged area thoroughly, then stick masking tape round the damaged place to make a form slightly wider and deeper than the missing piece. Pour the tinted epoxy mixture *(opposite page)* into the form until the mixture is slightly higher than the marble. Let the epoxy dry overnight, then remove the tape.

Simulating marble graining, a job that requires a steady hand, should be done before the epoxy dries. Dip a fine-tipped paintbrush in powdered pigment and brush streaks on to the new piece while the epoxy is still sticky.

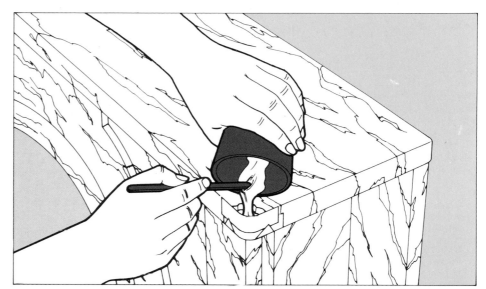

2 Sanding the epoxy. Misting the surrounding area of marble with water to prevent scratching, use a fine-grade wet and dry paper to smooth the epoxy patch with firm circular strokes. Sand the epoxy until it is level with the marble.

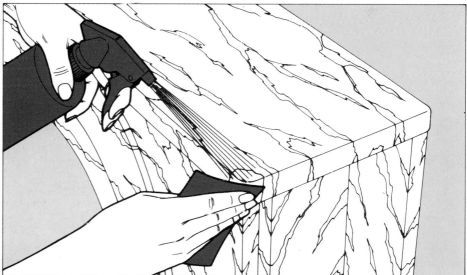

Cleaning Stained Marble

Marble fixtures that are in good condition are best maintained by regular washing with a mild detergent. You can repolish a small area of marble with tin oxide powder (commonly known as putty powder), which is available from masons' yards. (A large job requires the special tools and skill of an expert.) First wet the marble, then sprinkle with powder and buff vigorously with a buffing pad attached to an electric drill.

Several hard-to-remove stains that require more than a household cleanser can be erased from marble with the use of a poultice—a paste of powdered painter's whiting and a liquid chemical dictated by the nature of the stain. This paste is spread 15 mm thick over the stain and kept moist for 48 hours under plastic kitchen film secured with masking tape. To finish, scrape off the paste with a putty knife and rinse clean with water.

Organic stains can be caused by tea, coffee, ink, burning tobacco, soft drinks, flowers and coloured paper or fabric. They usually take the shape of the object that caused them—the bottom of a coffee cup, for instance. Make the poultice of 80 per cent whiting, 20 per cent hydrogen peroxide and a few drops of ammonia.

Other organic stains are caused by fatty or greasy substances—milk, butter or hand lotion, for example. Use a poultice of whiting with sufficient acetone added to form a thick paste; acetone, most familiar as nail-polish remover, is readily available at cosmetics counters.

Rust stains are orange to brown and generally take the shape of the metal object that caused them. If you find you are unable to remove a stain of this kind by rubbing it vigorously with a clean dry cloth, make a poultice of powdered household cleanser and water.

To remove stains caused by soot and smoke from a marble mantelpiece, use a poultice of whiting with baking soda and liquid bleach.

Replacing Cracked Glass

1 **Breaking out the damaged piece.** Lay the window flat with the smoother side of the stained glass facing up and a wooden support block under the cracked glass. Make several criss-crossing scores across the cracked piece, dipping the cutter in paraffin or household mineral oil for each score to avoid dulling the wheel. To make the scores, hold the cutter between your index and middle fingers; then, keeping your wrist locked and applying firm downward pressure, draw the cutter towards you in a continuous motion.

Set the window on edge, scores facing away from you, and use the ball on the cutter handle to rap the glass firmly until it breaks out of the lead.

2 **Cutting away the old lead.** Decide which side of the window is looked at less, lay the window with that side up and, round the open area, use a lead knife or a trimming knife to shave away the upper flange of the H-shaped came down to the crosspiece *(inset)*. Rub the lead lightly with a piece of steel wool so that the solder which is to be applied later will adhere.

Set the new piece of stained glass over the open area and use a fine-line felt-tipped pen to trace on the new glass an outline of the inside edge of the lead visible below. If the glass is so dark you cannot see the lead, trace a pattern on clear, stiff plastic and cut it out with scissors. Then outline the pattern on the new glass.

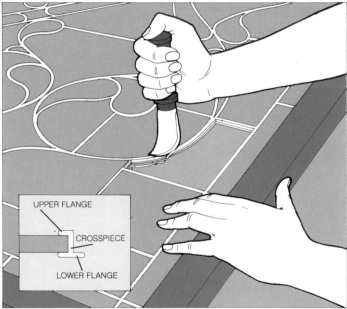

UPPER FLANGE
CROSSPIECE
LOWER FLANGE

3 **Cutting the new piece.** Working on top of several sheets of newspaper spread over a worktable, score a straight part of the outline from one edge of the glass to the other with a single stroke. Use a ruler if you need a guide for the cutter. Snap off the waste glass by placing your thumbs on top of the glass on either side of the score, making a fist with each hand below the glass, and twisting your wrists so that your thumbs press outwards to snap the glass along the score. To cut curves, make a few gently curved scores outside the guideline *(inset)* and snap off the outer sections one at a time.

If the glass does not snap easily, lift it and tap along the underside of the score with the ball end of the glass cutter until it becomes a visible fracture, then snap the glass. If you are working with a piece of glass that is too large for you to pick up, start by making straight scores and snapping them over the edge of the table.

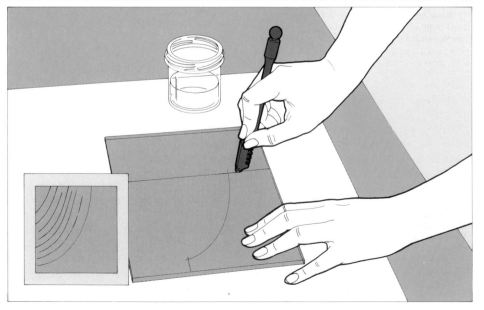

4 **Grozing for a perfect fit.** The new piece should slip easily into its place in the window, but if it does not, note where it binds. Use the tips of a pair of grozing pliers to nibble away bits of glass, no more than 1 or 2 mm at a time. Then set the fitted piece back in the window.

5 **Rebuilding the flange.** To replace the cut-away lead flange with a strip of solder, use a small brush to apply flux to the exposed lead crosspiece all around the new glass, then uncoil 125 mm of solder. Prepare the soldering iron by coating its tip with a thin layer of solder for the most effective heat diffusion. Touch the tip of the iron to the end of the uncoiled length of solder wherever you want to start the solder strip. As the solder melts on to the lead and glass, creating a new flange,

keep the iron moving—if you stop, the heat may crack the glass. Set the hot iron down only on a fireproof mat or in a holder. Excess solder can be cut away when cold. Clean the iron often by wiping its tip quickly across a damp sponge.

After soldering the new glass, cement it using one of the methods described on page 28, at the same time filling any loose spots along the came of the entire window. The new flange will fade in a few months to match the original lead.

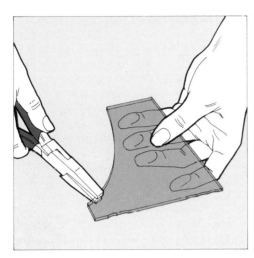

Reinforcing a Bowed Window

1 **Drilling holes in the frame.** Set the bowed window on a flat surface with the convex side facing up. Then, for the ends of the reinforcing bars, drill 6 mm holes in the inside edges of the frame, close to the glass, so that when the bar is laid across the flattened window, it will just be touching the lead came. Make the holes 6 mm deep on one side and just over 12 mm on the other.

Flatten the bowed area by gradually weighting it down with books or, if the bowing is not severe, by pressing on it with both hands. Caution: excessive pressure may crack the glass. Cut 6 mm round section steel bars to the width of the window plus 12 mm; use at least three parallel bars, and more for a large window.

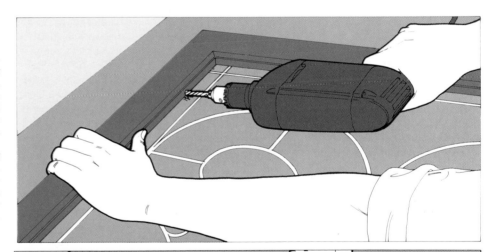

2 **Attaching the reinforcing bar.** Cut some 100 mm lengths of 16-gauge copper wire to use as ties for the bar. Lay them over the lead came at right angles to the direction of the bar, spaced at 80 mm intervals, and solder them into position. Insert one end of the bar into the deeper hole in the frame, lower it into position over the ties and slide it home into the hole on the other side of the frame. Grip the ends of the ties with pliers and twist them together firmly to fix the bar in place. Trim the ends and tuck them under the bar.

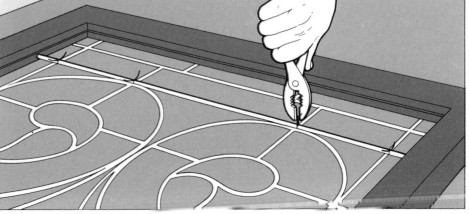

Rescuing the Elegance of Old Wood Trim

Original wooden mouldings—architraves, skirting, picture rails, panelling—are fundamental to the character and charm of old houses. Painstakingly shaped with hand planes, often from excellent timber, these elaborate mouldings testify to the value placed upon craftsmanship in a bygone age. But in most old houses the trim is in poor condition, with surfaces dulled or shapes concealed under layers of paint. The remedy is to cut back or strip away the old finishes, then finish the wood anew.

At its simplest, the work may involve only cleaning stained and varnished woodwork that has darkened with age to reveal the wood-grain pattern. Start with turpentine or white spirit to remove wax and grime; then, if necessary, use a strong cleanser, such as sugar soap, ammonia or washing soda. Methylated spirits and lacquer thinner can also be used to clean varnish. The first dissolves old shellac-based varnishes, and the second, lacquer; both should be used with caution. Turpentine or white spirit will clean lacquer and shellac. These substances can harm eyes and skin, so wear rubber gloves and goggles.

Unfortunately, most old mouldings are covered by layers of paint, which can be difficult and tedious to remove. Your objective will be either to expose the detail of the trim and repaint it, or to remove all the paint and revarnish the natural wood. In the majority of old houses, mouldings were cut from good-quality softwoods, particularly Douglas fir and Columbian pine, which may have beautiful grain and can look very attractive stripped and varnished. Balustrades, handrails, and occasionally door and wall trim too, were often shaped from fine hardwood. Before you decide whether to paint or varnish, strip away all the paint from a small section and consider whether the wood is good enough to merit varnishing, and worth the labour involved in preparing it properly.

If you intend to strip and varnish, you will have to remove every last vestige of paint. If you are repainting, you need only strip enough layers of paint to reveal the detail of the moulding, then sand and repaint. However, to be certain of the best results, it is always worthwhile stripping down to the bare wood and re-priming.

If the wood can be easily removed, it can be taken to a specialist firm for dipping in a caustic bath. Removing old and fragile wood is risky, however, and you may have to strip the wood *in situ*. You can either apply a chemical paint stripper to soften and loosen the paint and later scrape or peel it off, or you can soften the paint with heat and scrape it away immediately.

There are two main types of chemical stripper: those based on methylene dichloride, which come as a liquid or gel, and those based on sodium hydroxide (caustic soda) or other strong alkalis, which come as a ready-mixed paste or as a powder for mixing to a paste or jelly with water. Of the methylene-dichloride strippers, the semi-gel or gel types are best, because the liquid preparations run off vertical surfaces. The caustic-soda pastes cost more, but because they do not require scraping—they are simply peeled off or lifted off with a spatula, bringing the paint with them—they involve less work than the methylene-dichloride type. They are useful on delicate or intricate mouldings, which could be damaged by scraping, and for very thick layers of paint consisting of many coats. However, paste-type strippers do tend to "lift" the grain of the wood and they may also darken its colour.

Strippers of both types must be rinsed off the wood to neutralize the chemicals. Caustic pastes require liberal rinsing with water mixed with a little vinegar (which may increase the effect of lifting the grain); methylene-dichloride preparations are washed with either white spirit or water, depending on the product.

All strippers contain strong chemicals, so wear protective gloves and goggles. Methylene-dichloride strippers give off fumes that are harmful if inhaled and must be used only in a well-ventilated room. Always wear a face mask when mixing sodium-hydroxide powder with water.

Stripping large areas with chemicals can prove expensive. The alternative is to use a hot-air paint stripper or gas blow-torch, both of which will strip any solvent-based paints quickly, efficiently and economically. However, the limitations of these machines must be carefully considered. Neither will remove every last particle of paint, and so if you are revarnishing you will need to finish off with a light application of a chemical stripper. Both require careful handling on mouldings adjacent to windows, as the heat can cause the glass to crack. A blow-torch must be used with extreme caution at all times—careless use can easily start a fire—and can easily scorch the wood surface, which makes it an unwise choice if you are intending to varnish the stripped wood.

Once the work of stripping is complete, sand the wood lightly by hand, using progressively finer grades of abrasive paper, to smooth out any wood fibres "lifted" by the strippers and to ensure a clean finish. On flat surfaces, you can start with an orbital power sander and finish by hand with fine glasspaper. If you are varnishing, finish off by sanding in the direction of the grain to avoid scratch marks. If repainting, sand at a slight angle to the grain—this roughens the surface slightly and helps the paint to adhere.

Bare hardwood, particularly oak, may be stained with dark patches. Those that are not removed by sanding must be lightened with oxalic acid or household bleach. Spot bleaching may suffice, but usually you will have to apply bleach with a pad of fine steel wool over the whole piece. Rub until the spots disappear, then rinse with a sponge and water, allow to dry, and give a light final sanding.

If you are repainting stripped pine, seal any knots with shellac "knotting" to prevent resin weeping from the knots and discolouring the paint. This is not necessary if you are varnishing, in which case all that is needed is to apply the finish of your choice—probably either a clear varnish, or a cellulose sealer followed by wax polish.

Hardwoods can also be stained before sealing. The appearance of stripped and bleached hardwood can be surprising: raw oak is not dark but light brown, often with a grey or pink tinge; raw mahogany is not a deep rich red but varies from brown to tan. If you prefer this natural appearance, you can leave the wood unstained and finish with varnish, wax or oil (*chart, opposite page*). But to restore the mouldings to the deep colours of aged hardwood trim, first wipe or brush on a suitable shade of woodstain. For hardwoods, penetrating oil-based stains are best. Test the stain on a concealed area and allow to dry to see the final shade. To match the colour of an unstripped piece, you can generally mix different shades of the same brand of stain.

A Stripper or Cleaner for Every Job

Stripping Agent	Use	Remarks
CHEMICAL STRIPPERS Methylene-dichloride paint strippers	Effective on lacquers, varnishes, polyurethane, and all types of paint.	Fumes hazardous. Protect skin and eyes. May "lift" grain. Gel formulations best.
Caustic-paste paint strippers	Effective on all types of paint and varnish; ideal for mouldings and very thick paint.	Caustic—protect skin and eyes. Expensive. Can cause grain "lift" and may darken wood.
HEATING DEVICES Hot-air paint stripper	Removes built-up layers of solvent-based paints.	Not effective on emulsion paints. Some chemical clean-up needed. Caution when working near glass.
Blow-torch	Removes built-up layers of solvent-based paints.	As above, but cannot be used near glass. Can cause scorching. Fire hazard.
CLEANERS Methylated spirits	Cleans varnish; dissolves and removes shellac-based finishes.	Can be diluted with lacquer thinner to cut back rather than strip.
Sugar soap and ammoniated household cleaners	Clean and partially remove varnishes; degrease and cut back paintwork.	Can be diluted with hot water to vary their strength.

Choosing the right stripper. Use this chart after determining the quality and condition of the wood in your trim. To strip the wood bare, use either a chemical stripper from the start, or a heating device first with a chemical stripper for final cleaning. A blow-torch should be used with care, and preferably only when the surface will be repainted. If you plan to retain a stained finish, choose a suitable cleaner.

Finishes for Protection and Beauty

Finish	Durability	Moisture Resistance	Appearance	Usage	Remarks
HARD FINISHES Polyurethane varnish	Excellent	Excellent	Dries to a very high gloss. Also available in matt and satin finish. Somewhat synthetic look.	Softwoods and most hardwoods.	Sand between coats. Can be wax polished.
Alkyd resin varnish	Excellent	Excellent	High gloss	Softwoods and hardwoods.	Recoats easily.
SOFT FINISHES Wax polish (silicone or beeswax)	Fair if wood is sealed first.	Good	Soft satin lustre that improves with age and repolishing.	Most timbers, especially oak and pine.	Seal wood with a cellulose sealer before waxing. Needs occasional repolishing; easily marked.
Boiled linseed oil	Good	Good	Prized for its soft sheen. Darkens the timber.	Not suitable for softwoods. Good for oak and mahogany.	Recoats easily—needs additional applications at intervals.

Choosing the right finish. The first column of this chart lists the most commonly used finishes for wood trim, grouped in two categories: hard finishes, which stand up well to wear, and soft ones, valued mainly for their appearance. If the wood is subject to heavy wear, as in a chair rail or door architrave, or may be exposed to liquids or high humidity, give special weight to the durability of the finish (second column) and its resistance to moisture (third column). If trim is primarily decorative, make the appearance of the finish (fourth column) the main consideration. Some finishes are unsuitable for certain timbers (fifth column). The sixth column of the chart deals with special problems of application and maintenance for the different finishes.

Working with Chemical Strippers

Using a methylene-dichloride stripper. Cover the floor and ensure good ventilation. Wearing rubber gloves, brush stripper on to the wood with a stippling action *(below, left)*—back-and-forth brushwork damages the chemical's bond with the finish. Let the stripper stand for 20 minutes, until the paint liquefies into a sludge. Scrape the wood clean with a wide-bladed stripping knife or, if working on grooves or intricate edges, with a combination shave hook *(below, right)*. Use the edge of the shave hook—straight, pointed or curved—that matches the contour of the wood most closely. If the sludge does not come off in a single continuous ribbon, brush on another coat of the stripper and wait a little longer before you scrape the wood again with the shave hook.

Rinse the woodwork with the solution recommended by the manufacturer—most strippers can be rinsed with plain water, sometimes with a little vinegar added, or detergents, but some require white spirit or another solvent. Apply the rinse with an old paintbrush; use coarse steel wool, rubbing along the grain, to rinse off patches of stubborn paint.

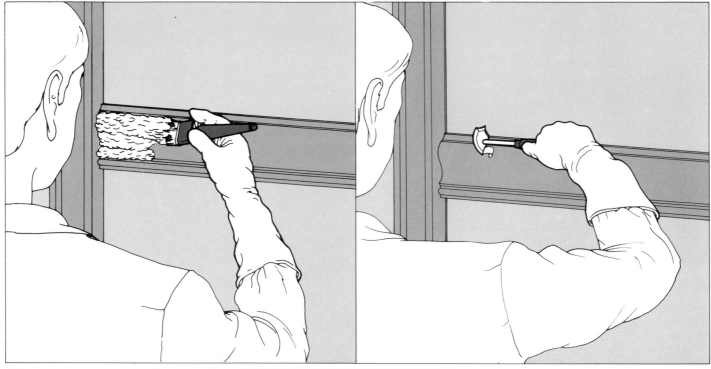

Using a caustic-paste stripper. Wearing rubber gloves, apply the paste thickly with a plastic spatula or a knife. Keep the paste moist by covering with polythene film or a special stripping blanket supplied with the paste. Allow time for the stripper to work—between 15 minutes and six hours, depending on the thickness of the old paint—then peel off the film or blanket (using a putty knife, if necessary) bringing the dissolved paint with it *(right)*. Clean the wood with water and vinegar and scrub with a soft scrubbing brush to remove any residue.

Follow the manufacturer's instructions closely. Some paste strippers do not require wrapping in film, but form a rubbery jelly which can be lifted with a spatula or peeled off with gloved hands.

Special Tools for Taking Off Paint

Using a hot-air gun. Switch on the hot-air paint stripper—a device resembling a hair dryer, available at tool merchants or D.I.Y. shops—and move it slowly back and forth, 50 to 100 mm away from the painted surface, until the paint begins to bubble up from the wood. If the gun has more than one heat setting, try at the lowest temperature first and raise the setting if the paint does not bubble up within a few seconds. Work evenly to avoid scorching the wood. Scrape the paint away with the same tools you would use with a chemical stripper.

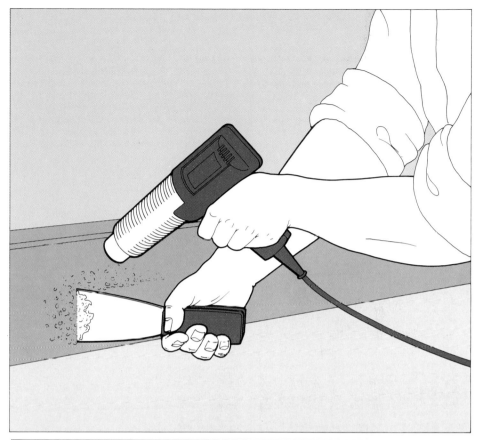

Finishing the job with a sander. Use an orbital sander and medium-grit sandpaper to sand traces of finish off flat moulding *(right)*. Then sand by hand back and forth with fine sandpaper. Follow the wood grain to remove any swirl marks. For rounded surfaces, use an electric drill fitted with a large, flexible-flap sanding wheel or a smaller, flapped sanding drum *(inset)*; both are available at hardware shops. Do not use a wheel with wire flaps. For finishing small, concave surfaces, glue a layer of felt round a short length of dowel, then hold a sheet of sandpaper round this to form a sanding block *(inset)*.

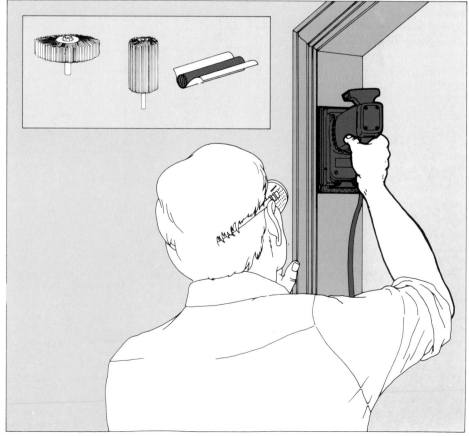

Freeing Fragile Woodwork for the Stripping Tank

Loosening a brittle moulding. First carefully separate the paint joints between the moulding and the wall, using putty knives. Insert the blade of one knife between the wall and the thickest edge of the piece of trim, then force in a second blade directly beneath the first. Lightly hammer a thin cold chisel—or old screwdriver—between the two blades, loosening the woodwork slightly. Work along the length of the moulding in this way. Use the cold chisel to prise the wood a little way from the wall, then hold the moulding with both hands and pull it clear. If it will not come away easily, or is very brittle, cut the fastening nails with a padsaw fitted with a hacksaw blade *(below, right)*. Once the moulding has been removed, pull the nails through the back of the moulding with pincers or pliers. Do not try to pound the nails out through the front of the moulding—you may splinter the delicate face of the wood.

As you remove the moulding, pencil a number on the back of each piece and enter that number on a sketch of the room. Later, scratch the numbers deeply into the end-grain of each moulding with a scriber or knife. Written marks will disappear in the stripping tank. To protect long mouldings during transport, lash them to a 100 by 50 mm board with cord or tape.

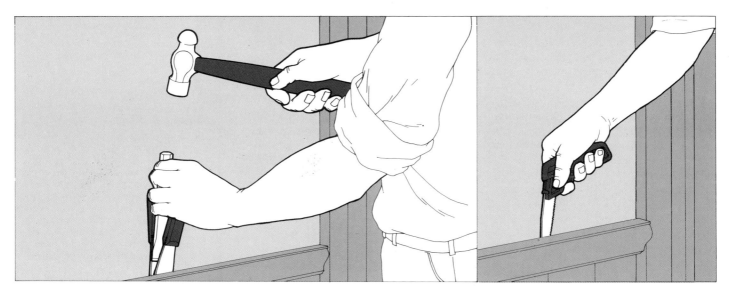

Filling a Dent and Shaping the Patch

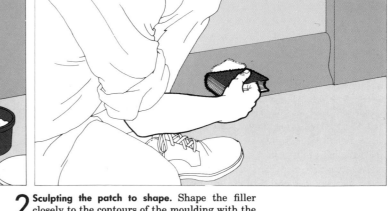

1 **Applying the filler.** Brush out all dust from the dent or crack to be filled, then apply the filler with a filling knife. For deep cracks, build up the filler in layers, allowing each layer to set before applying the next.

If the wood is to be painted, use a cellulose plaster filler; if it is to be stained or varnished, fill with wood stopping after first testing the colour on a piece of scrap timber.

2 **Sculpting the patch to shape.** Shape the filler closely to the contours of the moulding with the edge of a putty knife or with your fingers, but leave at least a slight bulge. After the patch is completely dry, sand it to shape with fine-grade sandpaper. A sanding block formed by wrapping sandpaper round an old deck of playing cards, as shown above, will conform to the contours of the trim and will permit you to apply even pressure to the various irregular surfaces.

Carving a Moulding to Match

When a section of wood trim is damaged beyond repair or is missing, it must be replaced. Many period-design mouldings are stocked by timber yards and joinery retailers, but sometimes your moulding will have to be duplicated from scratch.

For wide moulding, it may be possible to reconstruct the contour by gluing and pinning together several simple stock pieces. Most moulding contours, however complex, break down into a small number of classic shapes, and elaborate trim in old houses was commonly built up this way.

If you cannot replace your moulding with stock pieces, matching trim will have to be cut to shape. This can be done at a timber yard or joinery workshop, but with the right equipment you can make complex mouldings yourself. The ideal machine to use is a spindle moulder. But a cheaper and equally effective tool is an electric router mounted upside down in a special worktable *(below)*. Cutters for routers are available in a range of moulding shapes. Using two or more cutters in separate passes you can duplicate many contours precisely.

Select the cutters by matching them to a sample piece of your moulding. Alternatively, trace the moulding's profile on to a cardboard template or pick it up with a con-tour gauge—a tool with a row of tiny pins that will silhouette any contour the gauge is pressed against. If your moulding requires the use of a custom-ground cutter, it may be more economical for you to take the entire project to a professional.

You will often be able to duplicate the shape of your moulding in a single piece of timber. Some configurations, however, can cause problems. If there is a large variation in thickness between different parts of the moulding, the cutter may not project far enough for the deepest cuts. If the fence on your router table cannot be adjusted, it may be impossible to set the cutter far enough from the fence for some passes on wide mouldings. Such problems are overcome by building up the moulding from two or more pieces of timber. Plan the work so that the join falls inconspicuously in a recess or groove. Glue and pin the parts together before attaching the moulding.

To shape curved sections of timber—moulding for an arched doorway, or curved glazing bars for a fanlight—use a special type of cutter fitted with a pilot wheel above the cutting edge *(page 39)*. As the workpiece is fed past the cutter, the pilot wheel runs along the edge of the timber, acting as a guide. The depth of cut is determined by the diameter of the pilot wheel.

A mini spindle moulder. A portable plunging router mounted upside down in a special combination table forms a stationary spindle moulder able to cut intricate mouldings quickly and safely. The router's cutter projects through the hole in the centre of the table. To make the mouldings, lengths of timber are fed across the table along the guide fence to be shaped by the spinning cutter. Cutter height can be set on the depth scale of the router or by turning the knob of a fine-height adjuster, available as an accessory. The position of the guide fence on the table can be adjusted to determine the exact location of the cut. Hold-down devices, one mounted on the fence and the other running in a groove in the tabletop, hold the workpiece against the fence and table, and guard the cutter. The router is plugged into a push-button safety switch mounted on the leg of the table so that the machine can be turned on and off without reaching under the table.

Safety Rules for Routers

The cutter of a router spins at very high speeds and the machine must be operated with great care. Always observe the following safety precautions:

☐ Switch off before making any adjustments, and disconnect the power supply before changing cutters.

☐ Feed the workpiece past the cutter in one direction only, against the direction of rotation of the bit.

☐ Always use the guide fence (unless you are using a self-guiding cutter with a pilot wheel) and never operate the router without guards.

☐ Stand to the side of the board being cut, never behind it.

☐ Use a push stick or push block—a block of timber with one corner cut out and a handle attached—to guide narrow or thin pieces of wood past the cutter.

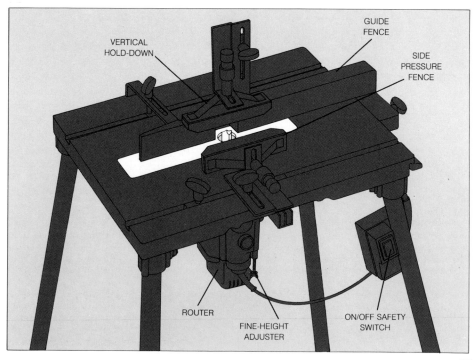

VERTICAL HOLD-DOWN

GUIDE FENCE

SIDE PRESSURE FENCE

ROUTER

FINE-HEIGHT ADJUSTER

ON/OFF SAFETY SWITCH

Shaping an Intricate Moulding

1 Using a set-up board. Trace the contours of the existing moulding on to a piece of stiff cardboard, then transfer the outline on to the end-grain of a 1 metre length of moulding timber. Place the board on the router table and, sighting along the table, set the cutter height and fence position so that the cut will be slightly outside the traced line *(right)*. Lock the vertical hold-down and side pressure fence in position and turn on the router. Push the stock a short distance over the cutter and then withdraw it. Switch off, check the results, and if necessary adjust the cutter and fence and try again. Repeat until the cut matches the outline. Now pass the set-up board all the way past the cutter *(Step 2, below)*.

A complex moulding will require two or more cuts with different cutters *(inset)*. Make the first cut in all the timber to be used before changing the cutter for the second pass, and use the same set-up board to set the fence and cutter position.

2 Feeding the workpiece. Switch on the router and feed the board to be shaped past the cutter in one continuous motion, taking care to stand to one side of the board and paying particular attention to the position of your hands. At the start of the pass use the left hand with fingers outstretched (but not splayed) to keep the board pressed against the fence and table, and use the right hand to push the board forwards *(below, left)*. As the left hand approaches the hold-down, transfer it to a point just in front of the hold-down. Then, as the right hand approaches the hold-down, use the left hand to continue the forward motion of the board and move the right hand in front of the hold-down. To finish the cut, press the board down and against the fence with the right hand and continue to pull the board through with the left hand *(below, right)*.

If the workpiece is less than 50 mm wide, use a home-made push stick held in the right hand to guide the last section towards the cutter. For long lengths of moulding, set up a table or trestle the same height as the router table to support the timber as it comes off the router table.

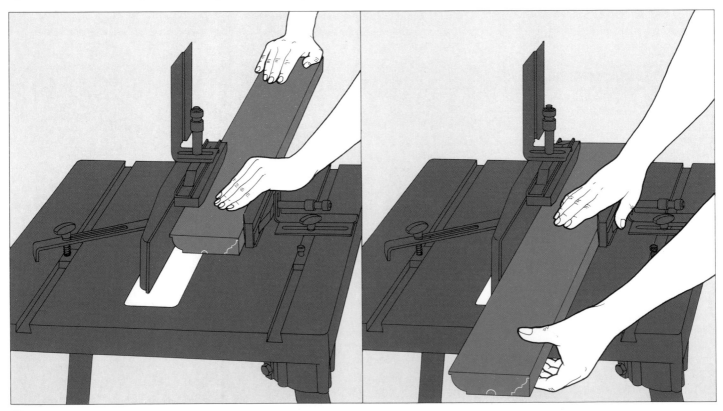

Shaping a Curved Moulding with a Self-Guiding Cutter

1 **Setting up the cutter.** Select a cutter and pilot wheel to match the contour of your moulding *(inset)* and secure them to the router. To make a guard for the cutter, cut a block of timber slightly thicker than the moulding, and nail it to an 8 mm plywood board of the same width with one semicircular end that projects beyond the timber. Place the semicircular end over the cutter and clamp the guard to the table.

Use a straight set-up board marked with the contour of your moulding to check the height of the cutter *(opposite page, Step 1)*. Prepare the curved section of timber to be shaped on a band-saw, cutting it 60 mm longer than required to allow for feeding on to and off the cutter. Smooth down the curved edges with a spokeshave.

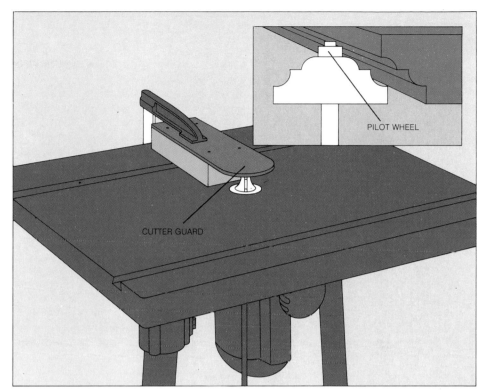

PILOT WHEEL

CUTTER GUARD

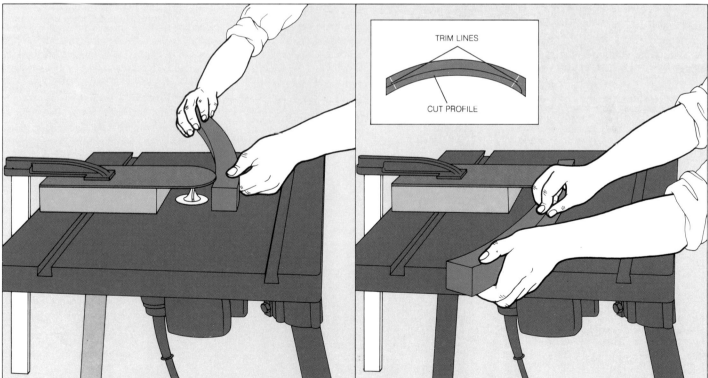

TRIM LINES

CUT PROFILE

2 **Shaping the moulding.** Switch on the router and hold the end of the workpiece about 30 mm away from the cutter *(above, left)*. Push the workpiece against the cutter with your left hand. As soon as the pilot wheel touches the edge, begin to move the workpiece round the cutter, using the right hand to provide the motion and the left to keep the workpiece pressed against the table and the cutter. As the right hand approaches and passes in front of the cutter, use it to apply pressure downwards and against the cutter; with your left hand pull the workpiece round to finish the pass *(above, right)*.

Before fixing the shaped moulding in position, mark across each end at the required angle and trim the moulding to length *(inset)*.

Sharp Profiles for Plaster Cornices

Of the characteristic decorative features of old houses, plaster mouldings are among those most likely to have suffered from neglect. Too often, the delicate design details have been obscured by built-up layers of distemper or paint, perhaps one or more centuries old, and damaged or missing pieces have been left unrepaired.

Cleaning off built-up layers of distemper and paint often requires nothing more than water, time and elbow grease. The water-based paints generally used can be softened by applying rags soaked in hot water with a little sugar soap added, and removed by a combination of brushing and scraping—an old toothbrush and a wooden modelling tool or pointed stick are suitable instruments. A steam gun of the type used for stripping wallpaper, available from tool-hire shops, can also be used to soften the paint. If paints which do not respond to hot water or steam have been applied, use chemical paint strippers *(page 32)*.

Minor damage such as small chips can be made good by filling and modelling with plaster. Small sections of damaged moulding can be duplicated by making a plaster cast from a mould. The mould is made from a section of the original moulding on the wall or ceiling, using a water-based clay (available at artists' suppliers), modelling clay or, if you wish to make several casts from the same mould, a thixotropic polysulphide "cold-pour" moulding compound which can be brushed on to the original *in situ* and built up in layers.

Larger sections of moulding can also be duplicated. "Plain-run" ceiling cornices with smooth continuous lines were originally made by pushing a metal template—known as a running mould—through wet plaster applied directly to the walls. You can use the same technique, but on the workbench, making and installing the new moulding in sections. Although marble is the ideal work surface, adequate alternatives are melamine-faced chipboard, or plywood sealed with shellac (this is available as button polish or knotting compound), then lubricated with a mixture of petroleum jelly and paraffin.

The most difficult part of this job is working with the plaster as it sets, and you should be prepared to make several attempts before you develop the knack of "running" a moulding. The plaster is first mixed to the consistency of single cream, and is shaped as it becomes stiff enough to be cut by the template. When the plaster becomes too stiff to work, discard it and mix a fresh batch. Before applying the new mix, run the template over the finished work a few times, as plaster tends to swell as it hardens.

Large sections of decorated ("enriched") moulding can be duplicated using a moulding compound, but this is a complex and delicate process which is best left to a skilled craftsman. There are many firms specializing in the refurbishment and restoration of ornamental plasterwork.

The plaster to use for all the operations shown here is moulding plaster, also called plaster of Paris. For running a moulding, use equal parts of plaster and white lime (hydrated lime), available from builders' merchants. To mix, sprinkle plaster or plaster and lime gradually into a bucket half-filled with clean cold water; do not stir, but allow the plaster to settle until you have an almost-full bucket with a thin layer of water covering the cracked, undulating surface of the plaster. Grease your hands with petroleum jelly, and with one hand whisk the plaster until it is creamy. After whisking, your hand should look as if it is wearing a white glove; if the mix does not adhere to your hand in this way, add more plaster. Note: the more you whisk the plaster or agitate it after mixing, the quicker it will set—that is, the less time you will have to work.

Once set, lengths of moulding are cut to size with a tenon saw and mitre box. Tile adhesive, or a mix of plaster with 3 parts PVA glue and 1 part water, hold each section in place with support from flat-headed brass or galvanized-iron screws driven into joists or studs. Joints between sections and the countersunk screw heads are concealed with plaster, the joints being first packed with hessian soaked in plaster.

Modelling an Ornamental Shape

Using a modelling tool. A special tool used by plasterers to round joints and fill cracks, known as a plasterer's small tool, can be used to press stiff plaster on to dampened, damaged moulding a teaspoonful or so at a time. The tool has a differently shaped blade at the opposite end, which can be used to sculpt the design. Use a moist soft-bristled watercolour brush to smooth the plaster, to refine the design and to remove tool marks.

Moulding a Small Section

1 **Making the mould.** Select a section of undamaged moulding that duplicates the damaged area, and clean or dust as necessary. Prepare a slab of clay about 20 mm thick and dust one face with French chalk to prevent it from sticking to the moulding. If the design is deep or complicated, dust the moulding also. Press the chalked face of the clay firmly over the moulding, using the side of the hand and the thumb to apply firm pressure. Scratch the back of the clay with a knife to create a keyed surface, then smear over it a 6 mm layer of plaster, embed a piece of hessian and add a second coat of plaster. After 30 minutes, use a putty knife to prise carefully along the plaster backing, thus removing the clay and plaster mould from the moulding.

If you are using a cold-pour moulding compound, prepare the surface of the moulding as above (or use the manufacturer's releasing agent), then brush on the compound in layers, allowing each layer to dry, until the mould is 6 mm thick. Then apply a plaster backing as for clay.

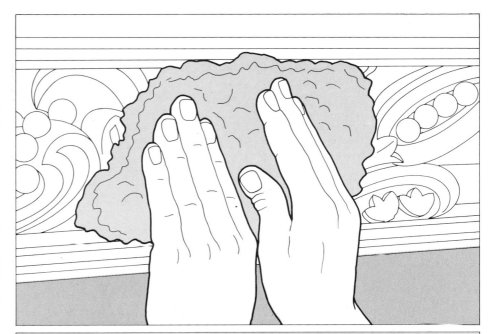

2 **Pouring the cast.** Into the clay mould pour a thin layer of plaster. Jog the mould so any air bubbles will rise, then press hessian on top of the plaster. After about three minutes, pour on a second layer of plaster and form a flat back by pulling the edge of a ruler across the top. Leave the cast to harden for about 30 minutes.

A cold-pour mould should be brushed with the manufacturer's releasing agent, or petroleum jelly mixed with paraffin, before the plaster is poured into it.

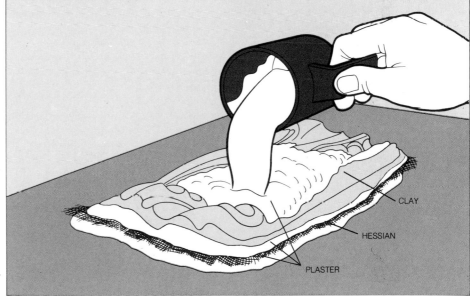

CLAY

HESSIAN

PLASTER

3 **Fitting the cast.** With a sharp wood chisel, cut away the damaged moulding to form a depression slightly smaller and shallower than the cast; check the fit of the cast, then shave down its back and edges with a forming plane until the cast slips into the moulding. Using a trimming knife, score the back of the cast and the area into which it will fit; this will help the adhesive hold fast. To the back of the cast, apply 3 mm of tile adhesive or PVA adhesive mixed with plaster—more, if it is needed to bring the cast out flush with the old moulding. Set the cast in place and slide it back and forth to even the adhesive. Use a modelling tool *(opposite)* and plaster to conceal the joints between the old and the new moulding.

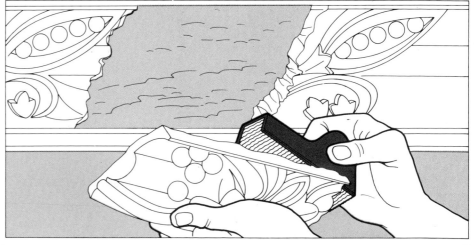

Running a Plaster Cornice

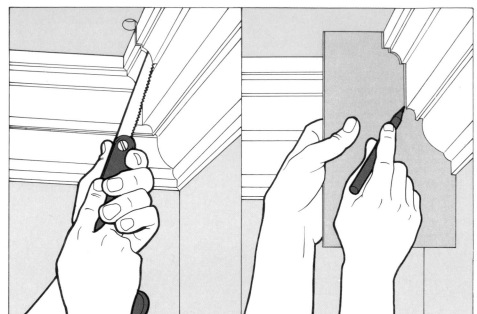

1 **Tracing the profile.** Drill a hole in the ceiling at the moulding's front edge and, starting there, use a keyhole saw to cut through the moulding from top to bottom *(right)*. Slide a piece of cardboard 40 mm longer and wider than the moulding into the kerf. With a sharp pencil, trace the moulding profile on the cardboard *(far right)*.

Cut a sheet of 1 mm-thick aluminium or zinc 40 mm longer and wider than the cardboard. Tape the cardboard on top of the aluminium or zinc—aligning the corner of the cardboard that entered the plaster with a right angle of the metal sheet—and place them on a flat surface.

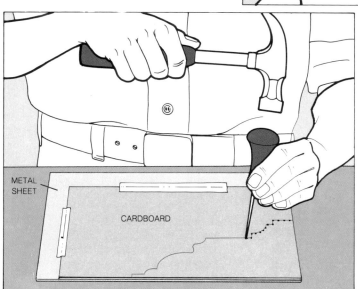

METAL SHEET

CARDBOARD

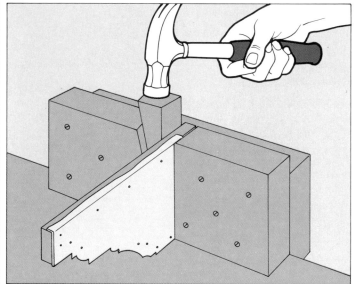

2 **Making the template.** Using an awl and a hammer, make pinpricks every 3 mm along the pencilled profile line. Remove the cardboard and, with tin snips, roughly cut the profile marked on the metal sheet. File the profile to the pinpricks and smooth with fine-grit wet and dry paper.

Place a scrap of 150 by 25 mm timber, 40 mm longer than the metal, below the metal sheet, aligning it in the same position as the cardboard had been. Trace the metal profile on the timber, then duplicate this line 6 mm inside the first. Cut along the second line with a power jigsaw. Reposition the metal on top of the wood, projecting 6 mm on the profile edge; nail it with brads every 12 mm along the profile and every 50 mm along the other edges. If necessary, bend excess metal over the top edge of the timber.

3 **Securing the template.** Set the template in a jig made of 150 by 50 mm timber and lock it in place by driving a wedge between the template and jig. To make the jig, cut three pieces of 150 by 50 mm timber: make them 300, 150 and 125 mm long. Cut a wedge 25 mm long at the top from the 150 mm piece. Screw the short pieces to the long piece, with the outside ends of the short pieces flush with the ends of the long piece and their lower edges 20 mm above the lower edge of the long piece.

Check that the template's top edge is square with the jig face, then tack a 20 by 50 mm diagonal brace from jig end to template end.

4 **Preparing the workbench.** With the jig snug against the front edge of the workbench, get a helper to hold a 225 by 25mm board upright against the far edge of the template while you mark its position on the table. Repeat at 150 mm intervals down the length of the board. Use these guide marks as you nail cleats to the bench along the back of the board. Then add diagonal braces from the top edge of the board to the workbench surface behind it.

Apply two coats of shellac to the work area of the board and the workbench, letting each coat dry, then brush a lubricant such as petroleum jelly mixed with paraffin on the board, bench, bench edge, template and jig.

5 **Making the run.** Pour a 12mm layer of plaster and lime, mixed to the consistency of single cream, on the workbench next to the upright board, then push the template and jig along the front edge of the bench, checking to make sure the template's far edge remains snugly against the board during the run. After each run, add more plaster. Work quickly, but always take the time to clean plaster from the template with a putty knife before making the next run.

Complete the job by filling any missed areas with plaster and making a final run. Allow 20 minutes for hardening, then score the end edges of the moulding with a wood chisel and pull the new moulding away from the board.

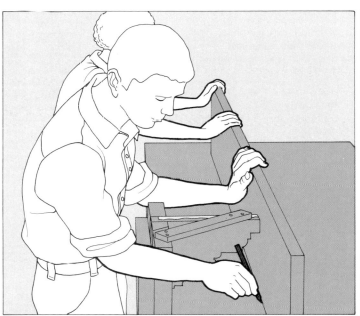
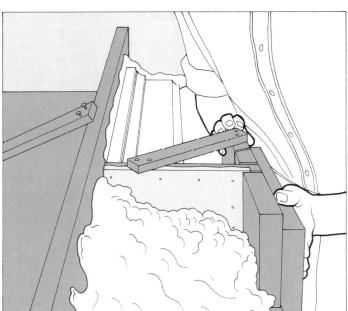

6 **Securing the new moulding.** Draw pencil lines on the ceiling and wall to mark the position of the top and bottom edges of the cornice. By tapping on the plaster, locate the position of the ceiling joists and wall studs, and mark their positions. If the wall is masonry, drill fixing holes in the walls at 300 mm intervals and insert wall plugs, marking their position on the wall below the cornice line. Fix three blocks of scrap timber to the wall along the pencil line to support the moulding during fixing. Coat the back of the moulding with tile adhesive or plaster and PVA. With a helper, lift the cornice into position, resting it on the scrap blocks. Drill holes through the plaster and drive flat-headed brass or galvanized-iron screws into the joists and studs or wall plugs. Allow a 10 mm gap between sections; stuff the joints with plaster-soaked hessian, then apply plaster with a modelling tool to conceal the screw heads and the joints.

Exposing Timber Ceiling Beams

To a modern purchaser, one of the most attractive interior features of a half-timbered house is often the timber ceiling beams that support the floorboards of a room above. However, not all the house's previous occupants may have been of quite the same opinion, and you may well find that the timber beams have disappeared behind a plain, flat ceiling of more recent construction erected by someone with different tastes.

Getting rid of such a ceiling is not difficult *(Step 1, below)*, but you should be prepared for a great deal of disruption and mess. Move all furniture out of the room you are working on, keep the door closed to prevent dust from spreading throughout the rest of the house, and wear goggles and a mask to avoid irritation. Before you begin work on the ceiling, you must also remember to turn the electricity off at the mains so that there is no risk of cutting into a live cable.

The exposed beams are likely to be at 450 mm centres, with a width of up to 75 mm and a depth of up to 225 mm. Where the beams span more than 3 metres, they may be notched into a wider cross-beam at one end of the room. Inspect both the beams and the underside of the floorboards for the familiar telltale signs of woodworm—tiny bore holes and small piles of bore dust—and probe with a knife or small screwdriver where you discover such evidence. If the wood feels firm when tested in this way, you can go on to treat it with insecticide. If the wood feels soft, however, you must seek professional advice—most probably, the entire beam will have to be cut out and replaced.

It may be that, when the house was built, the beams were left entirely exposed and that the ceiling was formed by the underside of the floorboards. Even with the floor above covered in thick carpet, this basic ceiling can transmit a disturbing amount of noise. The simplest solution is to install plasterboard sections between the beams and fill the space between the plasterboard and the underside of the floorboards with a soundproofing material such as glass fibre insulation mat *(overleaf, Step 6)*.

Use the type of plasterboard designed for maximum fire resistance. It is usually 9.5 or 12.7 mm thick and comes in a variety of widths and lengths—1800 by 900 mm sheets are the easiest to handle. You should also use the type of board with a slight taper running down its long edges. When two boards are butted together, the edges form a shallow trough that can be filled and smoothed for a seamless joint. The joint is reinforced with 50 mm-wide paper tape which is laid between two layers of joint filler. The filler can be obtained ready mixed or as a powder to which water must be added.

Use self-tapping dry-wall screws for securing the plasterboard. Dry-wall screws have crossheads and can be driven in with a spiral ratchet screwdriver or, more easily, with a hired electric screw gun. Alternatively, the plasterboard can be fixed in position with 30 mm plasterboard nails. Make sure that the fixings you use are sunk just below the surface of the plasterboard, leaving the paper intact.

1 Renovating the existing ceiling. Poke with a knife or screwdriver to determine the materials used in the construction of the existing ceiling. In the case of plaster and laths, make an initial opening by striking the ceiling with a hammer, then use a claw hammer or crowbar to pull down the laths and plaster *(below)*. Plasterboard sheets can be pulled away from the beams section by section. Carefully remove all nails remaining in the underside of the beams.

Protect your head and face by wearing goggles, a face mask and a helmet. Use a garden spray to keep down the dust in the atmosphere.

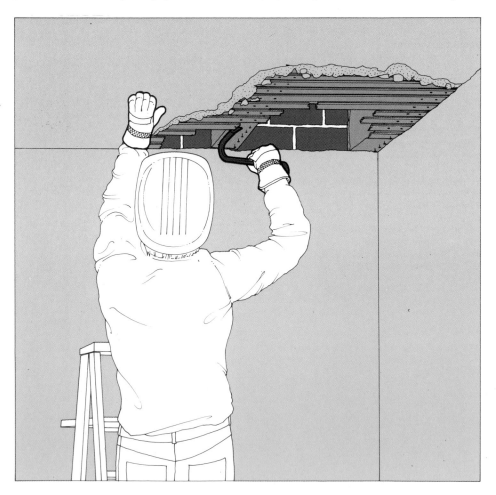

2 **Preparing the timber.** Remove dirt and dust from the exposed beams with a stiff brush *(right)*. Clean the underside of the floorboards, as well as the beams themselves, and work in straight, smooth strokes along the grain of the wood. Take off any old finish with a hot-air or chemical stripper *(page 34)* and smooth out rough spots using a power drill with a disc sander attachment.

3 **Applying preservative.** Apply a clear wood preservative to all the exposed timber, using either a brush or a pressurized garden spray *(right)*. Treat the underside of the floorboards as well as the beams, and pay particular attention to cracks, joints and end grain. If you wish to change the colour of the beams yet still retain the natural grain of the wood, leave the preservative to dry for about two days, then brush on a dye stain *(page 32)*. For an even colour, leave the stain on the surface for about five minutes and then wipe off any surplus with a piece of lint-free cloth or an old paintbrush.

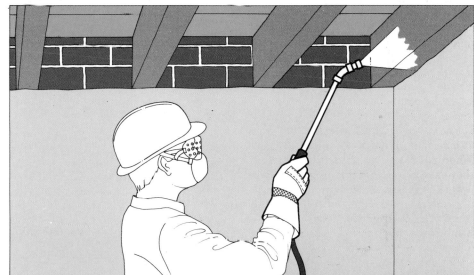

4 **Erecting the battens.** Fix 50 by 25 mm timber battens to the sides of the beams, leaving a gap of about 50 mm between the top of the battens and the underside of the floorboards. Use a straight-edge and spirit level to make sure that the battens are correctly aligned, and fix them with 50 mm No. 8 steel screws or 60 mm galvanized steel nails driven in at 150 mm intervals.

5 **Cutting the plasterboard.** Cut sections of plaster-board to fit between the beams, measuring each section to be filled before cutting to ensure a precise fit. To cut each section, first score across the width of the plasterboard sheet on the ivory side with a trimming knife. Stand the sheet on edge with the score line vertical and towards you and press on both sides of the line to snap the core, then turn the sheet round and cut through the grey backing *(right)*.

Where the beams are twisted or have irregular edges, first cut the plasterboard to the widest measurement between the beams, then hold the section in position and mark where trimming cuts are necessary. Alternatively, mark and cut a template from stiff paper stretched between the beams, and cut the plasterboard accordingly.

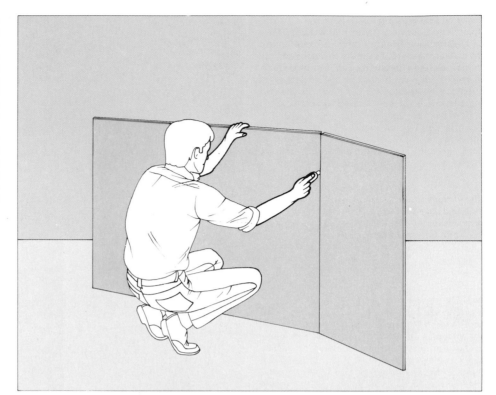

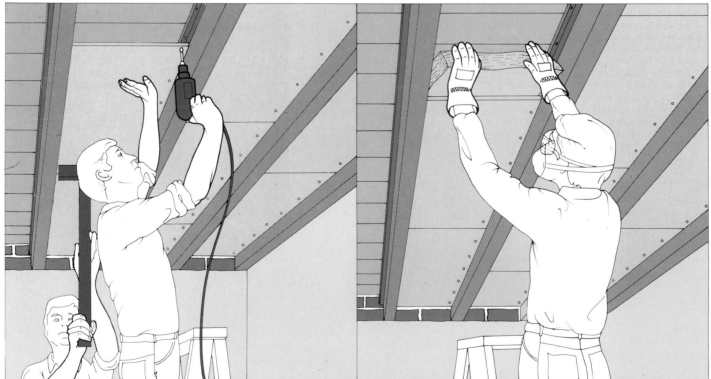

6 **Installing the new ceiling.** Lift the first plaster-board panel into position and get a helper to hold it steady with a "dead man"—a T-shaped timber support cut to fit between the beams —while you fix the panel to the battens *(above, left)*. Use self-tapping dry-wall screws, driving them in at 150 mm intervals with a power screw gun. Having fixed the first sheet, fill the space between the sheet and the underside of the floorboards with 50 mm thick slabs of glass fibre insulation *(above, right)*. Continue in this fashion until you come to the last panel in the row. Here you will have to reverse the sequence: first put up the insulation and hold it in place with 75 mm galvanized nails driven at 200 mm intervals into the sides of the battens, then fix the plasterboard as before. Fill the remaining rows, reversing the direction in which you are working for each row.

7 **Filling and taping the joints.** With a taping knife, apply joint filler to the seams between the plasterboard panels *(right)*. Hold the knife almost vertical at the start of each stroke and gradually angle it closer to the surface as you draw it along, forcing the filler into the depression formed by the tapered edges. Leave a smooth surface that more than fills the depression. While the filler is still wet, cover each joint with tape *(far right)*. Guiding the tape with one hand, run the blade of the taping knife along the joint to force the tape against the filler. Run the blade over the joint a second time to remove any air bubbles and most of the excess filler.

As you measure and cut each length of tape, dip it briefly into a bucket of water to make it pliable and easy to handle. After taping, cover the screw heads with joint filler, again using the taping knife for spreading and smoothing.

8 **Feathering the joints.** With a 200 mm jointing applicator, spread a second layer of filler over the first. Then, holding the applicator slightly off centre, draw it down the joint once again. Bear down on the applicator edge farthest from the joint to feather the filling on that side. Feather the other side of the filling in the same way.

Plaster over any bare masonry between the beam ends exposed by the removal of the existing ceiling, following the techniques demonstrated on pages 108–109. To conceal any unsightly gaps between the plasterboard and the beams, apply a skim coat of plaster across the whole surface of the plasterboard *(page 110)*.

The Enduring Beauty of Handsome Old Floors

Most old houses have wooden floors of a kind difficult to duplicate today and well worth considerable effort in reconditioning. They may be of expensive woods such as oak, beech or elm, or may be laid in parquetry patterns now costly to make. If the floors are of hardwood, the boards are probably beautifully coloured and grained. Even floors of less expensive pine or fir become handsome antiques if restored.

Because wood is a very durable flooring material, reconditioning may require no more than cosmetic work: sanding and refinishing. To remove paint and expose the original wood grain, to erase a surface stain or burn, or to restore the polish of a badly scuffed floor, hire a drum sander (one with a tilt-up lever for the drum) and a special edger for hard-to-get-at areas.

More often, repairs followed by refinishing will be needed; but the repairs may be quite simple. A squeaking floor—a minor but annoying ailment especially common in older houses—can have any of several causes. Adjacent floorboards may be rubbing against each other, for example, or they may have pulled away from the joists; the bridging between joists may be insufficient or missing entirely. If the joists beneath a floor are accessible, your job is relatively straightforward. You can steady a loose board by driving timber wedges between it and the joists, and a squeaky floor can be stabilized by the installation of solid bridging—timber blocks which are cut to fit between the joists and then nailed in a staggered pattern across the room.

If the ceiling under the floor is finished, the joists are relatively inaccessible. To eliminate squeaks from above, force powdered graphite, talcum powder or timber wedges into the joints; if squeaks remain, drive pairs of countersunk screws through pilot holes into the joists.

Other common defects in old flooring include gaps between skirting boards and the floor, wide cracks between floorboards, and holes left by the removal of pipes—often found near radiators. These too are easily repaired, with quadrant or scotia moulding, timber patches and plugs. Do not neglect such repairs: they not only restore your floor's original beauty, but also prevent dust and draughts coming up from below.

While these simple techniques provide remedies for many flooring problems, one or two spots may require more drastic surgery. Some sections of the floor may be completely missing, and others so badly warped or rotted that they must be prised out and replaced. In the case of parquet or wood-block flooring *(page 51)*, you will be unlikely to find exact replacements for the original rectangular pieces that make up your floor's pattern. Choose well-seasoned timber 2 or 3 mm thicker than your existing parquet and ask the timber yard to cut it to width. You can then cut off pieces to the required length. Stick new pieces in place with a latex adhesive and plane them to the level of the old floor.

Before removing sections of damaged floorboard, determine the location and direction of the joists (generally indicated by nail holes or the lines of end joints between boards), and plan to cut through the boards directly over a joist, so that you will have a nailing surface for the ends of the replacements. As you choose the sections of boards for removal, remember that end joints between boards must be staggered. And keep your patches as small as possible.

Square-edged boards face-nailed to joists are relatively easy to prise up and replace. Interlocking tongue and groove boards are often secret-nailed—that is, secured with concealed nails driven at an angle through their tongues—but can be eased out in sections with a chisel *(page 52)*.

The unusual size and look of old boards give your floor its character—but the same features make it difficult to find suitable replacements. One way round the problem is to use replacement boards taken from inconspicuous places in the house—cupboard floors, for example, or the areas under rugs or furniture—and to replace these boards with new wood. Another is to forage among local demolition, architectural salvage or second-hand timber merchants for old flooring; a third—the most expensive—is to have duplicate flooring custom-made at a mill. Whatever method you choose, you will still have the problem of matching the stain for the new boards with that on the old. This final stage of a refinishing job can be tricky: always experiment on scraps of flooring before staining a floor patch.

Quick Fixes for Gaps and Holes

Concealing gaps around the skirting. Cut sections of quadrant moulding to run round the entire room along the base of the skirting boards. For corner joints, mitre-cut the ends of the moulding at a 45-degree angle. Secure the quadrant moulding with panel pins driven horizontally through the moulding and into the skirting to ensure that any subsequent movement of the floorboards will not damage the moulding.

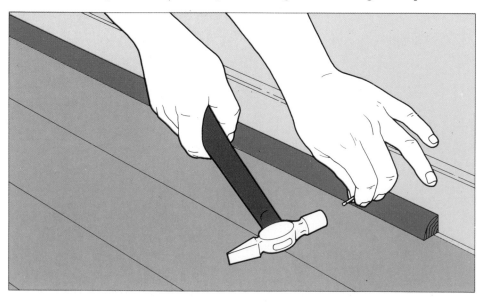

Plugging holes left by pipes. From a scrap piece of timber that matches the floorboards, cut a circular plug about 2 mm wider in diameter than the hole in your floor. Chamfer one end slightly with a chisel or coarse sandpaper, coat the chamfered end with PVA adhesive and hammer the plug into the hole, making sure that the grain of the plug is aligned with the grain of the board. Cut away the protruding surface of the plug with a plane or chisel *(inset)* and sand it smooth.

For knot-holes or other irregular shapes, first enlarge the hole in the floor, cutting a circle around it with a padsaw or keyhole saw, then proceed described as above.

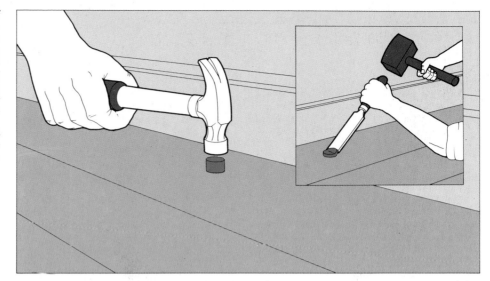

Filling Cracks Between Boards

1 **Shaping the strip.** Select a strip of timber about 100 mm longer and 3 mm wider than the crack that requires filling, and secure it to the edge of a workbench by driving a panel pin through each end. Bevel one edge of the strip with a smoothing plane to form a wedge, then cut it to length.

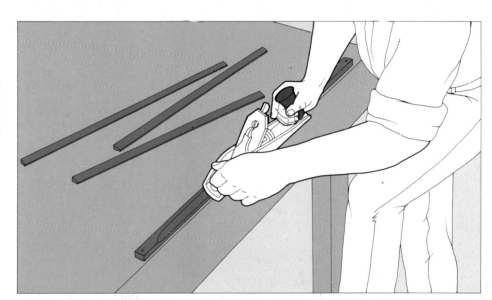

2 **Filling the gap.** Coat the narrow edge of the tapered strip with PVA adhesive, then push it into the crack and tap it down with a hammer and a block of wood. Plane it flush with the floor and fix it to any underlying joists with 40 mm panel pins. Punch the pins below the surface and smooth down the patched area with sandpaper.

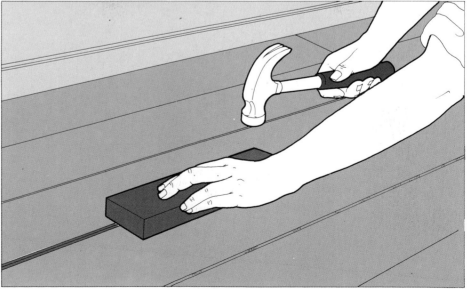

The Right Way to Sand a Floor

1 The first drum sanding. Wearing goggles and a face mask, start at a corner of the room, tilting the drum away from the floor before you start the motor; then, when the sander reaches full speed, lower the drum to the floor. On a parquet or herringbone-pattern floor, load medium paper in the sander and move diagonally across the floor; on floorboards, use coarse paper and move along the grain of the wood. Keep the sander in constant motion, always allowing it to pull you forwards at a steady pace.

At the far wall, tilt the drum up, swing the cord out of the way, and pull the sander back over the area you just sanded. When you return to the starting point, lift the drum and move the sander left or right to overlap the previous pass by at least 50 mm. Continue with forward and backward passes, occasionally turning off the sander to empty the dustbag. When you have sanded the entire room, run the sander along the unsanded strip against the wall.

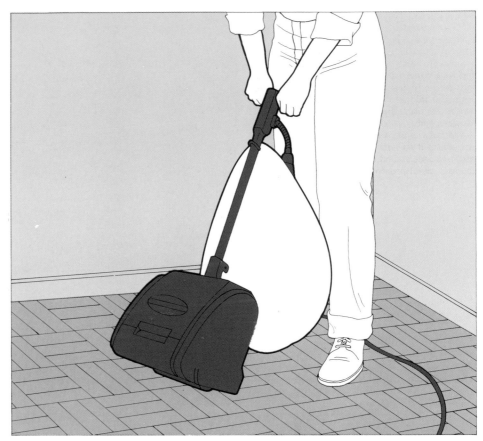

2 The first edge sanding. Use the edger, loaded with the appropriate paper for your floor, to sand the areas missed by the drum sander; the rotating disc of an edge sander can be moved in any direction on the wood.

Repeat the drum and edge sandings, using medium paper for a second sanding and fine paper for a third. On herringbone-pattern or parquet floors, do the second sanding on the opposite diagonal to the first and do the final sanding along the length of the room *(top inset)*. On floorboards, move the drum sander along the grain for each sanding *(bottom inset)*.

When you have completed all three of the sandings, remove the old finish in tight spots—under radiators and in corners, for instance—working along the grain with a sharp paint scraper. Then sand these areas by hand.

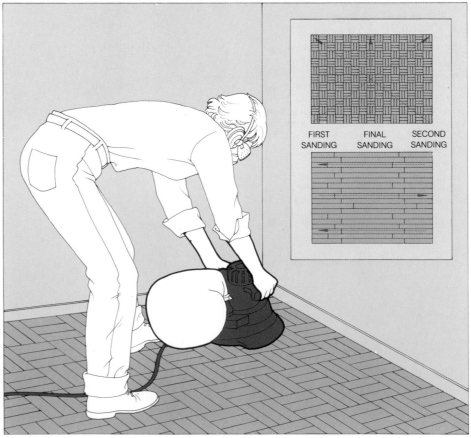

FIRST SANDING   FINAL SANDING   SECOND SANDING

Durable Patches for Damaged Parquet

1 **Removing damaged pieces.** Use a bolster chisel to split damaged pieces of parquet or wood block down the middle, then prise them out, taking care not to harm sound pieces of flooring. When the damaged area has been removed, soften any old adhesive with a hot-air gun or a hair drier and scrape it off with a putty knife. Where parquet has been nailed to timber floorboards, pull any nails that have worked through the wood and remain embedded in the subfloor.

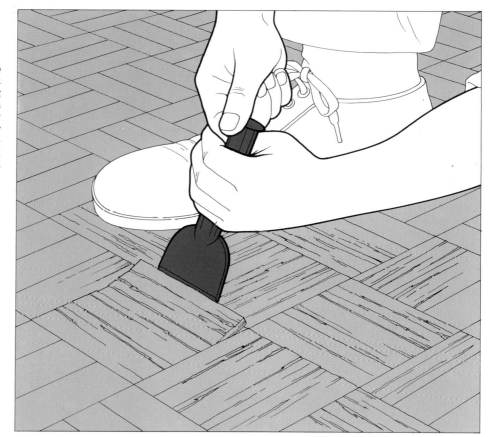

2 **Inserting new pieces.** To check that the replacement pieces fit snugly, fit them in position in a dry run, tapping them into place with a mallet. Take them up and make any adjustments to their edges with a block plane, then spread adhesive over the subfloor and tap them back into place. If the new flooring stands slightly proud of the old, allow the adhesive to dry, then plane the patched section flush with the original flooring, working diagonally across the patch with a smoothing plane or a jack plane *(right)*. Rub down with glass paper for a smooth finish.

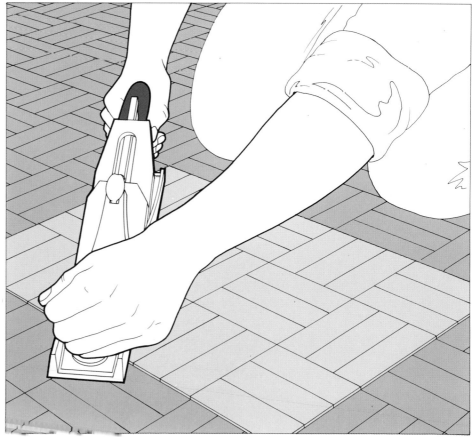

Fitting Replacements for Tongue and Groove Boards

1 Freeing the floorboards. If the end of the damaged section lies within the span of the floorboard, as shown here, chisel straight down over the centre of the nearest joist, with the bevel of the chisel facing the damaged area. About 25 mm closer to the damaged area, drive the chisel, bevel up, towards the vertical cut at a 30-degree angle. Repeat until you have cut through the board. To free a section of a floorboard from the joist at the end of the floorboard, omit the vertical cut; instead, chisel at an angle to cut away the end of the board. Free both ends of all sections to be removed.

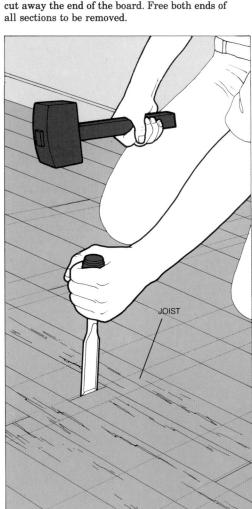

JOIST

2 Removing the boards. To avoid damage to tongues and grooves of undamaged boards, split each board to be removed into three strips. Starting at the middle of the damaged section, chisel two parallel incisions along each board to be removed. Rock the chisel blade in the incisions in order to split the board.

Insert a nail puller or old chisel into a split at the centre of the damaged area and carefully prise out first the middle strip, then the groove side, and finally the tongue side of the board. Working from the centre outwards, prise up the remaining boards in the same fashion, then remove or punch any exposed nails.

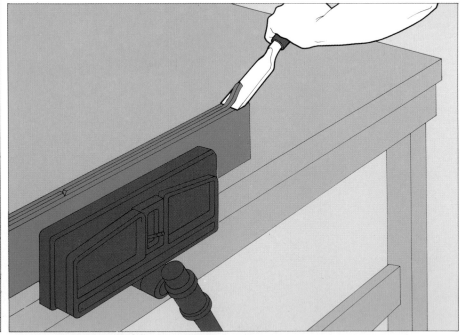

3 Cutting the tongue from a board. New sections of flooring must end over joists, the joints in adjacent rows must be staggered, and part of each new floorboard is generally fitted between two boards already in place. To prepare a board for fitting, secure it tongue side up in a vice and chisel off the tongue along the part that will fit between two boards. Make a vertical cut across the tongue to mark the section which is to be removed, and then tap the chisel, bevel down, against the end of the tongue to split it off only as far as this cut.

SCRAP PIECE

NEW BOARD

4 Inserting the new boards. Tilt the groove of the new board downwards alongside the tongue of the preceding course, fit the groove of a scrap of floorboard over an untrimmed section of the tongue and tap the scrap gently with a mallet to ease the board into place *(left)*.

To insert boards that do not require fitting between two boards already in place, use a piece of scrap wood fitted over the tongue of the new piece as a hammering block while you drive the board into place, positioning the grooved side of the new board over the tongue of the preceding course.

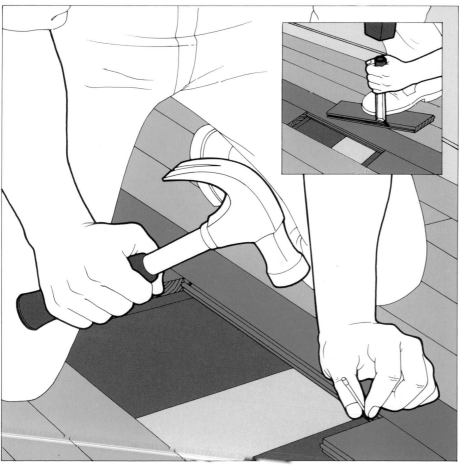

5 Secret-nailing a board in place. Drive and punch 37 mm lost-head nails at a 45-degree angle through the top corner of the tongue of the new board into each joist below the board. Wherever secret nailing is impossible—as at the ends of the board shown here—drill pilot holes and drive 37 mm lost-head nails down through the board face, 25 mm in from its edges. Punch the face nails and cover them with wood filler tinted to match the colour of the floorboard.

To fit the last board, use the chisel to remove the lower lip of the groove along its entire length *(inset)*, tap the board into place tongue first, and face-nail it to every joist.

Doors: Repairs and Renovation

Traditional panel doors, in which decorative panels are set into a solid timber framework of vertical stiles and horizontal rails, are among the most characteristic features of an old house. The problems associated with these doors are of two kinds: first, their operation may be impaired by defective hinges, warping, or settlement of the door frame; second, the door itself may have become structurally weakened or disfigured by loose joints or split panels.

The repairs necessary to correct the first type of problem—which affects flush doors as well as panel doors—are in most cases straightforward. If the door will not stay closed, check that the latch is operating properly *(page 24)* and is correctly aligned with the strike plate. A misalignment of only a few millimetres can be cured by filing the strike plate *(below)*. To rectify a more major misalignment, caused by warping of the door, you may have to prise the door stop from the jamb and reposition it against the closed door.

If the door sticks or catches against the jamb, first check the hinges. Retighten loose screws and fill worn screw holes with timber dowels *(opposite, top)*. Shimming out a lower hinge *(opposite, centre)* will often correct the alignment of a door that catches against the top of the jamb on the closing side.

Often, the cause of a sticking door is simply a build-up of paint on the edges, which can be removed with a shave hook and sandpaper. However, if neither scraping the paint nor adjusting the hinges will rectify the problem, you may have to use a plane. A smoothing or jack plane can be used to plane the top and closing edges without removing the door *(opposite, bottom)*; do not resort to planing the bottom edge of the door before first checking whether it is sagging because of loose or worn joints.

Strengthening joints and replacing a split panel call for more structural repairs *(pages 56–57)*. For both jobs the door must be taken off its hinges, and for clamping reglued joints you will need at least two sash cramps long enough to fit across the widths of the door.

Panels are either set into grooves in the rails and stiles or held in place by strips of decorative moulding; in some doors, both grooves and mouldings are used. On a door with loose joints, you can prise off one of the stiles and slide out the damaged panel. If the joints are sound, however, this procedure could weaken the door framework, and to remove the panel you will have to prise off the retaining strips of moulding or cut out the wall of the retaining groove with a router. After repairing the panel, replace the moulding strips or rebuild the groove wall with strips of matching moulding.

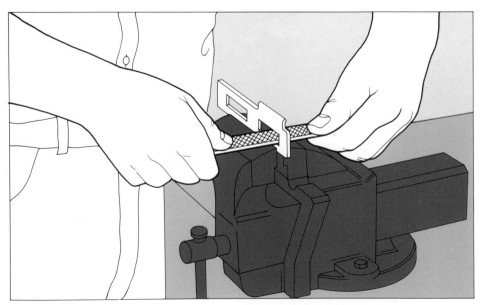

Adjusting a strike plate. Cover the strike plate with masking tape and mark the outline of the latch opening on the tape in pencil. Smear lipstick on to the tip of the latch, turn the door-handle to draw the latch in, and push the door closed; release the latch to mark the tape, then withdraw it and open the door. If the mark made on the tape indicates a misalignment of less than 4 mm, remove the strike plate, clamp it in a vice and file as necessary.

If the latch is misaligned by more than 4 mm, check for sagging hinges and distortion of the door frame. If it seems necessary, remount the strike plate so as to bring it into alignment with the latch, enlarging the mortise behind the opening with a wood chisel.

Repairing worn screw holes. Unscrew both hinges from the jamb and remove the door. Using a drill fitted with a 6 mm bit, drill out the worn screw holes. Cut 6 mm dowels to length, usually about 30 mm, coat them with glue, and tap them into the screw holes with a hammer. Allow the glue to dry, then drill pilot holes into the dowels and screw the hinges back into place.

Shimming a hinge. Loosen the screws fastening the hinge to the jamb and insert wedges under the bottom of the door to raise it slightly off the ground. Cut cardboard shims with slots for the screws and slide them behind the hinge leaf fixed to the jamb, then retighten the screws.

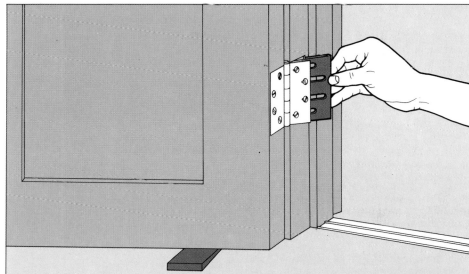

Planing the door edges. If the door sticks at the top or along part of the side jamb, wedge the door open and use a smoothing or jack plane to remove shavings from the edge that binds, leaving a gap of about 3 mm between the jamb and the closed door. If an entire side binds on the closing side or hinge side, remove the door and unscrew the hinges from the door. Mark a line 3 mm down from the hinge edge and have a helper hold the door on edge while you plane down to the line. Reattach the hinges and test the fit of the door; mark any points that require additional planing. When the fit is correct, deepen the hinge recesses with a chisel and replace the door.

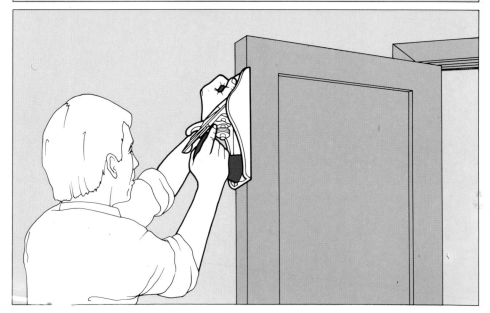

Securing the Joints of a Sagging Door

1 **Regluing the joints.** Remove the door from the frame and lay it flat across two sawhorses or on a workbench. On each side of the door affected by a loose joint, spread open all three joints to expose about 60 mm of the tenons; knock the joints apart using a mallet and a piece of fibreboard held against the inner edge of the door stile. Remove the old wedges from inside each mortise, loosening them with a chisel if necessary. Spread glue on to the exposed parts of the tenon and other inner surfaces.

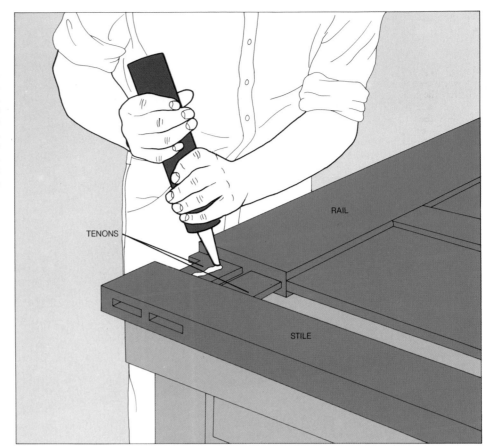

2 **Clamping and wedging.** Close the joints by knocking the door stile inwards with a mallet, holding a block of scrap timber against the stile to protect it. Clamp the joints at either end of each rail with two sash cramps. For each tenon, cut two timber wedges the same width as the thickness of the tenons; the wedges should be about 45 mm long, tapering from about 8 mm to 3 mm at the narrow end. Apply glue to both sides of the timber wedges, and insert them on either side of each tenon. Drive the wedges home with a hammer *(right)*.

If you do not have enough cramps to clamp all the rails, clamp and wedge the widest rail first, then clamp and wedge the other joints in turn.

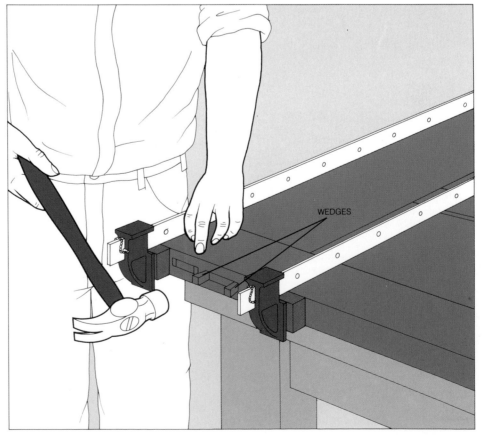

Repairing a
Split Panel

1 Freeing the panel. Lay the door flat on sawhorses or a workbench and determine by close inspection whether the panel is held in place by grooves in the rails and stiles, or by strips of moulding pinned to the rails and stiles. If the panel is held in grooves, cut away 8 mm from the inner edge of the stile *(right)*, using a plunging router with the side fence set to run along the door edge and the depth stop adjusted to avoid damage to the panel; clamp blocks of wood to the stile as stops for the router at the end of each pass. If necessary, reset the fence and rout again to expose the panel edge. Rout off the edges of stile and rails along the remaining edges of the panel, then lift it out. Where the side fence cannot be positioned, use a straight timber clamped to the door instead.

If the panel is held in place by strips of moulding, break the paint seal around the moulding with a trimming knife, prise off the mouldings with an old chisel, and lift out the panel. If the joints of the door are loose, open up the joints *(opposite page, Step 1)*, remove one of the stiles and slide out the panel.

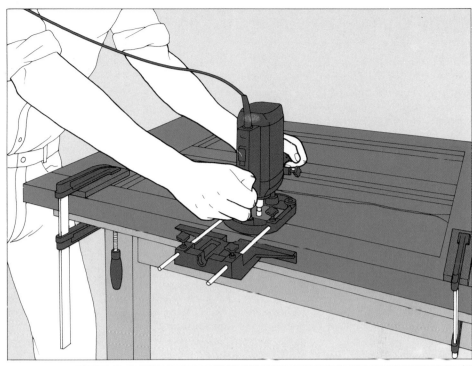

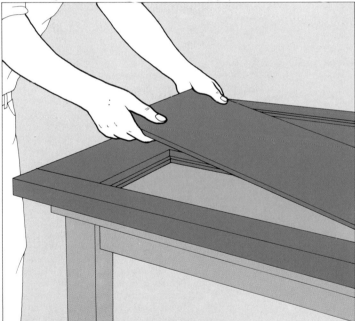

2 Replacing the repaired panel. Smear PVA glue on to the split edges of the panel, press the edges together and clamp with sash cramps. When the glue is dry, remove any excess that has oozed out of the join. Reposition the panel in the door.

If the panel cannot be glued, replace it with a new one. A plain panel in a painted door can be cut from plywood of the correct thickness; if the door is to be varnished, use matching solid timber, plywood faced with matching timber, or veneer a sheet of plywood to match.

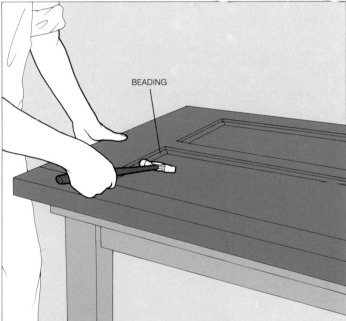

BEADING

3 Rebuilding the edges. Rebuild the edge removed by the router, using lengths of beading selected to match the existing panel surrounds. Cut the beading to fit the four edges, mitring the ends at 45 degrees, then press the beading tight against the panel and pin it to the rails and stiles with panel pins at 150 mm intervals. Never use glue to hold the panel in place, otherwise seasonal swelling and shrinking of the main timbers may cause it to split again.

If the panel was held in place by moulding strips, pin these back in position with panel pins. If you need to replace damaged mouldings, buy new ones of a matching profile or make your own *(pages 37–39)*.

Getting Windows to Work Right

The windows are usually high on the repair list for an old house, and with good reason—they are exposed to the ravages of the weather, their parts wear out from constant use and their operation is easily impaired by warping and sagging.

Most older houses have vertical sliding sash windows and all too often one of the sashes—generally the top (outer) one—is frozen shut. Typically, the sash is glued tight by layers of paint and can be freed by the method shown below. If the sash still refuses to move freely, the channels are probably blocked by a layer of dirt and paint. This layer can be removed with a scraper and sandpaper (opposite page, above), although you may find that you need to take the sash out of the window frame (opposite page, Step 1) in order to do a really thorough job.

If a sash sticks because one of the staff beads is bowed, set a wooden block against the side of the bead where it sticks, and tap the block gently with a hammer. If this fails to do the trick, prise the bead out with an old chisel, move it back slightly and re-nail it to the pulley stile.

Occasionally, a sash jams because mois-ture has loosened the glued mortise and tenon joints at the corners of the sash, allowing it to sag out of true. L-shaped steel brackets screwed on to the weakened corners will strengthen the joints (page 61). Never try to ease a reluctant sash by planing down its sides—no matter how small the amount of the wood you shave off, you are almost certainly going to end up with a sash that rattles.

Broken sash cords can be another cause of jamming, and can also cause the sash to fall to the bottom of the frame every time it is raised. If one cord breaks, it is likely that the other three are also in poor condition, so you should replace all of them at the same time (pages 59–60). Apply oil to the pivots of the sash-cord pulleys if they are not running smoothly.

New sash cord, available at hardware shops and builders' merchants, is sold in various thicknesses up to 12.5 mm, depending on the weight it has to support. Use synthetic cord, which is more durable than the old-fashioned waxed type. You can prevent the ends of the cord from fraying by using a lighted match to melt and seal the fibres.

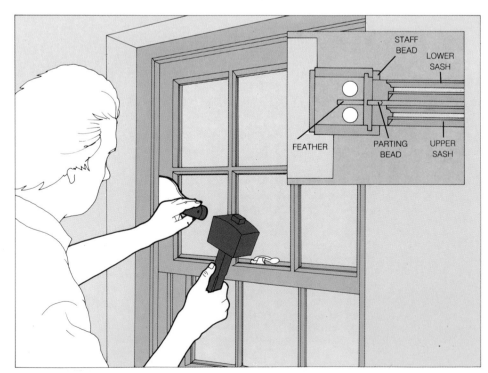

STAFF BEAD

LOWER SASH

FEATHER

PARTING BEAD

UPPER SASH

Loosening a Sticky Window

Freeing frozen sashes. Outside the house, try to free the upper sash by tapping a wide-bladed putty knife into the joints betwen the sash and the outer lining, working along the sides and then the top of the sash; if necessary, repeat the procedure between the lower sash and the parting beads. Inside the house, tap the blade between the upper sash and the parting beads and between the lower sash and the staff beads.

If the sashes remain frozen, go outside the house and wedge a crowbar between the lower sash and the sill. Place a timber block on the sill under the crowbar for leverage and prise the sash up, working first from one corner, then the other. To get at the upper sash with the crowbar, go inside the house and prise off the head staff bead with a wood chisel. Wedge the crowbar between the upper sash and the head lining, again using the timber block for leverage.

Easing tight sashes. Using a triangular shave hook or scraper, scrape off loose paint and debris from the inside of the sash channels. Clean the pulley stiles first, then the sides of the staff beads, parting beads and outer linings. Sand the channels smooth, using a wooden sanding block slightly narrower than the channels. Repaint if desired, then lubricate the channels with a candle or a block of beeswax. Alternatively, apply a silicone spray lubricant.

Replacing the Sash Cords

1 Removing the sashes. With the lower sash closed, cut the unbroken cord just above the top of the sash and lower the weight gently to the bottom of the pulley stile. Use a wood chisel to lever out the sill staff bead and the two side staff beads, starting at the centre of each length to avoid damaging the corner mitres. Remove the nails from the beads with pincers. Lift the lower sash out of the frame *(right)* and remove the ends of the cords. Each of the ends will either be nailed into a groove at the side of the sash or threaded through a hole and knotted.

To remove the upper sash, first lower the sash, cut the unbroken cords and lower the weights. Lever out the parting beads on both sides, using a wood chisel. Start at the sill end and work gradually upwards, prising the bead out a little at a time. Lift out the upper sash and remove the ends of the cords.

SASH CORD

2 **Taking out the weights.** Unscrew one pocket piece and prise it out of the pulley stile, using an old wood chisel. If the pocket piece is covered with paint, tap on the lower part of the pulley stile with a hammer until the outline of the pocket appears, then score round it with a trimming knife. Take out the sash weights inside the pocket and untie the ends of the old cord. Unscrew the pocket piece on the other side of the window frame and take out the weights in the same way.

3 **Fixing the new cords.** Feed one of the upper sash cords over its pulley until one end appears at the pocket, then tie on the sash weight with a double knot. Pull the other end of the cord to raise the weight up to the pulley, and pin the cord to the pulley stile to hold the weight temporarily in position. Rest the upper sash on the window sill, slightly angling one side towards you, and attach the cord to the frame by threading it through its slot and knotting it or by nailing it into its groove with four 19 mm broad-head galvanized nails. Attach the opposite cord in the same way, then position the upper sash in its channel and attach the lower sash cords *(below)*. Finally, replace the pocket pieces, parting beads and staff beads.

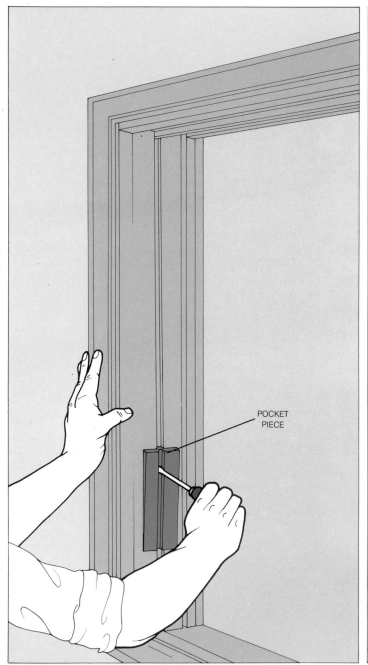

POCKET
PIECE

An Angle Bracket for a Weak-Jointed Sash

1 Marking the recess. Remove the sash from its frame and place it on a workbench with its outer side uppermost. Clean out the loose joint with a wire brush, then apply waterproof PVA or resin glue liberally to both sides of the tenon and force the joint closed with a sash cramp; tighten the cramp carefully to avoid cracking the glass. Place the bracket near the inside edge of the sash, making sure that the two halves of the joint are covered by the same number of screw holes, and draw the outline of the bracket in pencil.

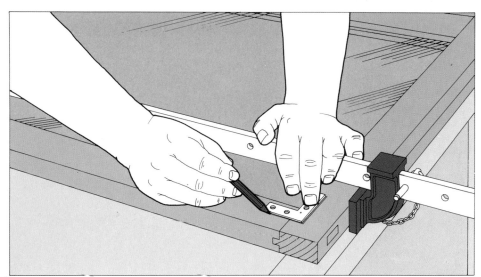

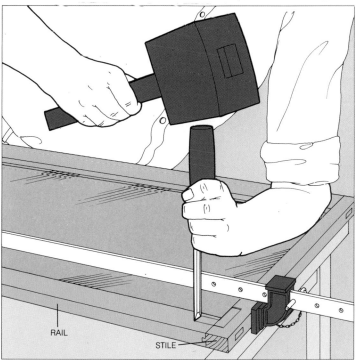

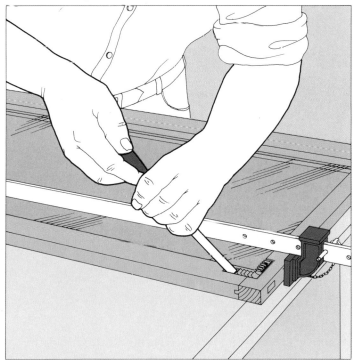

2 Cutting the outline. Using a mallet and bevel-edged chisel the same width as the bracket, make three cuts across the grain of the wood—one at either end of the bracket outline on the stile, and one at the end of the bracket outline on the rail *(above)*. Hold the chisel vertical with the bevel inwards and make each cut just inside the pencilled line, tapping the chisel to a depth slightly less than the thickness of the bracket. Then set the blade parallel with the grain of the wood and cut along the arms of the outline, this time making each cut on the line.

3 Finishing the recess. Set the chisel, bevel facing inwards, about 5 mm inside the cross-grain cut at the corner of the bracket outline. Angle the chisel towards the bevel side and tap it to a depth slightly less than the bracket thickness. Working back along the stile to the end of the outline, repeat this cut at 5 mm intervals. Make similar cuts inside the outline of the second arm of the bracket, then grip the chisel with both hands and pare along the grain to remove the wood chips and produce a smooth, even surface *(above)*.

Lay the bracket in the recess, check that it lies flush, then screw it in place. Fill the screw slots and any gaps round the edges of the bracket with a cellulose or resin filler, and sand the filler flush when it is dry.

Repairs for a Staircase Balustrade

Broken balusters or a shaky newel post at the bottom of a balustrade make a staircase unsafe, and require prompt repair. As matching replacements for the finely turned balusters and newel posts of an old staircase are hard to come by, in most cases you will have to work with the existing parts, taking care to make the repair as inconspicuous as possible. The only alternative is to remove the damaged piece and then get a custom-made copy turned for you by a professional joiner.

A loose baluster can usually be tightened by gluing and toenailing, or by inserting narrow wedges between the baluster end and its housing. A hairline fracture can be repaired by forcing in glue and then clamping or taping until the glue has dried. Repair a diagonal split with glue and two small screws, one at each end of the break, driven through the thinner section and into the thicker part.

A decorative baluster that has snapped cleanly at one of its narrow waists must be removed from the staircase before being repaired with a dowel (right). The technique for removing and replacing a baluster depends on the staircase construction. On a traditional "open-string" staircase, the lower end of each baluster is dovetailed into the tread, while on a "closed-string" staircase the baluster slots into a mortise in the outer string, the board that runs from the top to the bottom of the staircase and houses the outer ends of the treads.

The base of the newel post at the bottom of the balustrade is mortised to receive two tenons at the end of the outer string. Reinforce a shaky newel post with screws driven into the ends of the tenons (opposite page, below), and conceal the repair with cross-grain plugs that have been cut from timber that matches the colour and grain of the newel post.

Repairing a Broken Baluster

1 Removing the baluster. Mark a pencil line across the break in the baluster to enable you to match up the two pieces after they have been removed. On a closed-string staircase (below), wiggle each section loose, then pull the tenons free from their mortises; if they are firmly se-cured, saw off the sections flush with the string and the underside of the handrail. On an open-string staircase (inset), remove the lower section of the broken baluster by prising off the return moulding and nosing along the side of the tread, then pulling out the tenon.

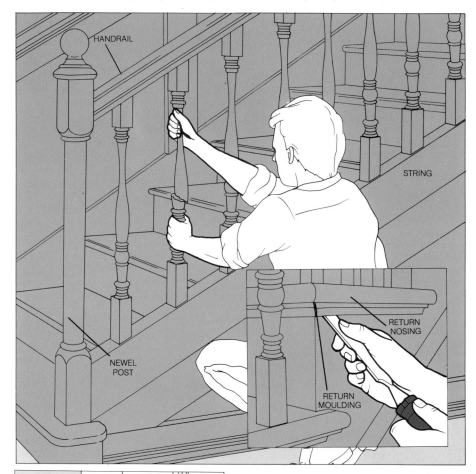

HANDRAIL

STRING

NEWEL POST

RETURN NOSING

RETURN MOULDING

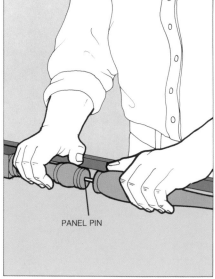

PANEL PIN

2 Marking for a dowel. Drive a 25 mm panel pin part way into the centre of one broken section, then snip off the pin's head at an angle with a pair of pincers. Align the two baluster sections along a straight batten pinned to the worktable and push them together to force the headless pin into the end of the second section (left). Pull the sections apart and remove the pin. If the baluster sections are not of the same width and cannot be aligned along a batten, clamp one piece vertically in a vice and then align the two sections by eye.

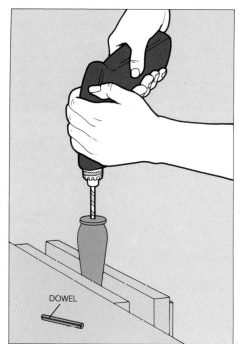

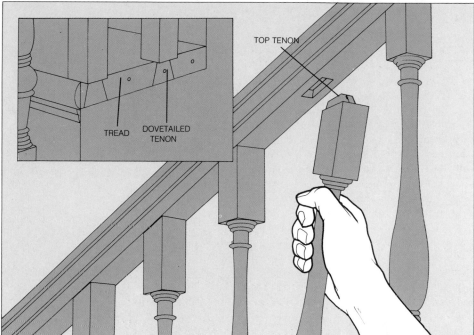

TOP TENON

TREAD   DOVETAILED
TENON

3 **Completing the repair.** Cut a 70 mm length of grooved dowel with a diameter no more than half the thickness of the broken surfaces, and chamfer its ends with a chisel. Using a bit of the same diameter as the dowel, drill holes 35 mm deep straight into the marks left by the panel pin in each section of baluster *(above)*. Coat the ends of the dowel and the broken surfaces of baluster with PVA adhesive, insert the dowel and push the broken surfaces together. Wipe off excess adhesive with a damp cloth and clamp with a sash cramp until the adhesive is dry. Remove any roughness round the new joint with a fine file and smooth down with sandpaper.

4 **Replacing the baluster.** To secure a baluster in a closed-string staircase, first saw off a triangular piece from the "upstairs" side of the top tenon, then coat the bottom tenon with PVA adhesive and push it into place with the baluster angled towards the top of the stairs. Apply more adhesive to the upper tenon and ease it into its mortise *(above)*, pushing up on the handrail if necessary. If the tenons have been sawn off during the re-

moval of the baluster, the repaired baluster should be toenailed in place.

To replace a baluster in an open-string staircase, coat both tenons with adhesive and push the upper tenon into its mortise under the handrail. Slide the lower dovetailed tenon into its original housing *(inset)* and nail it to the tread, then renail the return nosing and moulding along the side of the tread.

Tightening a Wobbly Newel Post

Making an invisible repair. Aiming directly at the end of the string, drill two pilot holes through the newel post, one above the other. Counterbore the holes to a depth of 20 mm, then drive home two No. 12 screws at least 100 mm long. Using a drill fitted with a plug-cutting attachment *(inset)* the same diameter as the counterbored holes, cut cross-grain plugs to conceal the screw heads. Apply PVA glue to the sides of the plugs, align their grain with that of the newel post, then hammer the plugs into the holes until only a millimetre or two protrudes. Cut off the plug ends with a chisel *(right)*, then smooth down with sandpaper.

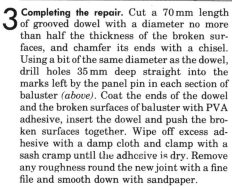

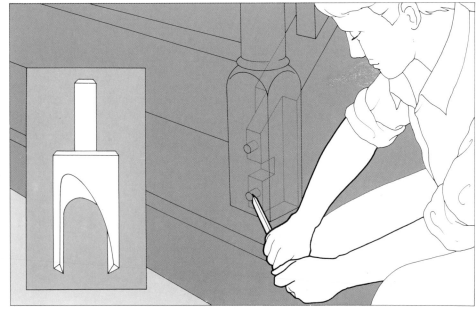

3 Making Do with Ageing Utilities

Joining new pipe to old. Two adjustable spanners are used to tighten the nuts of a union connector between adjacent lengths of steel and copper pipe. Horizontal sections of old steel or lead pipe are especially vulnerable to clogging and corrosion; transition fittings can be used to splice lengths of modern copper or plastic pipe into an old plumbing system without the need to renew a complete run of pipework.

The moment when the new owners of an old house are handed the keys is one of mingled joy and trepidation. Delight over the prospect of fine hardwood floors is tempered by concern about a dusty old fuse box. Anticipation of soft morning light through leaded glass in the pantry mixes with doubts about clanking pipes in the kitchen. Worries about the fitness of old utility systems can be a major concern: outdated systems are expensive to replace, and life in the house during such a repair can range from awkward to impossible.

A good house inspection will have laid these fears partially to rest—the plumbing is fairly sound, the fireplace and heating system are old but serviceable, the wiring may not be sufficient but at least it is safe—but doubts linger on. Household utility systems do have a limited life span. Yours will someday have to be replaced. In the meantime there are steps you can take to maintain and even improve the systems you have inherited.

Plumbing has undergone a number of changes since your old house was built, but the changes have largely been new developments in materials rather than fundamentally innovative ideas in design. The standardization of pipe sizes and layouts greatly simplifies plumbing repairs and makes it easy to find replacement parts. Plastic pipes and flexible copper tubing now make small replacement jobs simple; the development of a vast selection of adapter fittings allows you to repair any type of old piping material with almost any type of new material.

Similar innovations have contributed to the development of new heating systems, which are plainly cleaner, more effective and more convenient than their older counterparts. But replacing an old system is so expensive that it could be many years before the increased energy efficiency pays for itself. With the ever-uncertain costs of energy, it is not uncommon these days for an old-house buyer to learn to live with an old coal-burning boiler rather than make the expensive change to a more "modern" source of heat. Whatever the fuel, you can often improve the performance of an old heating system substantially by making simple repairs or catching up on neglected maintenance.

When it is the electrical system that is ailing, minor surgery may not be sufficient. If the materials and appliances show signs of wear, patching and replacing will only conceal potential dangers, and complete rewiring may be the only practical solution. However, if your preliminary survey has confirmed that the wiring system is sound, you will often be able to adapt its capacities to meet your requirements. And the installation of new switches and sockets—surprisingly uncomplicated projects—will have a rejuvenating effect, bringing light and energy to areas of an old house that were previously underused.

Keeping Fireplaces Safe, Clean and Efficient

Fireplaces are among the most aesthetically intriguing parts of an old house and they can be a practical asset as well: properly maintained and well fuelled, they can reduce energy costs by allowing a lower thermostat setting for the central heating system. Unfortunately, many old fireplaces are not safe—about 50,000 house fires are caused each year by flame and heat from faulty flues and chimneys.

Before using an old fireplace for the first time, conduct a smoke test (*opposite page, above*) to check the chimney for leaks caused by deterioration in the old mortar lining. If leaks are in evidence you should seek professional advice, since the chimney may have to be relined.

If the inside of the chimney is in good shape, you still must make sure it is clean; if it is not, it can cause a chimney fire. Such a blaze, burning with blast-furnace intensity, can spew flame and debris out of the fireplace and chimney top. Chimney fires occur most often when soot and creosote—a tarlike deposit—build up on flue walls and suddenly ignite. If the chimney has not been cleaned for some time, you should employ a sweep, who will use wire brushes to scrape off thick deposits. Thereafter carry out twice-yearly cleanings yourself, using polypropylene brushes and rod sections. This equipment can be obtained from specialist shops.

On the outside of the chimney, check the masonry and the flaunching—the mortar pyramid that holds the chimney pot in place. Repoint any crumbling joints (*page 100*) and patch or rebuild any cracked flaunching. If the stack is vulnerable to occasional downdraughts that can waft smoke into the room below, you can extend the flue above the stack with a cowl in place of your chimney pot; a builders' merchant will advise you on the most suitable model for your situation. Alternatively, install a simple dovecote top (*page 68*), which will serve the same purpose.

If the fireplace smokes chronically, you must improve the updraught. Installing an adjustable throat restrictor—a metal damper controlling the flow of warm air at the base of the flue—will encourage a fire to draw better. Another technique which will achieve the same effect is to reduce the size of the fireplace opening by lowering the lintel or—a much more simple method—by

raising the level of the back hearth with firebricks (*page 69*).

A special problem in many old houses is the fireplace that has been covered over. Returning such a fireplace to operation is usually a straightforward procedure, but after uncovering the opening you must systematically check each part of the fireplace and chimney and carry out any repairs which are necessary.

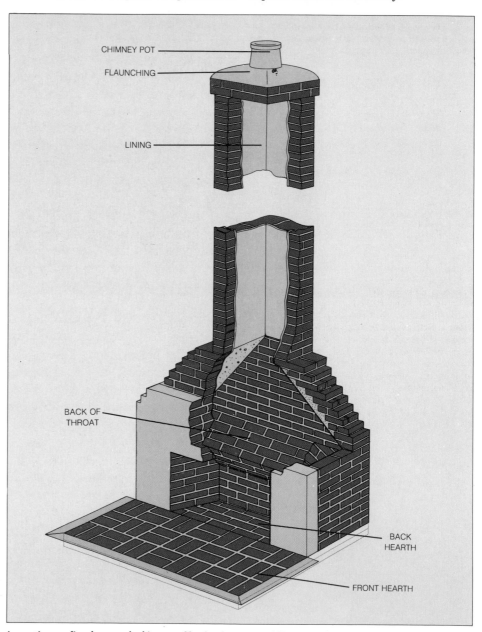

CHIMNEY POT

FLAUNCHING

LINING

BACK OF THROAT

BACK HEARTH

FRONT HEARTH

Inspecting a fireplace and chimney. Check the flue for blockages or faults in the masonry or lining by looking up the chimney; use a torch and a mirror to aid your inspection. The back of the throat should slope smoothly into the flue to allow smoke to rise directly upwards. Inspect the joints in the fireback, which may be of either individual firebricks or moulded sections of fire-resistant clay, and the joint between the back hearth and the decorative front hearth. Loose or crumbling mortar or cracks in the fireback can be repaired with fire cement (*opposite page*).

Outside the house, examine the exposed masonry of the chimney stack, the flashing at the base, the mortar flaunching round the chimney pot, and the pot itself. Grip the pot firmly with both hands to test whether it is secure. Caution: always work on the roof from a ladder equipped with a roof hook clamped over the ridge, or from scaffolding erected round the stack.

Conducting a smoke test. Cut a sheet of thick polythene to cover the fireplace opening. Place a smoke pellet in the empty fireplace and light it, then secure the polythene sheet across the fireplace opening with masking tape. Get a helper on the roof to cover the chimney top with a plastic bag as soon as smoke starts to appear. Check the length of the flue for smoke leaks, starting in the attic. Where the flue passes behind finished walls, look for leaks under skirting boards or round the frames of doors and windows. Get your helper to check the chimney out of doors.

Once the test is done, uncover the chimney top and let the smoke clear for at least 15 minutes before uncovering the fireplace opening.

Repairing firebrick joints. Chip out the crumbling mortar with a cold chisel and hammer, then brush off soot and debris with a wire brush. Using a cloth or brush dipped in water, dampen the raked-out joints and the surrounding area. Pack fire cement into the joints with a pointing trowel, then smooth the cement flush with the surrounding bricks using the edge of the trowel. Let the cement cure for 24 hours before you light a fire. The fire will darken the fresh cement to match the colour of the existing joints.

Repairing the Chimney Top

Renewing the flaunching. Working from scaffolding, rope the chimney pot securely to the stack to prevent it falling when the flaunching is removed. Wearing goggles to protect your eyes, chip away the cracked flaunching with a cold chisel and club hammer *(right)*, then brush off debris. Make sure that the pot is positioned centrally over the flue opening; cover any gaps between the edges of the pot and the flue walls by sliding pieces of slate under the pot. Then dampen the base of the pot and the top of the stack and trowel on mortar to form a sloping cap that extends from the edge of the brick to about 100 mm up the side of the pot. Keep the mortar damp for four days for proper curing.

If the chimney pot is cracked and needs replacing, work it loose when you have removed the flaunching. Even a small pot is surprisingly heavy: run a rope through it, tie it securely and lower the pot slowly to the ground.

Adding a dovecote cap. After removing the flaunching and chimney pot *(above)*, lay bricks at each corner of the chimney to a height of about 300 mm *(right, above)*. On a chimney whose top brick course overhangs the stack, the bricks must be set in from the edges so that they are directly over the main stack. Lay a bed of mortar over the top bricks of the stack, and allow the mortar to set overnight.

Mix a handful of brick chips into a small amount of mortar and trowel the mixture on top of the supports (the chips will keep the heavy dovecote cap from squeezing out the wet mortar). Set the cap—a flat slab of concrete cast slightly larger than the chimney—on the supports *(right, below)*. Check that the cap is horizontal using a spirit level, and adjust where necessary by tapping down the higher corners with a hammer.

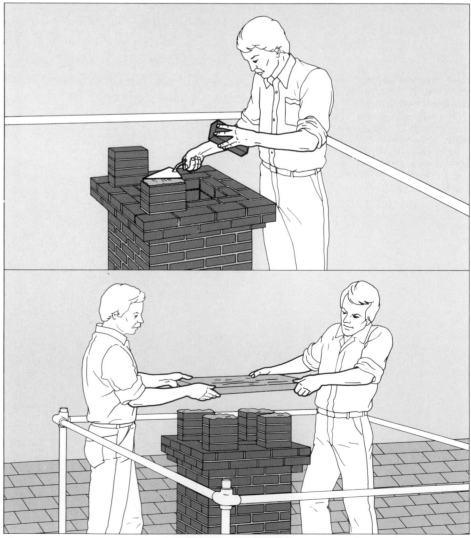

Raising the Hearth to Reduce the Opening

1 Measuring to reduce the opening. Tape a strip of aluminium foil across the top of the fireplace so that it overhangs the lintel and reduces the height of the opening by a distance equal to one course of firebricks. Then light a smoky fire or a smoke pellet. If smoke escapes into the room, lower the foil another brick course and repeat the test. When the smoking stops, leave the foil in place through several fires to be certain of its adjustment, then remove it.

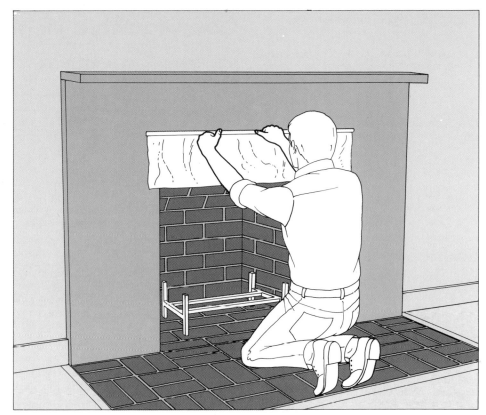

2 Laying firebricks. Lay up to three courses of firebricks over the back hearth, depending upon the outcome of the foil test *(Step 1)*. Set these bricks tightly together, but do not use mortar. To cut a brick to fit snugly against the back and sides of the fireplace, mark off the desired length with a ruler and pencil, then lay the brick on a stack of newspapers and cut along the line with a bolster and club hammer. While cutting firebricks, wear goggles to protect your eyes.

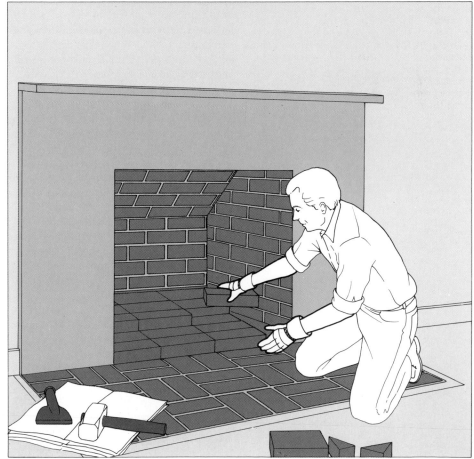

Coaxing More Heat from the System

If an old heating system is hopelessly incapable of maintaining comfort, a new system may be needed. But you can coax a surprising amount of additional heat from even the oldest systems by catching up on regular maintenance and repairs that were neglected over the years, and by installing a circulating pump to boost the flow of hot water.

Many of the commonest heating problems are caused by faulty radiators. Each radiator has two valves, the flow valve on the pipe that brings water to the radiator, and the return valve. These valves are usually located at the bottom of the radiator on opposite sides, although on old radiators the flow valve may be at the top. The smooth cover of the return valve is known as the lockshield, and the larger, knurled cover of the flow valve is known as the wheelhead. To check that the covers have been secured to the correct valves, start the system from scratch—the flow valve is on the pipe that heats up first, and should be covered by the wheelhead.

Leaking radiator valves can be simply resealed with PTFE tape, available from any plumbers' merchant *(opposite page, above)*. Trapped air that prevents a radiator from heating up properly can usually be released through the air vent at the top of the radiator, or by "pulling through" hot water to eliminate an air lock in the pipes *(opposite page, below)*. Corrosion inside radiators or pipes—often indicated by a need for frequent venting and a smell of rotten eggs as air escapes—should be treated with a proprietary corrosion inhibitor added to the feed and expansion tank according to the manufacturer's instructions.

If some radiators give off more heat than others, check that the system is properly balanced. Open all the radiator valves and allow the system to reach its usual operating temperature. Using a clip-on radiator thermometer, check the temperature of each radiator, then close down the hotter radiators by turning the return valves one complete revolution clockwise. Check the temperatures again after 15 minutes and repeat as necessary until all the radiators are approximately the same temperature.

If the rooms remain cold even when the radiators are functioning correctly, get a heating engineer to check the capacity of your boiler—radiators added on to an existing system by previous owners may require the installation of a new boiler. If only certain rooms remain cold, individual radiators can be replaced with new ones of a larger capacity—your heating contractor will advise you on the appropriate replacement for the size of your room. The new radiators can often be installed without altering the existing pipework.

Other methods by which you can improve the efficiency of your heating system involve the installation of new components. Replacing existing flow valves with thermostatic radiator valves (TRVs) will allow separate rooms to be heated to different temperatures *(page 72)*. And installing a pump to boost the flow of water will greatly improve the performance of an old heating system that relied on convection only for the circulation of warmth to the radiators *(page 73)*.

To enable your heating contractor to supply the correct pump for your needs, prepare a plan that includes room sizes, the number of radiators and the diameter of the pipe on which the pump is to be installed. On a heating system which has separate circuits for the radiators and the hot water cylinder, with four pipes connected to the boiler, the pump should be installed on the flow pipe leading from the boiler to the radiators. If the radiators and hot water cylinder are on the same circuit, with only two pipes connected to the boiler, seek professional advice. The pump can either be connected by a plug to a switched socket outlet, or wired by an electrician to a room thermostat or programmer.

Before installing new fittings, you must drain the system *(box, opposite page)*. The TRV and circulating pump on the following pages are fitted to copper pipe; specially designed TRVs are available for screwing on to the threaded ends of steel pipe, but before installing a pump on a steel pipework system, you must first replace the relevant section with copper pipe and transition fittings *(page 76)*.

Tuning a Troublesome Radiator

Resealing a valve. Remove both valve covers—these are usually held in place by a single central screw. Then close both valves by turning the spindles clockwise with the knurled flow valve cover. Using a spanner, turn the gland packing nut anticlockwise, easing it up the spindle to expose the stuffing box. Remove old packing with a screwdriver, then wrap two or three turns of twisted PTFE tape round the spindle base and pack it into the stuffing box with the screwdriver (*right*). Replace the gland nut and tighten it until the spindle is difficult to turn with the knurled valve cover, then loosen it until the spindle will turn with only slight resistance. Open both valves to their original positions; replace the covers.

If you have leaks round other screw-together parts of the valve, try tightening them. If it seems necessary, replace the valve using the plumbing techniques shown on page 72.

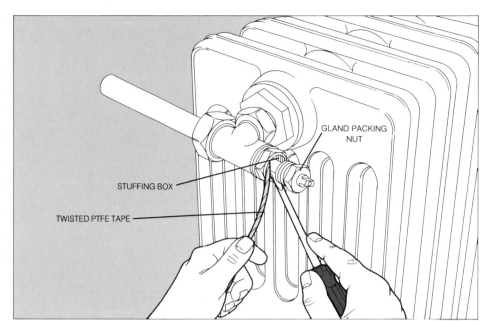

GLAND PACKING NUT

STUFFING BOX

TWISTED PTFE TAPE

Venting trapped air. To release air trapped at the top of a radiator, hold a container ready to catch water and turn the square spindle of the air vent anticlockwise with a venting key. When all the trapped air has been released and water spurts out, close the vent

To release air trapped in the pipes, close the flow valve and open the air vent. Allow about half a litre of water to run out into a container, then close the air vent and repeat the procedure with the flow valve open and the return valve closed. If the radiator still fails to heat up properly, close all the other radiator valves in the system and repeat the operation.

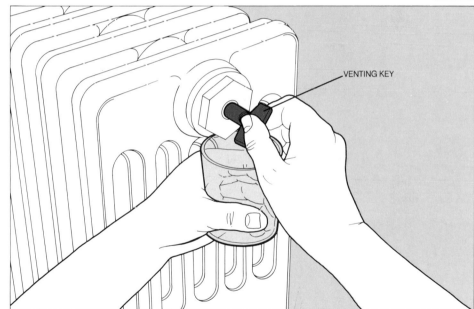

VENTING KEY

Draining and Refilling the System

Emptying the heating system of water is the essential first step in the installation of any new or replacement fittings, and involves the following procedures:

☐ Turn off the boiler—and the pump if one is fitted—and open all radiator valves throughout the system

☐ Shut off the water supply by closing the mains stop tap or by tying up the float arm of the feed and expansion tank.

☐ Attach a hose-pipe leading to an outside drain to the lowest drain-off tap in the system, and then open this drain-off tap with a spanner.

☐ When no more water runs out of the hose, open the air vents of the radiators on the top floor of the house. If water escapes, close the vents and wait a few minutes, then open them again.

☐ Leave the top-floor radiator vents open to allow any remaining water to percolate down and out of the hose. Follow the same procedure for the radiators on each floor of the house, working from the top downwards until no more water remains anywhere in the system.

After the new fitting has been installed in the system, close all radiator vents and restore the water supply. As the system is refilling, open each vent in turn and close it when the escaping water is free of air bubbles; start at the bottom of the house and work upwards.

Installing Thermostatic Radiator Valves

1 **Removing the old valve.** Drain the system and remove the wheelhead cover from the flow valve. Using an adjustable spanner, slacken the union and compression nuts that secure the valve to the radiator and the flow pipe. Remove the valve, then unscrew the union tailpiece and union nut from the radiator with a special valve key.

Cut through the compression ring on the flow pipe with a junior hacksaw, taking care not to damage the pipe, then pull both the nut and the ring off the pipe. If the ring is tightly compressed on the pipe, lever it off with a screwdriver.

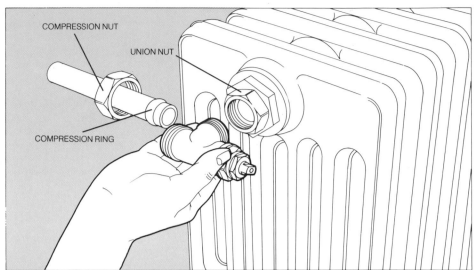

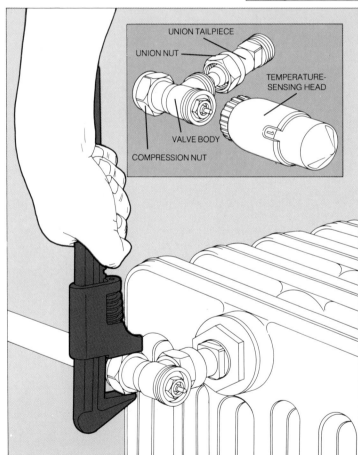

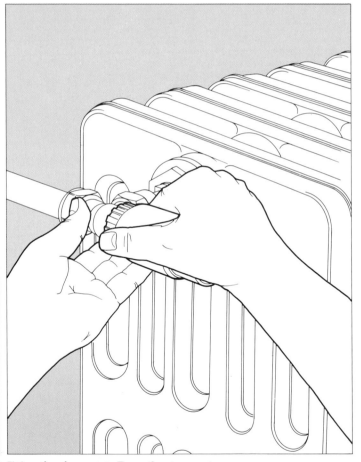

2 **Fitting the new valve.** Unscrew the temperature-sensing head from the TRV *(inset)*. Wind two or three turns of PTFE tape clockwise round the threads of the new union tailpiece, then unscrew it from the valve body and screw it to the radiator, tightening with an adjustable spanner. Slip the new compression nut and ring over the flow pipe and smear jointing compound on to the ring and the valve's union face. Hand-tighten the compression and union nuts on to their respective threads. Using a spanner, tighten first the compression nut *(above)* and then the union nut.

3 **Fitting the thermostat.** Turn the temperature-sensing head so that the highest number appears in the window, and attach it to the valve body by hand-tightening the large knurled nut under the head *(above)*. Following the same procedure, install TRVs on other radiators before refilling and starting up the system. Set the controls at first to their lowest reading, turning them up one number every hour until the rooms are at the required temperatures.

Adding a Circulating Pump

1 Breaking into the pipe. Having drained the system, secure the two pump valves to the pump using the washers and union nuts provided. Measure the distance between the tube stops inside the entry pipes of the pump valves *(inset, A)*. Mark this length in a convenient location on the flow pipe from the boiler to the radiators, noting the manufacturer's recommendations carefully if fitting to a horizontal flow pipe. Cut out the marked section of pipe with a hacksaw *(right)* or a tube cutter, and remove any burrs with a file.

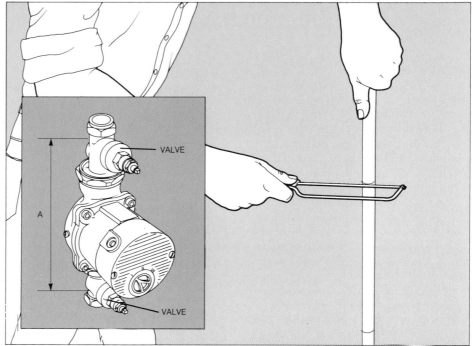

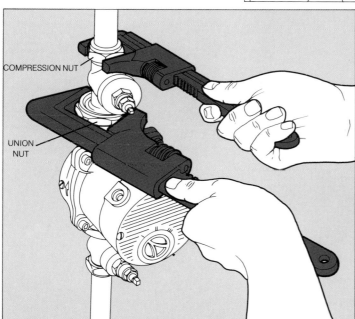

2 Mounting the pump. Remove the valves from the pump, and remove the compression nuts and rings from the valves. Slide one nut and ring over a sawn-off end of pipe, smear a small amount of jointing compound on the ring, and secure the valve by hand-tightening the nut. Fit the second valve in the same way. Position the pump with its directional arrow pointing away from the boiler. Use two large adjustable spanners to tighten the compression nuts and valve union nuts *(above)*, then open the pump valves fully with a spanner and refill the system. Check that the joints of the valves are watertight.

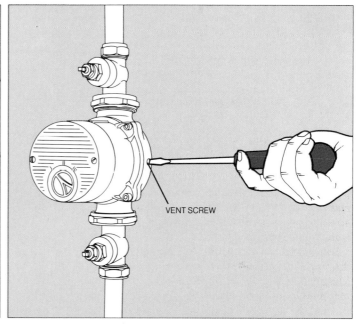

3 Venting the pump. Drain the system again to flush out any debris. If you are adding corrosion inhibitor, pour this into the feed and expansion tank as you refill and vent the system. Vent the pump by turning the vent screw anticlockwise one half-turn with a flat-bladed screwdriver *(above)*—when water escapes from under the screw head, retighten the screw. Wire the pump to a plug or to a room thermostat or programmer according to the manufacturer's instructions; if in doubt, get a professional electrician to make the wiring connections.

Renovating the Plumbing, a Little at a Time

Plumbing in many old houses is either obsolete or well on its way to becoming so. But the wholesale replacement of pipes is a big job that may mean having to tear into interior—and sometimes also exterior—walls. Unless your plans call for a major renovation of the house, you can extend the useful life of the plumbing you have for some time to come by patching it and renovating it piece by piece.

The most visible components of a plumbing system—the baths, sinks, washbasins and toilets—long outlast the pipes to which they are attached. The working parts of these fixtures—taps, toilet valves and the like—have remained basically the same for years. In most cases modern parts can be used to repair old equipment.

A far more serious problem in old plumbing systems is the deterioration of pipes. Although the lead supply pipes used in all houses prior to the Second World War do not corrode, they should be replaced by copper or CPVC when the occasion arises. The galvanized steel pipes that were widely used during the 1940s and 1950s last no more than 40 years before rust and corrosion rupture or clog them. Cast iron (the most common material for old drainpipes) has proved more durable, but it too can rust over the years. Steel piping eventually must be replaced, but the first leaks can be patched for the time being with the semi-permanent patches that are shown on the right and opposite: slip fittings for leaks in straight runs and fibreglass bandages for leaks round joints and fittings.

Leaks round the joints of cast-iron drainpipes should be recaulked with lead. Though this job calls for working with molten metal, the straightforward configuration of the joints makes it a rather simple task. Old cast-iron piping is connected with lead-caulked socket-and-spigot joints. Each pipe section is made with a bell-shaped hub at one end and a plain spigot at the other end.

To join pipe sections, the spigot of one piece is inserted into the hub of the next, the joint is packed with caulking yarn—an oil-impregnated, ropelike fibre—and the space over the yarn is filled with molten lead. The lead is then caulked—that is, pounded into the joint—so that it will form a tight seal. Small leaks in these joints sometimes can be repaired by simply tamp-

ing down and reshaping the soft lead with a hammer and chisel or by packing the joint with lead wool, a shredded lead product similar to steel wool.

If these simple measures are not sufficient to stop the leak, the leaking joint must be recaulked from scratch. You will need to hire a propane cylinder and torch, a cast-iron lead pot, an iron ladle, and yarning and caulking irons—offset, chisel-like tools that are used to pack down the yarn and lead. To recaulk a joint in a horizontal pipe, you also will need a fireproof joint runner to direct the molten lead, since you cannot pour it directly into the hub of a pipe in this position.

Wear long sleeves, gloves and safety goggles when you pour hot lead, and make sure the joint is completely dry before you begin. Any moisture in the hub will turn into steam when heated and will send molten lead splattering out of the joint. If the pipe seems at all damp, dry it by heating the outside with a propane torch. Stand behind the joint when pouring the lead and fill the cavity with one continuous pour.

Minor leaks in lead pipes can be successfully repaired by using a fibreglass bandage (opposite page). Alternatively, you can opt to replace leaky sections of lead pipe with copper by using a special compression transition fitting (page 77, below).

Simple Patches for Small Leaks

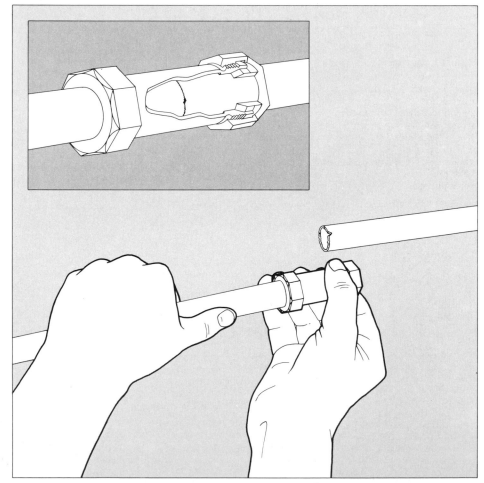

Installing a slip fitting. Using a hacksaw, cut through the pipe at the point of damage. Loosen the compression nuts on the fitting, pull one section of the pipe aside and slip the fitting on to it (above). Realign the two cut ends, centre the fit-

ting over the damaged area, then tighten the compression nut at each end of the fitting using two spanners (page 73, Step 2).

Use a steel fitting for leaks in steel pipes and a copper one for copper pipes.

Bandaging with fibreglass. To apply a fibreglass pipe patch, clean rust and flaking paint from around the area which is leaking, then mix about 50 ml of epoxy adhesive and butter it on the pipe 100 mm on either side of the damaged section, as well as over the damage, with a wooden spatula. Wrap a strip of glass fibre cloth around the pipe, embedding it in the adhesive. After the adhesive has hardened, spread a second layer over the glass fibre cloth.

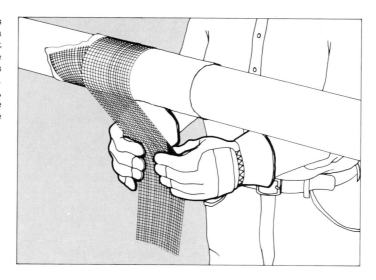

Recaulking a Joint in Cast-Iron Pipe

1 Packing the yarn. Prise the old lead and caulking yarn from round the leaking joint with a thin chisel or an old screwdriver. If it does not come out easily, heat the joint with a propane torch to soften the lead. Repack the hub with three full turns of yarn, ramming it down tightly with a hammer and an offset yarning iron designed for this purpose, leaving at least 25 mm of space at the top. Make sure that no strands of yarn reach into this space.

Light the propane torch and melt approximately 500 g of lead in the lead pot for every 25 mm of pipe diameter.

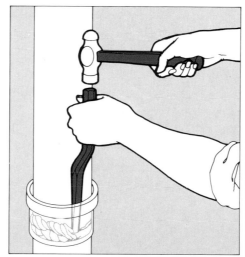

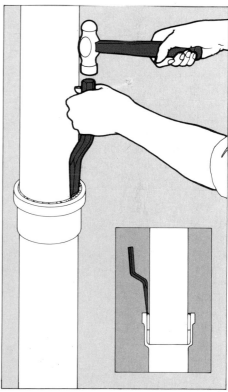

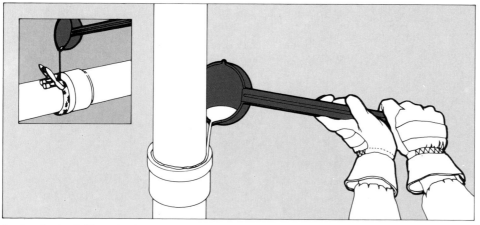

2 Pouring the lead. Heat the ladle in the flame, then use the ladle to push aside any dross or scum that has accumulated on top of the molten lead and dip out a ladleful. Pour the lead carefully over the yarn until it reaches the rim and curves slightly at the top. If the first ladleful does not fill the space, add more lead immediately. If you are pouring lead into a horizontal or pitched joint *(inset)*, clamp a fireproof joint runner snugly round the pipe and push it tightly against the hub in order to channel the lead into the hub. Keep the clamped ends on top; pour the lead between these ends. Wait until the lead has hardened before removing the runner.

3 Caulking the lead. After the lead has cooled for at least two minutes, position the tip of an inside caulking iron, its bevelled edge facing outwards, against the spigot, and hammer the lead firmly into the joint with a ball-pein hammer. Drive the lead down until it is flush with the rim.

To compress the joint, hold an outside caulking iron *(inset)* between the inside of the hub and the lead and tap it with a hammer until the top of the lead bulges slightly. (A caulking iron resembles a yarning iron, but is shorter and is bevelled.)

Replacing Lengths of Worn-Out Piping

If so much of the pipe in your house has deteriorated that simple repairs are impractical, you will have to cut out the bad sections and replace them with new. The first pipes to deteriorate—the horizontal sections—are, luckily, the easiest to reach. Vertical pipes, which run up through finished walls, are cleared continuously by gravity. Mineral precipitations and rust drop down and collect in the horizontal pipes below. These generally run through an unfinished cellar or beneath floorboards, where they are accessible.

Defective piping can be replaced by new pipes of identical material, but it may be better to make new installations with durable plastic or copper piping. Copper has until recently been the best replacement for steel or lead and is still favoured for hot water and central heating systems. Latterly, however, CPVC has become accepted as a material that is versatile, inexpensive and exceptionally easy to work with.

To splice copper or plastic pipe into a steel or lead system, you need one or two of the transition fittings described on the right. Once you install such fittings, you can join all the new piping together with standard couplings designed for that particular type of pipe.

Larger transition fittings are available to splice sections of plastic pipe into a cast-iron soil and waste system. But if you have only a short section of soil or waste pipe to replace, it might be more convenient to use cast-iron piping with special couplings known as no-hub fittings (page 78). Before you cut into a heavy vertical soil or waste pipe, make sure it is supported above. In most cases, such a plumbing stack is attached to horizontal branch pipes that are anchored to the house structure. However, if you must cut into a vent pipe that goes straight up through the roof and has no fixtures or branch piping, secure it with a pipe clamp braced by 100 by 50 mm timber, above the place where you will cut.

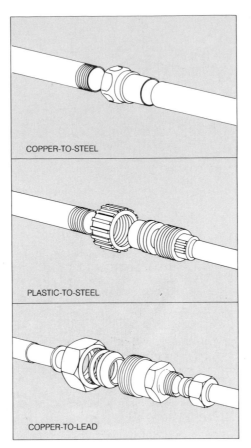

COPPER-TO-STEEL

PLASTIC-TO-STEEL

COPPER-TO-LEAD

Three fittings. These couplings make it possible to graft pipes of new materials to old. A copper-to-steel fitting (left, above) is made of copper or brass, with interior threads at the wider end to screw on to the existing steel pipe and a smooth bore at the other for soldering to unthreaded copper. A variation of this fitting, known as a boiler union, consists of three pieces: a threaded connector for the steel pipe, a smooth-bored connector for the copper and a nut to join the two which enables you to connect and disconnect pipes easily.

Plastic-to-steel coupling (left, centre), known as a union connector, consists of an internally threaded brass socket for the steel pipe, and an externally threaded plastic connector which is solvent-welded to the plastic pipe. The two connectors are clamped together with a large knurled nut. Union connectors are also available for joining copper to plastic and copper to steel.

For joining copper to lead pipes, use lead pipe connectors (left, below). Made of brass, these connectors attach with compression nuts and rings and have a copper liner which inserts into the lead pipe to prevent it from collapsing when the compression nut is tightened.

Where steel pipe is so deteriorated that the fitting must be hacksawed off, use the slip fitting shown on page 74 to join the unthreaded ends.

Four Ways to Connect Pipes

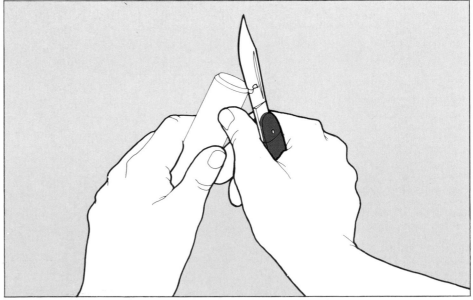

Solvent-welding a plastic connector. Use a penknife to bevel the outside of the plastic pipe end slightly so that it will not push the solvent cement from the joint. Paint the correct solvent cement for the type of plastic pipe you are using round the outside of the pipe and push the pipe into the plastic fitting, twisting the parts to spread the cement evenly. As you do this, enough cement should be forced out of the fitting for a smooth bead to form round the joint. If this does not happen, you must pull the pipe and fitting apart immediately—the cement will harden in seconds. Apply a thicker coat of cement and join the parts again.

Soldering a copper connector. Use steel wool or emery cloth to scour the inside of the fitting and the outside of the pipe as far as it will go into the fitting. Dry the pipes and fittings thoroughly. Apply a thin coat of soldering flux to both surfaces with a small brush. Slip the copper pipe into the connector and heat the pipe and fitting with a butane or propane torch. When both the fitting and the pipe are hot enough to melt the solder on contact, remove the torch and touch the solder to the joint between the two. Feed solder into the joint until a bead appears round the rim. Whenever possible, do the soldering on a workbench that is protected by a fireproof pad. If you must solder pipes in place near any wooden framing in walls, tape a fireproof pad behind the work and keep a fire extinguisher handy.

Because heat from soldering can damage traditional packing, wrap two or three turns of PTFE tape round the threaded end of the pipe before screwing on the fitting.

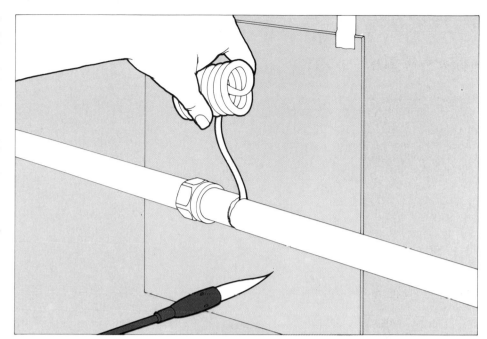

Installing a plastic-to-steel connector. Slide the knurled nut well up on to the steel pipe, then wind two or three turns of PTFE tape clockwise round the threads of the steel pipe. Screw on the internally threaded steel connector and tighten it with an adjustable spanner. Solvent-weld the plastic connector to the plastic pipe *(opposite page, below)*. Align the steel and plastic connectors, place the rubber washer between them and tighten the knurled nut on to the plastic connector, using an adjustable wrench to make the final turn *(right)*.

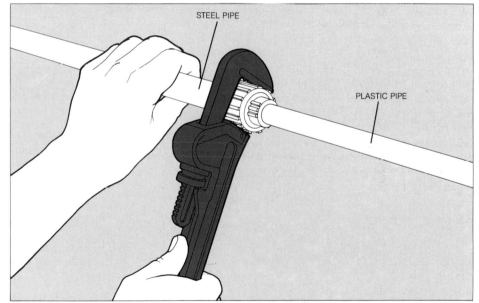

STEEL PIPE

PLASTIC PIPE

Installing a "lead" fitting. After cutting off the old lead pipe with a hacksaw, smooth the inside and outside of the cut end with a sharp knife. Slip the larger compression nut, washer and compression ring over the end of the lead pipe, then push the copper liner into the lead pipe until its flange stops against the pipe end. Slip the body of the fitting over the lead pipe *(right)* until its tube stop meets the flange of the liner, then hand-tighten the larger compression nut on to the body. Slip the smaller compression nut and ring over the end of the copper pipe, push the copper pipe into the fitting, then hand-tighten the compression nut on to the fitting. Finally, use two adjustable spanners, turning against each other, to tighten both the compression nuts.

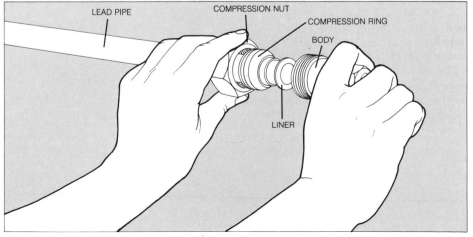

LEAD PIPE   COMPRESSION NUT
                                    COMPRESSION RING
                                    BODY

                        LINER

Replacing a Section of Cast-Iron Pipe

1 Cutting the iron pipe. Wrap the chain of a pipe cutter round the pipe and tighten the knob that holds the cutter in place. Then work the tool back and forth until the pipe separates. Cut through the pipe above and below the damaged section and pull the cut piece out. Stuff toilet paper into the lower cut end of the stack to prevent sewer gas from escaping. Use the pipe cutter to cut a new section of pipe 20 mm shorter than the distance between the cut ends.

2 Replacing the pipe section. Slip the flexible neoprene sleeves of a no-hub fitting over the cut ends of the existing pipe and slide the steel clamping straps on to the new section of pipe. Then fold the sleeves back on themselves, push the new section of pipe into place and unfold the sleeves so that the joints are covered.

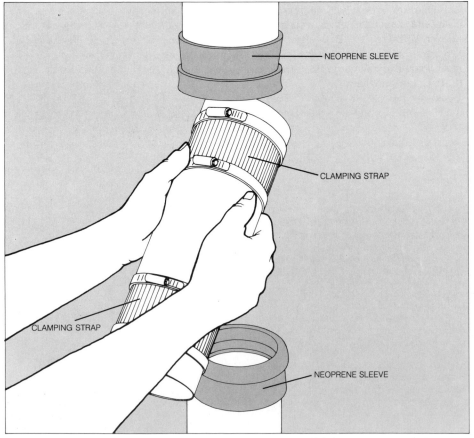

NEOPRENE SLEEVE

CLAMPING STRAP

CLAMPING STRAP

NEOPRENE SLEEVE

3 **Assembling the joint.** Slide the steel straps over the neoprene sleeves. Tighten the straps with a socket spanner or with the special plumber's T-handled torque-wrench socket tool illustrated on the right. After a week, check the joint and re-tighten the clamps if necessary.

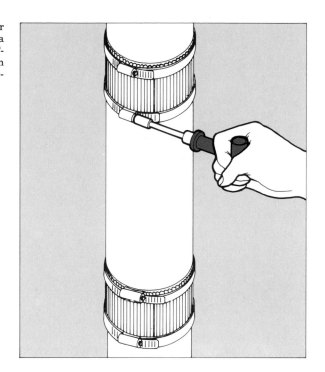

Making the Drains Flow Freely

Generally, a single clogged waste can be unblocked easily with a plunger, a plumber's auger or even a bent coat hanger. But if there is more than one fixture draining slowly, the trouble will most probably be found to lie in the main drain or its branches.

First establish how far down your system the obstruction is lodged. A blockage in the main soil and waste stack will affect only those fixtures that enter the pipe above it; fixtures below the blockage will drain normally. Look for easy access to the pipe within the house; you may find a cleaning eye located on the soil stack, from which you can auger out the obstruction. If there is no cleaning eye, or if all the ground-floor fixtures are blocked, however, you will have to work from the inspection chamber situated outside the house *(page 17)*.

The traditional, and still the simplest, tool for clearing a main drain is a set of drain rods, short sections of cane which screw together to form a long flexible probe. These are available from tool-hire shops, along with a number of different attachments which enable you to cope with various obstructions.

Working at first with a rubber plunger fitted to the head, push the rod back and forth in the drain, adding more sections until you clear the drain or encounter the obstruction. Dislodge a stubborn blockage with a metal corkscrew head. When the drain is clear of obstructions, flush it out with plenty of water.

Finally, wash and disinfect the drain rods and the head.

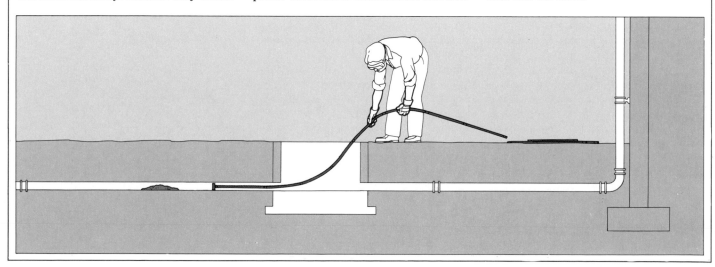

Safe Circuits for the Household Wiring

Your initial survey of the wiring *(page 16)* will reveal major faults or the presence of an ageing electrical system that must be professionally rewired at the very earliest opportunity. However, even if the house has been recently rewired you will invariably have to repair superficial damage to fittings, ensure that your appliances can be accommodated on the existing circuits, and add new sockets and switches.

Repairing damaged sockets is quite a straightforward procedure *(opposite page)*. Surface-mounted fittings are particularly vulnerable to damage and may need replacing entirely; in the case of flush-mounted fittings, whose mounting boxes are recessed into the wall, you will usually have to replace the face plate only. If a damaged socket is of the unswitched type, replace it with a safer, switched model.

To check the safety of the electrical circuits, first inspect the fuses inside the consumer unit. The capacity of each circuit is determined by the thickness of its wire and is guarded by a fuse that prevents more current from entering the circuit than its wires can safely carry. If your consumer unit contains traditional rewirable fuses, which consist of short lengths of wire secured between two screw terminals, make sure each fuse has the right rating for its circuit by comparing the existing fuse wire with a wire of the correct rating *(opposite page, above)*. If someone has attempted to upgrade the system by taking the dangerous short cut of substituting a heavier gauge fuse wire for the one specified on the fuse case, replace the substituted wire with wire of the correct rating. (The modern cartridge-type fuses, which contain colour-coded cartridges instead of fuse wire, come in different sizes according to their current rating, making it impossible to insert a cartridge of incorrect rating.)

The circuits must also be checked to ensure that your electrical equipment—washing machines, heating units, power tools and kitchen appliances—will not cause overloading. Make a map of all the circuits in the house by removing the fuses one at a time and observing which outlets and fixtures are affected. Add together the wattage—this is printed or stamped on appliances or bulbs—connected to each circuit and divide by 240 to estimate amperes. Compare these figures to the amperage on the fuse for each circuit. The total amperage for appliances that will be used simultaneously on one circuit must not exceed the amperage specified for the circuit. If possible, redistribute loads from heavily used circuits to lightly used ones.

Modern consumer units may be fitted with individual switches for each circuit—known as miniature circuit breakers or MCBs—which serve the same purpose as fuses. When an overload occurs, a tripping mechanism automatically switches off the power to that circuit. A similar device, the high-sensitivity residual current circuit breaker or RCCB *(opposite page, left)* switches off the power in the event of your touching a live wire, and should be installed to protect all sockets or circuits supplying appliances that are used outdoors.

Having carried out the above procedures to ensure the safety of your wiring, you will probably wish to make some adjustments to the number and location of the existing sockets and switches to meet your specific needs. Perhaps the two most common improvements to the wiring of an old house are installing a second switch for a light, and adding a new socket outlet. Techniques for routing new cable and for making electrical connections are described on the following pages

In Australia and New Zealand all work on electrical installations must be carried out by a qualified electrician.

Essential Safeguards to Protect Against Shocks

Electric shock is always dangerous and can be fatal. Before working on any electrical device, you must make absolutely sure that no current is flowing in or near it. A convenient way to double-check is with a mains-tester screwdriver *(right)*. Between the blade of this inexpensive tool and a metal cap on top of its hollow plastic handle are a high-value resistor, a spring and a small neon bulb.

Before working on any electrical fitting or appliance, turn off the power at the consumer unit and remove the fuse that protects the circuit. Test that the fitting is not working, then place a finger over the metal cap of the screwdriver and touch the blade to all wires, terminals and other metal parts. If the bulb glows, current is still flowing. Find the correct fuse and remove it; if you cannot do this, call an electrician.

Note: before beginning work, check that the screwdriver itself is operating correctly by testing it on one of the power points of a light fitting.

Protect yourself further by following these additional safety rules:

☐ Never touch any plumbing or gas pipes while you work with electricity. Make sure the floor is dry, or stand on a piece of dry chipboard.

☐ Label the consumer unit with a notice so that no one will restore power to a circuit while you are working.

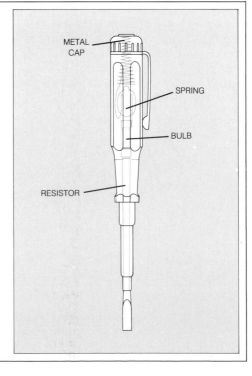

METAL CAP

SPRING

BULB

RESISTOR

The Residual Current Circuit Breaker

Although modern wiring regulations have greatly reduced the risk of accidental shocks, many situations remain potentially dangerous. High-powered tools and metal-surfaced appliances, especially if they are to be operated in damp conditions, pose the greatest threat. When a fault develops in the insulation of an appliance, electricity will seek the quickest route to earth. With moisture reducing resistance to electrical current, that route can be a fatal one—through you, the operator.

The residual current circuit breaker, or RCCB for short, is wired to a consumer unit, power circuit or individual socket outlet. It will cut off the current when earth leakage creates an imbalance between the inward and outward flow of electricity. Wiring regulations now require that any circuit or socket used for outdoor electrical equipment be protected by an RCCB that will switch off the power when earth leakage exceeds 30 milliamps (mA). It is well worth extending this protection so as to cover washing machines, irons and any portable appliance.

The RCCB shown below can protect an entire socket outlet circuit; other models are available to suit your safety needs, including ones that are incorporated in individual socket outlets.

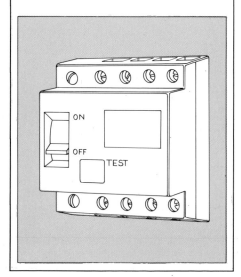

Checking and Replacing Fuse Wire

Rewiring a fuse. Remove a fuse from the consumer unit and compare the size of the wire already in the fuse to a wire of the appropriate rating on a fuse wire card. If the two wires do not match up, unscrew the terminals, remove the old wire and thread a wire of the correct amperage through the fuse. Wind the free end clockwise round the terminal, tighten the screw, then gently tighten the wire to eliminate any slack and connect it to the second terminal in the same way. Cut off the excess wire and plug the fuse back into the consumer unit.

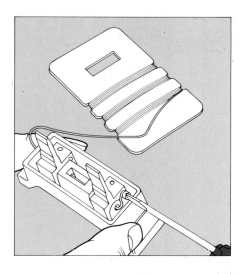

Replacing a Damaged Socket

1 Removing the old socket. Turn off the power at the mains and remove the appropriate fuse. Unscrew the socket face plate and disconnect the single conductors or twisted pairs of conductors from the terminals, then unscrew the damaged mounting box from the wall and pull it free of the cables. With a screwdriver, knock out a hole in the back of the new mounting box to receive the cable.

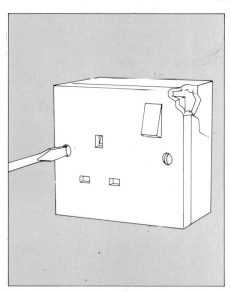

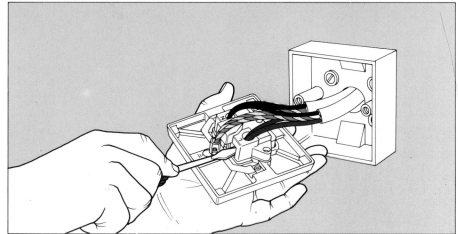

2 Wiring and fitting the new socket. Feed the cables through the hole in the back of the mounting box. Place the box against the wall, line up the fixing holes with the plugged holes already in the wall and screw the box in position. Connect the conductors to the terminals at the back of the new socket face plate: red to L, black to N, and green and yellow to E or ⊕. Fit the face plate over the box, making sure that the conductors are not cramped, and screw it in place. Restore the power and test the new socket with a socket tester or an appliance.

Routing New Cable

Extending your wiring to supply a new socket outlet or switch involves running lengths of cable from a suitable point in your power or lighting circuit to the new fitting. For safety reasons, the cable must be properly shielded from damage, never just laid loose under a carpet or clipped to a skirting board.

The simplest method of installing cable is to run it through plastic trunking mounted on the surface of walls and ceilings. For the living quarters of a house, however, where you will wish to conceal your wiring, the techniques shown here will provide a more satisfactory solution.

Concealing cable in plaster. Carefully outline a chase wide enough to receive the oval PVC conduit that will house your cable. Using a bolster and club hammer, cut away within the outline *(below, left)*, removing plaster to a depth of about 15 mm; where necessary, use a narrow cold chisel or old auger to extend the chase behind skirting boards. Cut a length of conduit to fit the chase and secure it in position with cable clips every 300 mm, then feed your cable through the conduit. Plaster over the conduit to just below surface level *(below, right)*. Allow this plaster to dry, then level the chase carefully with a cellulose filler and sand the surface smooth.

Note: cut a chase vertically or horizontally from a fitting, never diagonally. The concealed cable can then be easily located during subsequent repairs or improvements.

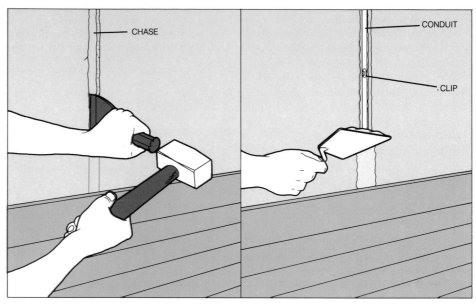

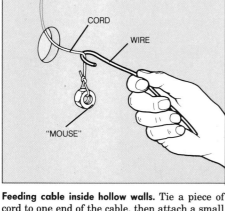

Feeding cable inside hollow walls. Tie a piece of cord to one end of the cable, then attach a small heavy weight—a "mouse"—to the free end of the cord. Working from an attic or from between floors, lower the mouse inside the hollow wall down to the opening you have made for a switch or socket. Get a helper to pull the cord through the opening with a hooked wire, and carefully draw down the cable *(above)*.

Where a nogging in a partition wall prevents this technique from working, drill holes on either side of the nogging and fish out the cable. Then cut a chase in the plasterboard over the nogging and chisel a groove to take the cable. Feed the cable into the wall beneath the obstruction and plaster over the chase.

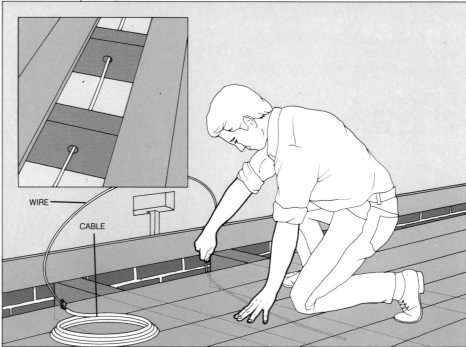

Running cable under floorboards. Where possible, route cable under floorboards in the same direction as joists. Carefully prise up the boards next to the wall at each side of the room; if the boards are tongued and grooved, first split between them with a bolster. Then cut a length of stiff galvanized steel wire, long enough to span the floor. Hook one end of it to the cable and push the other end under the boards from one gap to the other *(above)*. Pull the cable under the floor and up through the second gap.

Where your wiring must cross joists, drill holes for the cable at least 50 mm below the top of each joist *(inset)*. In an unfloored attic, cable can be laid across joists but in such cases must be protected by steel capping.

A Second Switch for an Essential Light

A bedside switch for a ceiling light, or an upstairs switch for a hall light at the foot of a steep staircase, can add to your comfort and your safety. Adding a second switch to an existing single-switch system involves three straightforward steps: running a length of cable between the existing switch and the location you have chosen for a second switch, replacing the former one-way switch with a two-way switch and installing a new two-way switch

The cable that connects switches in a two-way system has three conductors and an earth wire instead of the more conventional two plus earth. Their colours are different too: red, yellow and blue, instead of the usual red and black. Always use cable that is at least $1\,mm^2$, and sleeve the exposed end of the earth wire with green and yellow PVC.

If the switchplate on your existing switch has three terminals (marked L1, L2 and C) instead of the usual two, there is no need to replace it with a new switchplate. Your second switch can be either surface-mounted or flush-mounted. The surface-mounted second switch shown here is fixed to a partition wall with screws and toggle bolts; for flush-mounting on a partition wall, you will need a mounting box with specially designed flanges. A box flush-mounted in a masonry wall must be set in a recess *(page 84)*.

Installing a Two-Way Switch System

1 Adapting the existing box. Prepare your route for the three-core and earth cable between the planned location of the new switch and that of the existing switch *(opposite page)*. Turn off the power and remove the lighting circuit fuse, then unscrew the switchplate from the old mounting box and disconnect the wires. Using an old screwdriver, knock out one of the metal discs in the mounting box to provide access for the new cable *(right)*. Fit a rubber bush to the new hole *(inset)*, bring the cable to the box and feed one end through the access hole.

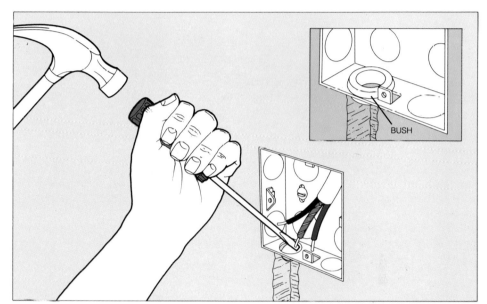

BUSH

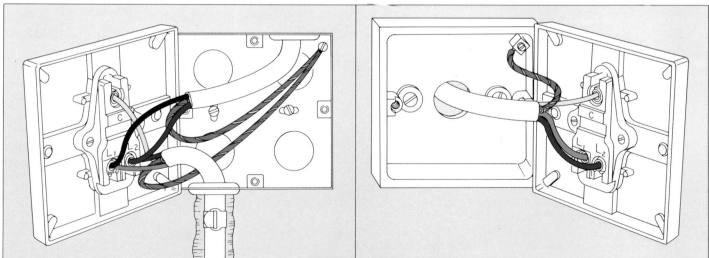

2 Wiring the switches. At the existing mounting box *(above, left)*, connect the wires of the two cables to a new two-way switchplate. Twist the ends of the two red conductors together and screw them into terminal L2; likewise connect the blue and black conductors to L1. Connect the single yellow conductor to the terminal marked "C" or "common". Sleeve the earth wires in green and yellow PVC and connect them to the earth terminal in the box. At the new box *(above, right)*, punch the appropriate access hole; fit a metal box with a rubber bush. Feed the three-core and earth cable into the hole and screw the box to the wall. Connect the red wire to terminal L2, the blue to L1 and the yellow to "C" or "common". Sleeve the earth wire and connect it to the earth terminal. Screw the switchplates to the boxes, replace the circuit fuse and restore the power.

New Sockets Where You Need Them

An old house is unlikely to be equipped with an adequate number of socket outlets, and in exactly the locations you require. Fortunately, installing new sockets is a relatively straightforward job.

Look first for simple solutions to inadequate wiring. Any single socket in the house, for instance, can be replaced with a double one without further investigation into your wiring system. The wires you find behind the single socket, whether they come from one, two or three cables, will be connected to the new double socket in the same way—red to the L terminal, black to N and earth to the terminal marked E or ⏚.

A new socket in a new location involves laying cable *(page 82)* and requires a basic understanding of how your power sockets are wired. Since 1947, sockets have been located along what is known as a ring final circuit. The circuit cable feeds into the first socket, then continues out and along to the next and so on until it eventually leads back to the consumer unit. From each socket on a ring final circuit you may run a cable for one additional socket, which is then said to be on a "spur".

First find a convenient socket from which to run your spur, then remove the switchplate and check that there are two cables wired to the terminals. Three cables indicate that a spur already runs from that socket; one cable means that the socket is itself on a spur. Since earlier wiring regulations permitted more than one socket on a spur, check the sockets adjacent to the one you have chosen. If both have two cables, you can assume that your socket is safely situated on the ring final circuit.

Each new socket you install may be either single or double, but bear in mind two regulations: the total number of spur sockets may not exceed the number of sockets located on the ring final circuit, and the floor area served by any one ring final circuit must not be greater than 100 square metres. If in doubt about where to install a spur, consult an electrician.

Adding a New Socket on a Spur

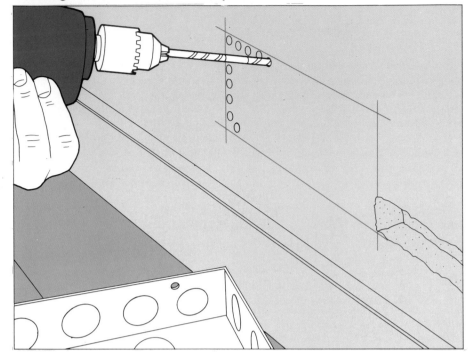

1 **Preparing the wall for a new socket.** Having prepared your cable route, switch off the power at the mains and remove the circuit fuse. Place the mounting box of the new socket in position against the wall and draw round it with a pencil. Drill holes just inside the outline to the depth of the box; a piece of tape on the bit serves as a useful depth gauge. Then, using a bolster and club hammer, knock out the plaster and masonry to the depth of the drill holes.

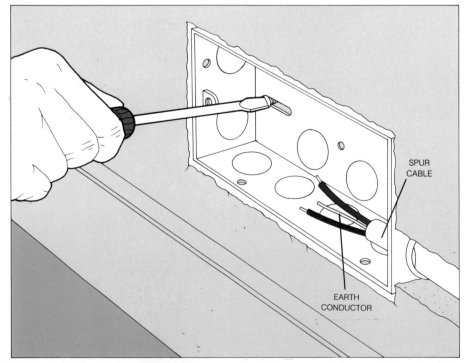

SPUR CABLE

EARTH CONDUCTOR

2 **Fixing the new box in place.** Punch out an access hole in the box to accept the new cable, and fit this hole with a rubber bush. Place the box in its recess and mark the location for mounting screws on the wall; then remove the box, drill holes for screws and insert wall plugs. Feed the cable through the access hole, refit the box and secure it to the recess with screws. Sleeve the bare earth conductor with green and yellow PVC, leaving 5 to 10 mm exposed at its end.

3 Adapting the existing socket. Unscrew the existing switchplate from its mounting box and disconnect the three pairs of matching wires from their terminals. Punch out an access hole in the box, fit it with a rubber bush and feed through the spur cable. Slide green and yellow sleeving over any bare earth conductors.

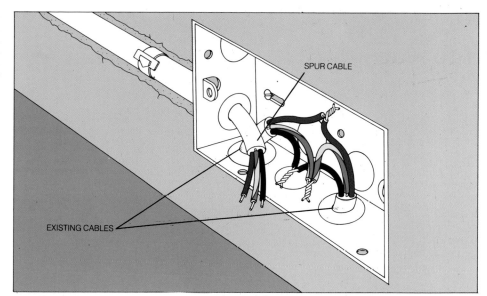

SPUR CABLE

EXISTING CABLES

4 Rewiring the existing socket. Match up the like-coloured wires from the spur cable with those of the existing cable. Screw each group of three wires into its respective terminal in the back of the switchplate—red to L, black to N and earth to E or ⏚. Replace the switchplate, taking care not to crush any wires.

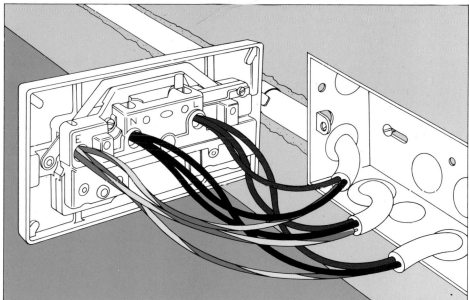

5 Wiring the new socket. Attach the red, black and sleeved green and yellow earth wires to the terminals marked respectively L, N and E or ⏚ on the back of the switchplate. Screw the switchplate to the box. Restore the power and test both old and new sockets before permanently fixing the cable and making good with plaster.

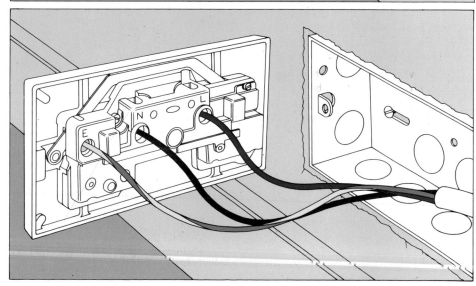

4 First Aid for Structural Faults

Support for a timber ground floor. Mortared into its housing in a basement wall, a new timber joist provides rigid support for old floorboards above. Resting against the wall are the adjustable steel props used to jack up the joist to the correct height and eliminate any sag in the floor.

Faults in the structure of an old house are seldom as threatening as they seem when you first notice them. Of course, all major flaws require fixing, but many can wait years, if necessary, for repair. A floor may sag, a rafter may weaken or a wall may remain cracked for decades without threatening the overall stability of a house. For the sake of both your comfort and your finances, it makes good sense to list the necessary repairs in order of priority, and tackle them accordingly.

Deterioration in the roof covering—slipped or broken tiles or slates, leaks in the flashing between roofing slopes or between roofing material and masonry—and broken gutters and downpipes need prompt attention to prevent water soaking into the fabric of the house. Repairs for these faults involve working at a considerable height, and safety is paramount. Ladders must be set on firm, level ground, and fitted with stays to hold them away from overhanging eaves, or hooks that clamp over the ridge tiles on a roof. For extensive work on the roof, hire scaffolding or a scaffold tower.

Although exterior walls are generally the least trouble-prone structural part of a house, continual exposure to the elements inevitably takes its toll. The sand and lime mortar commonly used to bond stones or bricks in the walls of old houses was more flexible and less likely to crack than modern mortar strengthened with cement, but over time it may crumble and become eroded. Cracks in rendering and timber cladding must be sealed before water can seep in through them, and crumbling plaster on internal walls and ceilings—a typical result of such penetration—must be hacked off and replaced.

Rising damp in the exterior walls, as distinct from penetrating damp, is caused by water soaking up from the ground. All houses built since the 1920s should incorporate a damp-proof course—a layer of impermeable material built into the walls just above ground level—but settlement of the house foundations may have caused a traditional DPC of slate to crack or deteriorate. A new DPC can be installed by injecting a chemical fluid with hired equipment.

Where regular maintenance has been neglected, rot will almost certainly have developed in joist ends, window frames and other timbers. Dry rot, which attacks timber in poorly ventilated indoor spaces, is the more serious form—it can spread rapidly to masonry and other materials, and requires prompt professional treatment. Wet rot, which attacks timber with a higher moisture content both outdoors and indoors, can be treated by replacing the affected timbers and repairing the source of damp. The other major enemy of timber in old houses is woodworm, a term used to describe the larvae of various wood-boring insects, which can be treated with an insecticidal fluid.

These problems may seem daunting, but it is unlikely that a single house will be affected by all of them. Age, construction and location are variable factors, and often time has left old houses strong, lacking only a new rafter or some fresh mortar to make them whole again.

Making the Roof Watertight

The simplest roof problems to detect and remedy—and problems that potentially endanger all other systems in the house—are leaks in the broad expanse of the roof itself. Only a bit harder to find and fix are leaks under flashing—the metal strips sealing joints where roof slopes converge or where roof meets wall or chimney.

It is usually easy to spot slates, tiles or wooden shingles that are cracked, rotten, or missing altogether. If large areas of the roof need attention, or if the damage is so severe that complete reroofing is required, you should call in a professional. However, smaller areas of three or four damaged units can be simply repaired by installing replacement tiles, shingles or slates (pages 89–90). If you find that the timber battens beneath the missing or damaged units have been damaged by water penetration, remove the affected sections by sawing at a 45-degree angle directly above the rafters and nail new sections in place.

Leaks in vulnerable places, such as the valleys between roof slopes and the joints round dormer walls, pipes and vents, can be difficult to pinpoint. Examine flashing to see that it is unbroken and that its edges are properly sealed. From inside an unfinished attic, look for daylight and mark where it enters by poking a wire through.

In an emergency, leaks in flashing or roof fabric can be stopped by brushing or spraying on a proprietary liquid rubber preparation. Some of these sealing compounds are formulated for use in wet conditions, so you can actually repair a leak during a downpour—do not, however, attempt to climb on to a pitched roof during wet weather. More permanent repairs to cracks and small holes in flashing can be made with self-adhesive flashing tape of heavy-duty aluminium foil or polythene backed with a bitumen-based adhesive, sold in rolls of various widths. To ensure a perfect seal, apply a bitumen primer before sticking on the tape (page 91).

If damage to valley flashing is extensive, the entire section of flashing must be replaced—a complex task involving lifting large numbers of tiles and replacing the corroded metal lining with a new one. This is a job best left to a specialist.

Where a roof abuts a chimney stack or wall, the flashing is usually fixed into the mortar joints of the masonry. Repair flashing that has worked loose by raking out the old crumbling mortar and repointing the joints with new mortar.

You may also have to resort to mortar and trowel if ridge tiles—the specially shaped tiles mounted on the apex of the roof—have become loose (below). Prompt repair is essential, not only to guard against water penetration but because loose ridge tiles could become very dangerous if dislodged by storm-force winds.

Once you have determined what repairs your roof requires, gather the materials and tools you need. A special slate ripper is handy for cutting nails concealed beneath slates, tiles or shingles. Flashing tape, bitumen primer, liquid rubber and new flashing may all be on your shopping list. New flashing may be of traditional materials—lead or copper—but aluminium, zinc, laminated bitumen-asbestos and bituminous felt are also available. Try to avoid joining different metals to eliminate the possibility of galvanic corrosion, which sometimes occurs when dissimilar metals touch each other.

Finally, always be careful when you work on a roof. Make sure it is completely dry, and wear non-slip shoes. Let professionals do the work on very steep roofs. Except on flat roofs or those with the shallowest of pitches, use a climbing support such as a ladder stabilized with special ladder hooks that clamp over the ridge. As an alternative, a roof ladder or "duckboard"—a plank with horizontal cleats attached—improves your footing and distributes your weight on slippery, brittle slates and tiles when it is anchored firmly at the peak with ladder hooks. Protect passers-by from the risk of falling tools or materials by cordoning off the area.

Rebedding a Ridge Tile

Setting the tile in mortar. Carefully lift off the loose ridge tile and clear away the old mortar from the ridge of the roof with a club hammer and bolster. Carry the ridge tile down to the ground and chip off the mortar with the edge of a bricklayer's trowel. Prepare fresh mortar by blending 1 part cement and 4 parts sand with just enough water to make a stiff mix.

Dampen the top course of roof tiles and apply the new mortar to form a bed about 50 mm wide on both sides of the ridge, following the lines of the old mortar. Mortar the ends of the adjacent ridge tiles and set the cleaned ridge tile in position (left). Tap the tile gently with the trowel handle to level it, then smooth down the joints at each side and along the bottom.

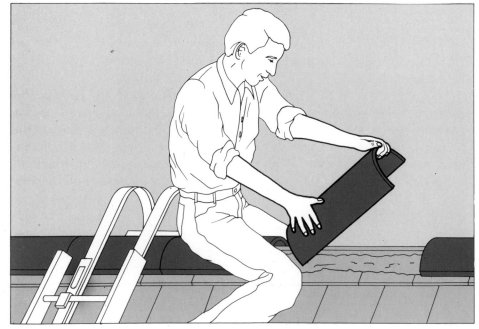

Replacing Damaged Slates

1 Using a slate ripper. Slide the arrow-shaped head of a slate ripper under a broken slate and hook one of the cutting notches round one of the two holding nails. Cut the nail with a sharp downward hammer blow on the raised handle of the slate ripper. Repeat on the other nail. If you do not have a slate ripper, wear gloves and use a long hacksaw blade to cut the nails.

After cutting the nails, slide out the broken piece without disturbing adjacent slates.

2 Securing a replacement slate. Cut a "tingle", a 50 mm-wide strip of metal flashing that is long enough to extend several centimetres under the course above and about 25 mm below the replacement slate. Nail it to a batten through the joint between the two slates lying underneath the replacement *(below, left)*, using nails of the same metal. Slide the new slate into position and bend the projecting tab up and over the bottom edge of the new slate to fix it in position *(below, right)*.

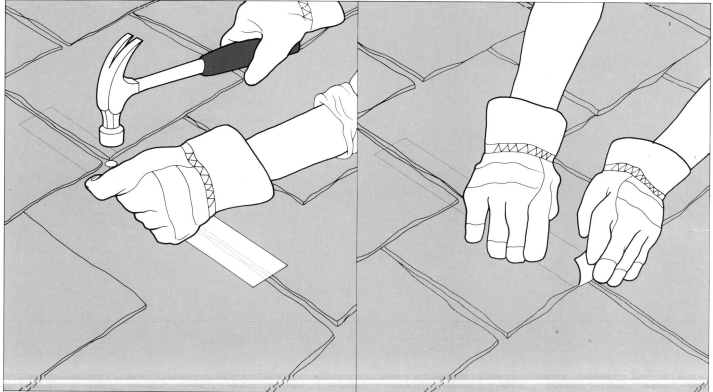

Replacing Tiles

Wedging and lifting. To remove a tile, cut two wedges from 100 by 25 mm timber and use them to raise the tiles in the row above the damaged one; if the tiles have an interlocking profile, also wedge up the tile to the left of the damaged one. Take hold of the damaged tile *(right)* and lift it so that the nibs—the hook-like projections found on the underside of the tile at the top—are free of the batten, then remove the tile. To fit the new tile, hook the nibs over the batten and remove the timber wedges.

To remove a tile nailed to a batten—usually in one in every four courses of tiles—first remove the upper tiles to reveal the nail, then pull the nail out with pincers or a claw hammer. Nail a new tile in place and replace the upper tiles.

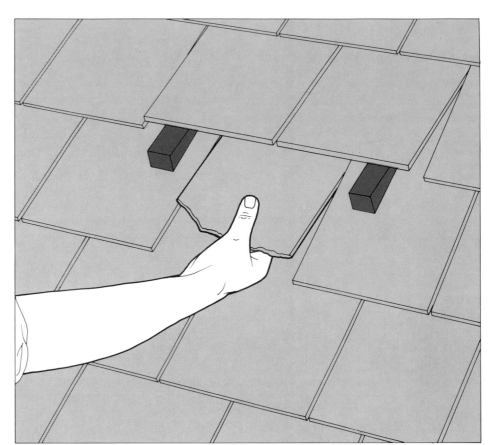

Fitting New Wooden Shingles

Hammering the shingle home. After removing all the remnants of the damaged shingle—splitting it with a chisel and cutting the holding nails if necessary—use a hammer and block to tap a new shingle into position. Cut the replacement shingle 12 mm narrower than the space it will fill to allow for expansion. If the new shingle is too long, pull it out and trim the excess length from the thin end. When the shingle is in line with the others in its course, secure it with two galvanized roofing nails just below the edge of the overlying course. Cover the nail heads with non-hardening mastic.

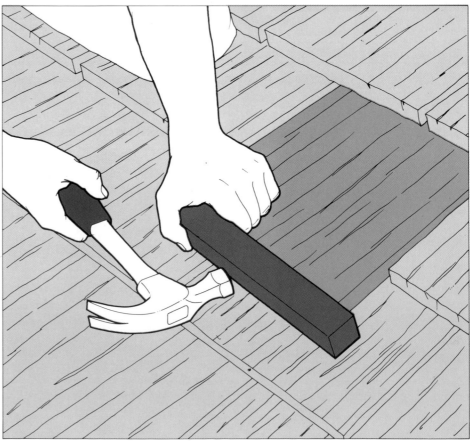

Repairs for Leaks in Flashing

Resetting flashing in a mortar joint. If flashing is loose where it is set into a masonry wall or chimney, pull out the upper part of the flashing—the apron—and rake the old mortar out of the joint to a depth of 35 mm, using a club hammer and bolster (*right*). Push the lip of the apron flashing back into the raked-out joint and hold it in place with wedges made from folded-over strips of the same flashing material (*inset*) or from hardwood. Repoint the joint (*page 100*) with a mortar mix of 1 part cement to 4 of sand.

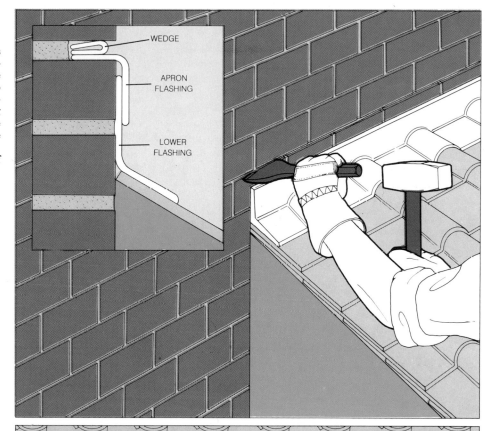

Patching with flashing tape. Clean the flashing round the damaged area thoroughly with wire wool and wipe clean. Paint on a coat of bitumen primer, extending 75 mm all round the tear, and leave to dry for an hour. Cut a length of self-adhesive flashing tape with a trimming knife to make a patch large enough to cover the damaged area and extend for 50 mm all round it. Peel off the backing paper and press the tape down into place, using a wooden wallpaper-seam roller or cloth pad to smooth out any air bubbles trapped beneath the patch (*inset*).

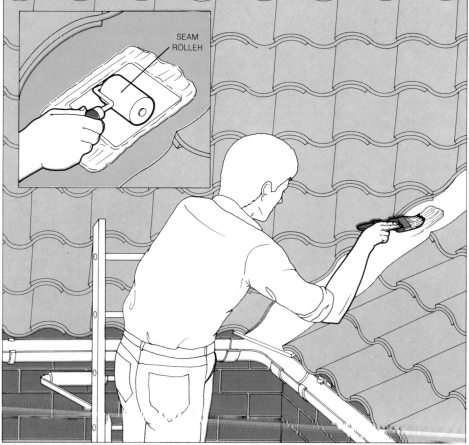

Making Good the Eaves and Gutters

Rainwater pouring over the edge of a blocked gutter or through broken joints between gutters and downpipes can cause extensive damage both to the wall fabric and to the adjacent fascia boards, soffits or rafter ends. Damp stains on the walls and rot in the timbers are usually sure indications of faults in the guttering, which are particularly common in old houses that have not been properly maintained.

Clean out leaves and debris from a blocked gutter with a garden trowel and a stiff brush, then flush with a garden hose to check that the gutter is not sagging and that water flows freely towards the downpipe. Blocked downpipes can be cleared with a flexible drain rod or length of hosepipe. To prevent future blockages, fit a wire cage—obtainable from builders' merchants—into the entrance of the downpipe, and clear the gutter of debris regularly.

Most old guttering is made of cast iron. Corroded areas should be brushed with a wire brush, then coated with a rust inhibitor and one or two coats of bituminous paint to provide a waterproof seal. Fixings that have rusted or pulled away should be replaced with galvanized nuts and bolts, and leaking joints can be repaired by dismantling the joints and renewing the sealing compound. Repair minor cracks with adhesive-backed foil strips or fibreglass patches *(page 96)*, available from DIY stores or car repair shops. Sections of badly damaged or corroded guttering are best replaced with plastic guttering.

When working from a ladder, ensure that the base of the ladder is resting on firm ground or scaffold boards, and secure the ladder to a window mullion or another convenient fastening for extra stability. Ladders that extend above the height of the guttering should be fitted with stays to hold them away from the wall. For extensive areas of work, hire a scaffold tower.

To remove old guttering, undo the nuts and bolts that secure the joints between sections—or chip off the bolt heads with a cold chisel if they are badly corroded—and lower each section to the ground with a rope. Dismantle downpipes in sections from the top downwards, again using ropes to support their weight.

With the fascia boards exposed, you can cut away and replace any rotted sections *(below and opposite)*. Coat new sections of timber with preservative, or use pressure-treated timber. New UPVC guttering is sold by various manufacturers, and installation is straightforward *(pages 94–95)*.

Repairing Rotted Fascia Boards and Rafter Ends

1 **Cutting away the damaged wood.** Look for nail heads in the fascia board to locate the rafter end nearest the damaged section of fascia. Drill a pilot hole next to the rafter end, then use a jigsaw or keyhole saw to cut through the board *(right)*. If the damaged section is midway along the wall, make a second saw cut on the other side of the section. Use a chisel if necessary to complete the cuts, then prise the damaged section away from the rafter ends. Cut away any rotted section of soffit in the same way.

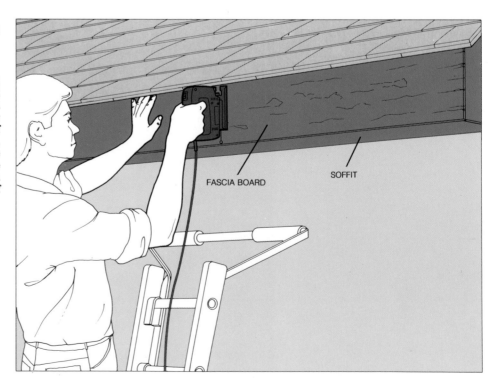

FASCIA BOARD

SOFFIT

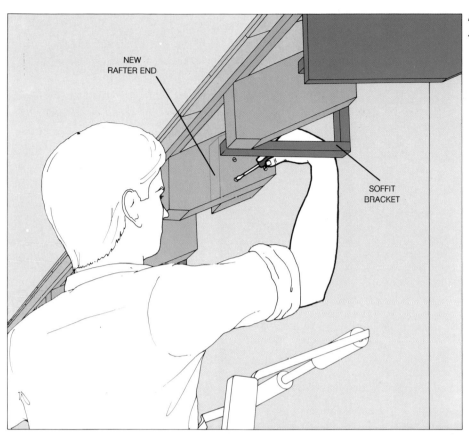

2 **Doubling damaged rafter ends.** If a rafter end has rotted, cut a piece of timber of the same width and thickness to match the shape of the rafter from its overhanging end back to the wall. Coat the timber liberally with preservative. Prise off the soffit bracket attached to the damaged rafter, then saw off the rotted end. Depending on the extent of damage, you may have to remove a number of tiles above the rafter. Hold the replacement section in position alongside the sawn-off rafter and mark positions for the screws that will secure it to the sound section of rafter; drill pilot holes at the marked positions, then secure the new section with galvanized screws *(left)*. Replace the soffit bracket, using new timber cut to the same dimensions if it is rotted.

NEW RAFTER END

SOFFIT BRACKET

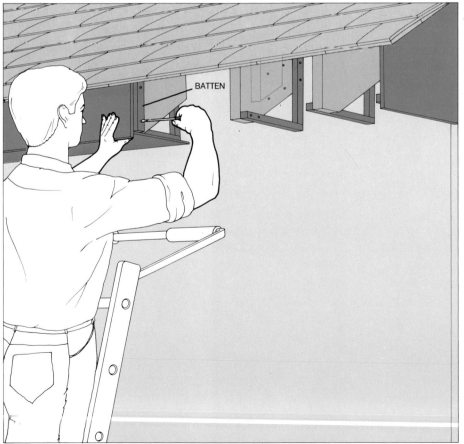

3 **Attaching new fascia boards.** Cut 50 by 50 mm battens to fit to the sides of the rafters to which the cut ends of the existing fascia or soffit boards are secured. Secure the battens flush with the rafter ends with galvanized screws *(left)*. Cut a replacement section of fascia or soffit board to the required dimensions, apply exterior-grade glue to the ends, then secure the section by screwing it to the battens and to the rafter ends or soffit brackets that it crosses.

BATTEN

Installing Plastic Guttering

1 **Fixing the gutter outlet.** To determine the position of the gutter outlet, drop a plumb line from the fascia board so that the plumb bob is aligned with the centre of the drain into which the downpipe will discharge. Drive a nail part way into the fascia board to mark the position of the outlet, then drive another nail into the opposite end of the fascia board. Tie a taut string between the nails and check for level. If the manufacturer's instructions recommend that the guttering be installed at an incline, adjust the position of one of the nails so that the string slopes at least 5 mm in every 3 metres towards the outlet position. Align the centre of the outlet beneath the nail driven into the fascia board, then secure the outlet firmly to the fascia board with 25 mm sherardized screws *(right)*.

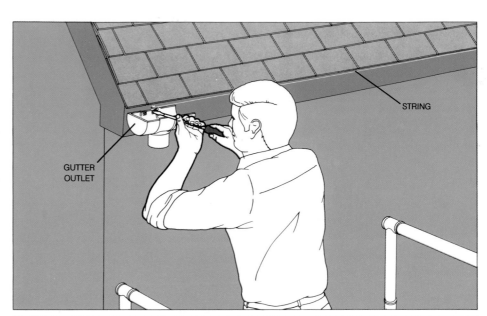

2 **Securing the brackets.** Using the string as a guide, mark positions for brackets at intervals of no more than 1 metre; below steep roof pitches and in areas of heavy rain or snowfall, the intervals must be no more than 750 mm. Screw the brackets to the fascia board, then remove the string and nails.

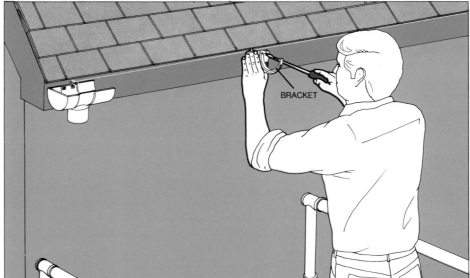

3 **Attaching the gutter.** Cut sections of straight guttering to fit along the fascia board using a fine-toothed hacksaw and remove burrs with a file. To attach the guttering, first hook the rear top edge under the retaining lip of each bracket, then support the bracket with your thumb while pulling down the front top edge until it snaps into position *(right)*. Join successive lengths of guttering with union fittings according to the manufacturer's instructions, observing carefully the end positions marked on the unions that allow for heat expansion. Fit any angle or corner fittings at the end of straight runs in the same way.

Fitting a Plastic Downpipe

1 **Connecting the offset bends.** To assemble the swan's neck that will channel rainwater from the overhanging gutter outlet to the downpipe, first hold a pipe clip against the wall and measure the horizontal distance between the centre of the gutter outlet and the centre of the clip *(below)*. Lay the offset bends on the ground at this distance apart *(A, inset)*, and measure the diagonal distance between the two bends (B). Cut a length of connecting pipe to this distance, smooth the edges, and assemble the swan's neck according to the manufacturer's instructions, using solvent cement if required.

2 **Securing the swan's neck.** Fit the socket at the top of the swan's neck over the spigot of the gutter outlet, and the socket of a length of downpipe over the spigot at the bottom of the swan's neck. Allow a 10 mm expansion gap between the end of each spigot and the bottom of each socket. Mark on the wall the location for the first clip at the height of the collar on the downpipe, then remove the swan's neck and downpipe. Drill and plug holes at the marked location, and secure the downpipe section to the wall with a pipe clip according to the manufacturer's instructions. Fit the top of the swan's neck over the outlet, push it up as far as it will go *(below)*, then lower the bottom of the swan's neck into the downpipe.

3 **Completing the downpipe.** Fit the top of the next section of downpipe over the bottom of the first section, check for plumb, then secure it to the wall with a pipe clip. As each section is installed, fit additional support clips at intervals of no more than 2 metres. Measure the bottom section of downpipe by holding it against the last secured section and marking off the length required *(right)*. To channel rainwater away from the bottom of the wall, secure a shoe fitting over the end of the final downpipe section with a clip *(inset)*.

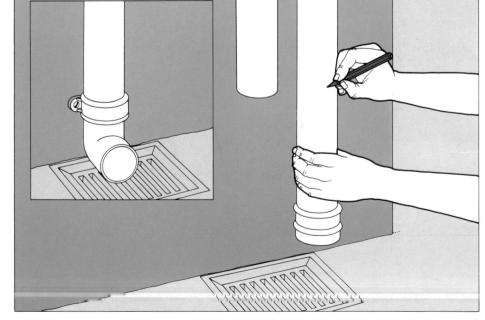

Bandaging Surface Cracks with Fibreglass

Deteriorated and damaged surfaces are ubiquitous in the old house. Inside it, years of settling and door slamming crack plaster. Outside, rain and sun chip away at concrete and rendering, rot wood and eat into metal. Traditionally, such surfaces are repaired by filling or coating them with a like material: patching plaster for walls, mortar for masonry, a soldered patch for metal. But many home owners have found fibreglass patches more effective for some of these repair jobs.

A patch of fibreglass is quite literally a bandage—a piece of tough cloth held to the skin of a roof, wall, gutter or sill with adhesive. Instead of filling cracks, it bridges them and, because it is waterproof and remains slightly pliable, it prevents the damage from recurring with the next rain or the next slam of a door.

While fibreglass patches can be used on practically any surface, you still may need traditional patching materials for some jobs. Fibreglass seldom matches the material it is applied to, so you should use it only in places that will be painted or where appearance is unimportant.

Several types of glass fibre are available, but the one used for most household patching jobs is known as chopped strand mat. Readily obtainable from hardware shops and D.I.Y. centres, this felt-like fabric is generally sold either by the roll or the metre. Widths range from 25 mm to 900 mm, and patches of the fabric can be overlapped for larger areas.

To secure the patch, you must paint first the surface, then the patch itself, with an epoxy or polyester resin which has been mixed with a hardener. Add the hardener to the resin according to the manufacturer's instructions and mix until the two components are thoroughly blended; take care, however, not to create air bubbles, which will weaken the mixed resin. To smooth the patch down, use a small trowel or a curved piece of plastic laminate. You will also need a paintbrush 75 mm or smaller to spread the mixed resin (use a brush you can throw away—the resin is impossible to remove), a pair of scissors to cut the fabric and a supply of rags and solvent for cleaning up.

Before applying a fibreglass patch, make sure your surface is clean and dry. Scrape away any loose paint or, for metal surfaces, use a wire brush to remove rust or corrosion. Powdery surfaces, such as concrete or plaster, should be wiped with a damp rag. If they still feel dusty when dry, give them a coat of clear varnish.

Both the resin and the hardener are caustic, inflammable and toxic, so be sure to take the necessary precautions. Wear rubber gloves and work only in well-ventilated areas, away from any flames. If you are sanding the patch, wear a face mask and goggles to protect yourself against the fine glass fibres that will be released into the air.

If you are patching concrete or rendering, stipple the final coat with a brush or textured roller to match the surrounding surface. Allow the fibreglass patch to dry for at least 24 hours before painting.

Patching a Flat Surface

1 Applying the mixed resin. Paint the mixed resin over the crack, spreading it evenly with smooth brush strokes. Cover the crack and the wall round it to a width 50 mm greater than the width of your fabric and at least 50 mm beyond each end of the crack. Cut the fabric with scissors to the length of the crack plus 25 mm. With your fingers, press the fabric lightly on to the resin. If you find that you need more than one piece of fabric, lap the second piece at least 35 mm over the edge of the first.

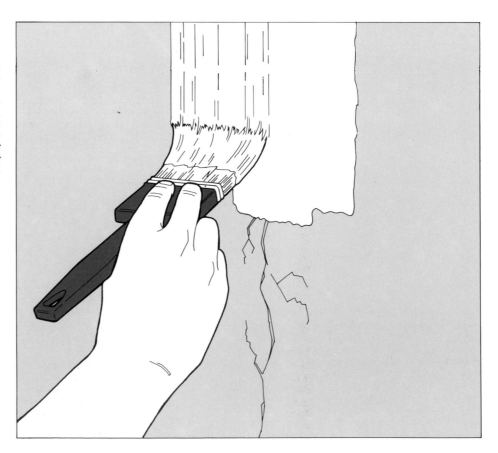

2 **Embedding the fabric.** Hold the smoothing tool almost at a right angle to the wall, across the centre of the fabric. Working out towards the ends, scrape the tool over the fabric to push it well into the resin. Hold the tool with both hands, thumbs underneath and fingers close together near the centre, to keep it stiff. Keep the concave edge up as you sweep it downwards; turn it over for upsweeps. After embedding the cloth, make sure that the resin is completely dry before brushing on the second coat.

3 **Smoothing the final coat.** Immediately after applying the second coat of resin, run the smoothing tool lightly out from the centre to the sides of the patch. Go over the patch two or three times to smooth it and feather the edges of the resin. On textured surfaces, stipple the final coat with a brush or paint roller.

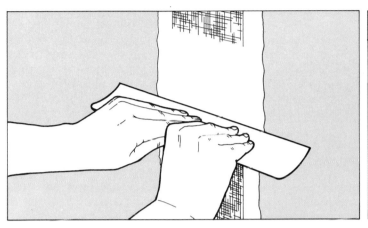
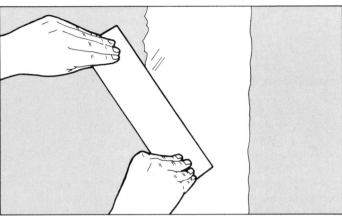

Special Techniques for Corners and Curves

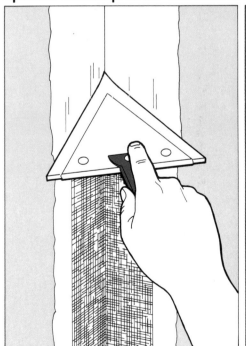
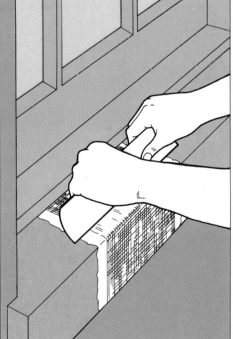

Patching an interior corner. After applying the mixed resin, fold a single piece of the fabric and press it into the corner. Then embed the fabric with the point of the cornering tool. First work up and down the corner, then smooth the fabric out towards the edges on each side.

Patching an exterior corner. After spreading the resin, stretch the fabric smoothly round the corner from one surface to the next. Embed the fabric by working from the corner out to the edges on both sides. Finally, feather the edges of the resin as in Step 3, above.

Patching a curved surface. For contours where a smoothing tool cannot reach—inside a rusted gutter, for example—you can embed the fabric with a paintbrush. Though the patch will not be as smooth as on a flat surface, it will seal tightly and weatherproof the surface.

Maintaining Exterior Masonry

External walls of brick and stone are generally extremely durable and require very little maintenance beyond occasional re-pointing of the mortar joints. However, the walls of an old house will frequently have become soiled or stained by atmospheric pollution and unsightly deposits, and will require cleaning before any repair work can be carried out.

Light soiling can often be shifted simply with water from a garden hose and soft brushing with a fibre or special bronze-wire brush and a mild detergent. For more stubborn areas you can use a hired press-ure washer—a machine that jets water out at up to 60 bar. Start with a low press-ure spray, avoid saturating the wall com-pletely, and do not use on soft or crumbling stone, brick or mortar.

Spilt paint from painting trim can be re-moved with a commercial water-rinsing masonry paint stripper. Scrub oil and tar stains with an emulsifying degreaser and rinse well. Organic growth—lichen and algae—can be removed with a pressure washer or by brushing or scraping with wooden scrapers. Efflorescence—whitish mineral-salt deposits on brick—can be left to weather away or alternatively brushed with a dry fibre brush.

Whichever cleaning method you use, a gentle approach is essential. Over-vigorous scrubbing and unskilled use of powerful cleaning agents can cause irreparable damage. Heavy all-over soiling should only be tackled by specialists on the advice of a reputable professional, who may prescribe sophisticated water-mist sprays that can soften dirt without saturating the fabric of the building, or acid-based cleaners that must be applied by trained operators. Only as a last resort should brick ever be sand-blasted, as this process seriously damages the surface and may necessitate applying a silicone sealer, which can block the pores of the masonry and cause frost damage and other harmful effects.

Masonry walls that have been painted are best repainted. Stripping an entire wall with paint stripper is very arduous and is likely to leave the wall with a variega-ted appearance. Specialist companies can tackle a job of this kind, but the expense is likely to be high.

Repairing crumbling mortar joints (page 100) is another skilled and also time-consuming job, and damaged areas larger than a few square metres should be left to a professional. The mortar usually used in old houses—a mix of lime and sand, some-times with cement added—is lighter in colour and more flexible than modern mor-tars which contain a high proportion of cement. Repointing with a mortar that is too strong can cause cracking through the stones and bricks; in addition, brittle cement mortar has a tendency to crack and shrink, trapping moisture behind and lead-ing to damp and frost damage. For these reasons, it is advisable to repoint an old wall with a mixed mortar—relatively high in lime for flexibility and colour but also containing some cement for strength. Ratios can be varied to suit particular wall materials and positions (chart, page 101).

Until you become experienced, keeping mortar stains off the surface of the brick or stone is difficult. A commercial mortar-stain remover based on hydrochloric acid can be applied when the mortar has dried, but its handling and use demand extreme caution. Wear goggles and protective cloth-ing. Follow the manufacturer's instruc-tions regarding diluting (always adding acid to water). Apply to the wall with a long-handled brush and rinse thoroughly, preferably with a pressure washer.

Cracks in a masonry wall are often structurally harmless, merely indicating that some settlement of the foundations has occurred, but you should check with a surveyor to ensure that they are station-ary. Cracked joints can be simply repoin-ted, and cracked bricks replaced (page 101). Cracked stones in an ashlar wall, where the stones are cut to form neat blocks laid in regular courses, can sometimes be re-placed in the same manner as bricks, but consult a skilled stonemason. If matching stones are not available, specialist firms can reinforce or reface existing stone—much as a dentist crowns a tooth. In a rubblestone wall—one with irregularly shaped stones laid randomly—it is only necessary to replace stones that are so badly damaged as to be structurally un-sound, and this should not be attempted without expert advice.

Surface Cleaning for Stone or Brick

Scrubbing masonry. Wet the wall with cold water from a garden hose; brush with a soft fibre brush or a special masonry wire brush that has bronze wires, available from builders' merchants. Do not use a steel-wire brush: this will damage the masonry and may cause rust stains. To avoid washing old mortar out of the joints, scrub with a circular motion, and try never to scrub back and forth along a mortar line.

If plain water does not shift the stains, use a little mild detergent—preferably a neutral pH masonry detergent—in a bucket of warm water. Rinse the wall well with clean water.

Using a pressure washer. Connect a pressure washer to your house cold-water supply with a garden hose. Set the pressure at the lowest level and wet down the entire wall to soften the dirt. Then set the pressure to 21 bar and, starting at the top, apply the spray to the wall, a small area at a time. If necessary, increase the pressure gradually, but do not exceed 42 bar. Stand well back from the wall when spraying with the pressure washer; to reach high areas, lay a scaffold board between two stepladders.

Caution: if the spray begins to abrade the surface of the masonry or flush mortar out of the joints, use lower pressure and, if necessary, stop using the machine altogether. Do not hold the spray on any one area for longer than necessary, and avoid saturating the fabric of the wall. Before using the pressure washer, check that the drains round the house are not blocked.

Using paint stripper. After wetting the wall, apply masonry paint stripper with an old paintbrush. Take care to brush in one direction—away from yourself—at all times. Wear goggles, a cap, gloves and long sleeves for protection. Allow the stripper to work for 15 to 30 minutes before agitating with a long-handled brush. Then, standing on a ladder, rinse off the stripper thoroughly with a pressure washer or garden hose aimed down and away from yourself.

Repointing Brick and Coursed Stone Walls

1 **Cutting back the old mortar.** Wearing goggles to protect your eyes, remove crumbling mortar from the joints with a club hammer and cold chisel. Lime mortar, which is usually light-coloured and has a sandy, granular feel, should be chipped out to a depth of 25 mm. Remove cement mortar to a depth of 15 mm.

2 **Renewing the joint.** Spray the joint lightly with water. Place a small pile of mortar on a hawk and hold it up to the work. Cut and pick up a small "sausage" of mortar with the back of a pointing trowel and press the mortar into the joint. For long horizontal joints, a window trowel, also known as a joint filler, may be more convenient than a pointing trowel.

Work from top to bottom and left to right, taking care not to stain the bricks with new mortar. After filling the joints in an area of about 1 square metre, shape the mortar *(below)* before moving on to the next section.

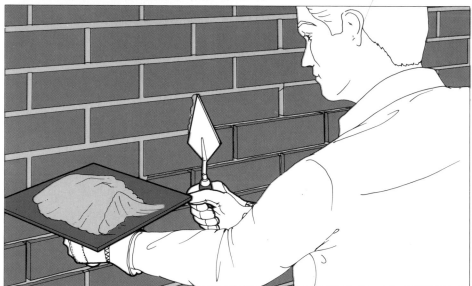

3 **Shaping the joints.** Finish the new joints to match the original ones; check under the eaves or in sheltered areas for a guide. For concave joints, press the mortar into the joints with a convex bricklayer's jointer *(right)* or a teaspoon. Use a V-jointer for V-shaped joints. For flush joints, build the joint with a slight excess of mortar and scrape it off with a trowel when it has set slightly.

Restoring Fractured Masonry

Replacing a damaged brick. Chisel out the mortar round a spalled or cracked brick, then split the brick into several pieces to remove it *(left)*. Chisel out any mortar behind the brick, being careful not to damage nearby bricks; wire-brush the pocket left by the old brick. If there is no cavity behind the brick you have removed, cut 25 mm off the back of a new brick with a bolster and club hammer so that the brick will have ample room at the back; wet the pocket and mortar its sides, then mortar each side of the brick. Hold the brick on a board and push it off the board and into the pocket with your hand; tap the brick into position, using the butt of a trowel handle. Mortar the joints *(opposite page, Steps 2–3)*.

Mixing the Right Mortar

Type of wall	Sheltered position	Moderately exposed position	Severely exposed position
STONE			
durable and moderately durable	1:3:10	1:2:8	1:1:6
poorly durable	0:1:3	0:2:5	1:3:10
BRICK IN LIME MORTAR			
strong and moderately durable	1:3:10	1:2:8	1:1:6
poorly durable	0:2:5	0:2:5	1:3:10
BRICK IN CEMENT-LIME MORTAR			
strong, durable	1:1:6	1:1:6	1:1:6
moderately durable	1:2:8	1:2:8	1:2:8

A mortar mix for every old wall. The chart above gives the proportions by volume of Portland cement, hydrated lime and builders' sand to use for various building materials in different situations. The strength of the mortar used should always be slightly weaker than the masonry, but must be adjusted according to the wall's position: a wall exposed to wind and rain needs a tougher mortar than one sheltered by nearby buildings or natural features. When mixing, wear gloves and a long-sleeved shirt to protect your skin, and slowly add just enough water to give a consistency like that of soft butter. To check that the colour of the mortar conforms with the existing joints, mix a small batch and spread it on a piece of scrap wood or an old brick, and let it dry for 12 hours. If it is too dark, try using a lighter-coloured sand, or a more expensive white Portland cement instead of grey, or even increase the amount of lime by ½ or 1 part. If the mortar is too light, use darker sand or add a very small quantity of soot or a mineral oxide pigment.

Repairs for Rendering

Properly applied and cured, rendering is a practically indestructible covering for a house. The material dries concrete hard and has no seams or joints to admit water. Over the years, however, it is likely to develop small cracks and holes, which must be repaired promptly to prevent water penetration.

Fill fine cracks with an exterior-grade filler, larger cracks and patches with mortar. Glass fibre matting embedded in a special bitumen base coat *(page 96)* can also be used to repair cracks, but the matting must be painted over—and if the surrounding rendering is not painted, you will have to paint the entire wall.

You can mix mortar for rendering yourself using 1 part Portland cement, 1 part hydrated lime and 6 parts sand, but for small patching jobs it is just as economical to buy it in ready-mixed dry form. Add just enough water to give it a uniform, plastic texture that leaves a fairly heavy residue on your glove but still holds together when picked up and squeezed. Always wear gloves to protect your hands from the lime, and wear goggles to protect your eyes when you pour out the dry mix.

While the rendering is still damp, you can give a patch a textured finish by rubbing in small circular strokes with a wooden float. To create a finer texture, attach a piece of carpet or plastic foam to the base of the float; for a coarser finish, score the surface with a broom. If the surrounding area is pebble-dashed, press matching pebbles on to the patch when it is wet and push them in lightly with a float.

It is best to patch rendering on a humid, overcast day when the temperature is between 10° and 30°C. In any case, the night before you apply the rendering, wet down the area to be patched and then spray it again just before you begin.

Filling a Crack

Packing in the mortar. With a club hammer and cold chisel, enlarge the crack until it is 6 to 10 mm wide throughout its length. Mix up enough mortar to fill the crack. With a brush, dampen in and around the crack with water containing a little PVA bonding agent. Use a pointing trowel to pack the mortar into the crack until it is slightly proud of the surface. When firm but not set, scrape it flush with the rendering. Allow to harden for 24 hours.

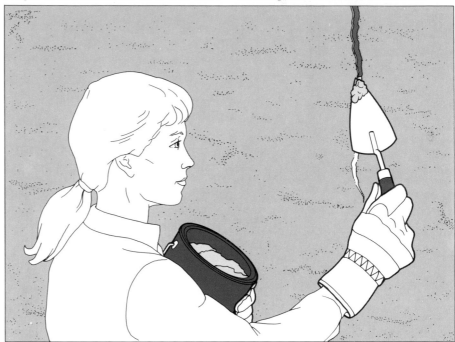

Patching a Small Area

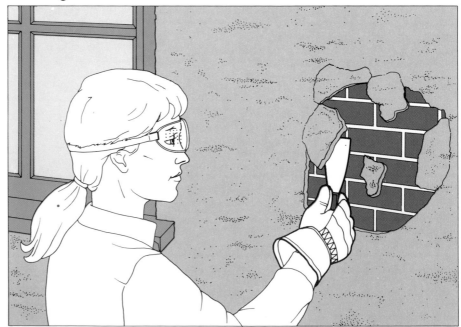

1 Removing the damaged rendering. With a trowel or stripping knife, scrape away all loose and flaking rendering until you reach sound edges and firm material underneath; if necessary, remove all of the rendering to expose the masonry. Undercut the old rendering round the edges of the patch, then brush away all dust and debris with a wire brush. Soak the area and cover it overnight with damp sacking propped in position with lengths of timber.

2 Applying the new mortar. Load a small amount of mortar on to a hawk, then spread the mortar over the patch with a plasterer's steel trowel. Sweep the trowel upwards from the hawk and on to the wall, pressing the mortar firmly into the backing. If the masonry is exposed, build up the new render in two layers, applying a first coat to within about 10 mm of the surface. When this has stiffened but is not yet set hard, score lines in the patch with the edge of the trowel to provide a "key" for the top coat. Allow to set for two days. Moisten the area and apply the second coat, working the render well into the edges.

3 Levelling off. Use a straight piece of timber to level off the mortar, starting at the bottom and drawing the timber upwards with a side-to-side sawing motion. Fill in any shallow depressions and level off again if necessary. Polish the surface smooth with a steel float, feathering the edges to merge with the surrounding render. Alternatively, texture the surface of the mortar while it is still damp to match the existing render.

Making Timber Cladding Weathertight

To provide effective protection, all exterior walls need to be weathertight. Masonry walls have built-in weather-resistance: for so long as the bricks and mortar are intact, they will keep out the cold and wet. External timber cladding, however, needs a protective layer to ward off the damaging effects of water and ultraviolet light, and this coating must be reapplied regularly.

In most old houses external cladding will be painted, although in some cases it will have been treated with creosote or another tar-based substance, or perhaps an external woodstain designed to protect and colour the wood. Changing the type of finish is not practicable: stripping paint involves enormous labour and may leave a variegated surface, and painting over a tarred surface is unlikely to be successful.

Before you repaint the outside of a wooden house, wash it down well with a garden hose, using a mild detergent and a scrubbing brush where the dirt is thick. Scrape off any loose or peeling paint, if necessary, using a hot-air gun (page 35) to help with stubborn areas. Then give the surface a complete examination. Dark stains, blistering, cracking and rust streaks around nail heads all show that moisture is getting into the wood. Unless the source is tracked down and fixed, your new paint will not last.

If the damage is near a kitchen or a bath-room, you may need a vent or extractor fan to stop moist air from attacking the cladding from inside. Make sure the gutters are in good condition so they channel rainwater away from the walls (pages 92–95). Use a caulking gun and sealant liberally to fill gaps round windows, doors and any other interruptions in the wall surface.

Once the walls are clean and sealed, any boards that have rotted through should be replaced. Often it is simplest to replace the entire length of a board, but short sections can be cut out and a new piece then nailed in place. Traditional weatherboarding—overlapping horizontal boards—can be cut through with a tenon saw and a thin-bladed compass saw (opposite page, below). A similar technique is used for shiplap interlocking boards; for tongue and groove boards, the simplest course is to cut along the centre of the affected board and remove it in two halves, using a padsaw fitted with a hacksaw blade to cut through the fixing nails where they cannot be pulled out with pincers.

In cases of slight or surface damage, you can save a board by scraping it bare, letting it dry for several days, and treating it with wood preservative. Cracks and splits in boards can be stopped with sealant or, if they are large, filled with a sliver of timber planed to a wedge shape and glued into place (opposite page, above).

Preparing for Paint

Removing nail rust. Sand a rust-stained area by hand with medium-grade wet and dry paper or steel wool until all of the rust is removed. Then sand the nail head itself to remove any build-up of rust. Use a nail punch to countersink the nail head. Coat the nail head and the area round it with paint primer. After the area is dry, fill the countersunk hole with exterior wood filler.

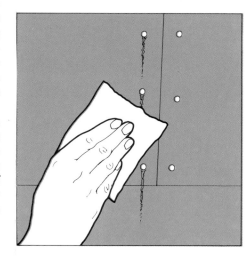

Caulking the joints. Put a cartridge of sealant into a caulking gun and slice off the tip of the cartridge to make an opening about 6 mm in diameter. Starting in an unobtrusive spot (under a window sill or above a door), pull the trigger of the gun slightly, experimenting with varying pressures to obtain the desired width of bead. Pull the tip slowly along the joint while squeezing out just enough sealant to fill the joint but without overflowing. (If it does not flow smoothly, warm the cartridge slightly in warm water.)

Use a wet cloth to keep the outside of the cartridge nozzle clear of sealant. Release the trigger just before reaching the end of the seam. Bed the sealant into the joint and give a slightly concave shape to its surface, using a wet finger or a damp cloth. Clean away any excess sealant from the joint with a second wet cloth.

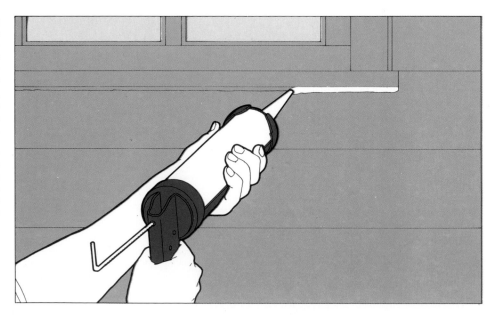

Filling large cracks. Pin a timber batten slightly thicker than the widest part of the crack to the workbench, and plane it to a wedge shape using the technique shown on page 49. Trim the wedge to the length of the crack, coat it with exterior woodworking glue and gently hammer it into the gap with a mallet. Fill the thin ends of the crack, where the wedge cannot fit, with glue or sealant. When the glue has dried, pare off the protruding part of the wedge with a mallet and chisel *(right)*. Keep the chisel blade's bevel towards the wall to prevent the blade from digging into the board. Finish by planing the wedge flush with the surface of the board.

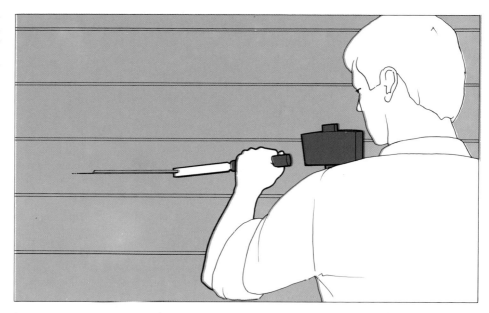

Replacing Sections of Cladding

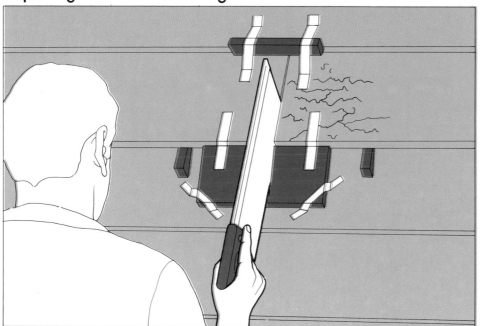

1 Cutting out damaged weatherboarding. Locate the nearest stud or batten on either side of the damaged area by looking for nail heads. Tap wedges under the board to separate it from the one below, then use a tenon saw to cut through it. Make the cut as close as possible to the stud—the right-hand edge of the stud to the left of the damaged area, and vice versa. Protect the boards above and below with scraps of wood temporarily held in place with adhesive tape.

2 Finishing the cut. Move the wedges to the top of the damaged piece to protect the board above, then finish the cut using a compass saw with the handle reversed *(above)*. Use a padsaw fitted with a hacksaw blade to cut through any nails under the damaged section and remove the section. Following the technique shown on page 93 for replacing a section of fascia board, screw timber battens to the sides of the studs; then nail a replacement section to the battens.

To remove a section of shiplap cladding, first drill a pilot hole near the top of the damaged board, then use a compass saw to cut upwards. Keep the saw at a steep angle to avoid damaging the edge of the board above. Saw downwards with a tenon saw, again finishing the cut with the compass saw held at a steep angle to avoid damaging the tongue of the board below.

Restoring External Sills

Projecting beyond the vertical face of the house walls, external window sills are particularly vulnerable to the action of the elements. Traditional stone sills are eroded by decades of exposure to rain, and both stone and newer concrete sills can crack as a result of frost damage or the settling of foundations. Timber sills quickly succumb to rot once water has penetrated their protective coat of paint or varnish.

Test timber sills for rot by probing with a sharp penknife. Strip paint from affected parts and cut out the rotten wood with a saw or, for small sections, a chisel and mallet. Fill small areas, cracks and depressions with wood stopping, larger ones with a new piece of timber cut to shape and secured with exterior woodworking glue. Small cracks in stone and concrete sills can be repaired with mortar. Enlarge the crack to a width of 25 mm with a cold chisel and hammer, brush away dust and fragments, then paint the interior of the channel with PVA bonding agent before filling with a stiff mortar of 1 part cement and 4 parts soft sand. Cracks can also be bridged with a fibreglass bandage *(page 96)*.

To fill a depression, chisel out a pit with vertical walls and a uniform depth of about 20 mm. Paint the interior with PVA bonding agent and fill with mortar, holding a batten against edge sections as a form, then smooth the surface with a steel float. Cover the repair with polythene and allow to cure for a few days; paint with exterior masonry paint when thoroughly dry.

A stone sill that is extensively damaged can be repaired by chipping away the entire front section and replacing it with a concrete cast made in a timber box frame called a "shuttering box" assembled against the wall *(right)*. If a number of sills need repairing, hire an electric mini jackhammer to remove the damaged parts. Screws driven into the remnants of the sill, or the masonry behind it, help to form a bond between the existing material and the new concrete poured into the box. To conceal any contrast in colour and texture between the new sill and the old, paint the entire sill with exterior masonry paint.

Casting a New Concrete Sill

1 **Cutting back the old sill.** Wearing goggles and stout shoes, chop away the damaged front of the old sill with a club hammer and cold chisel. Using a hammer drill with a No. 10 masonry bit, drill holes into the rear of the sill at 100 mm intervals; insert No. 10 plastic plugs, then partially drive in 75 mm No. 10 screws *(below)*. The shank projecting, which will anchor the new concrete, should measure two-thirds of the depth of the replacement portion.

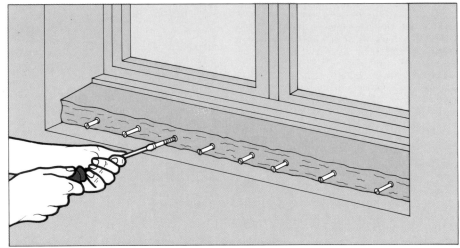

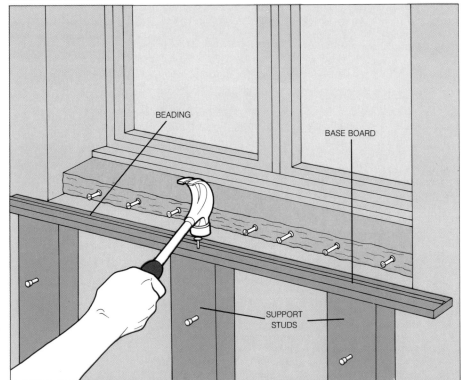

2 **Making the shuttering-box base.** Cut a base board from 25 mm softwood or 19 mm plywood to span the opening, plus a 75 mm overhang at each end. Make the depth of the board equal to the distance the new sill will project out beyond the face of the wall. To create a drip groove under the new sill, pin a strip of window beading along the base board 25 mm in from the front edge.

Cut three 100 by 50 mm vertical timber studs to reach from ground level to the underside of the base board at the sill height. Nail the studs to the wall at 400 mm intervals, using masonry nails driven into the mortar joints; to make removal easy, do not drive the nails fully home. Place the base of the box in position on the studs and secure with 50 mm wire nails driven through the base into the stud tops.

3 **Completing the shuttering.** Cut the front wall from shuttering ply or 25 mm-thick softwood, making its length equal to that of the base and its width equal to the desired height of the front edge of the sill plus the thickness of the base board. To allow for a drainage slope, the height of the sill should be 10 mm less at the front than at the back. Nail the front wall in position with 50 mm wire nails driven into the edge of the baseboard at 100 mm intervals. Cut two sloping side walls to size, making their top edges match the planned slope of the sill, and secure these side walls in position with nails driven into the end-grain of the base board and the front wall *(right)*.

For sills with a large overhang, fix battens to the wall with masonry nails to provide extra support for the side walls *(inset)*.

BATTEN

4 **Pouring the concrete.** Apply a coat of PVA bonding agent to the exposed face of the old sill. Then prepare a wet concrete mix of 1 part cement, 2 parts sharp sand and 1 part fine aggregate; alternatively, buy bags of dry-mixed concrete. Grease inside the shuttering box with a proprietary releasing agent or clean oil, then pour the mix into the box and pack it down with a trowel to fill any gaps and dispel air bubbles. To produce a smooth finish, vibrate the sides by tapping them gently with a hammer. With a steel float, level the concrete flush with the sides of the box. Cover with polythene.

After 24 hours, carefully prise off the front and sides of the box to aid curing. A day later, remove the studs and the base board and make good any blemishes with a fresh mix of concrete. If the rear of the new sill adjoins the bottom of the window frame, wait about three days, then caulk the joint between them.

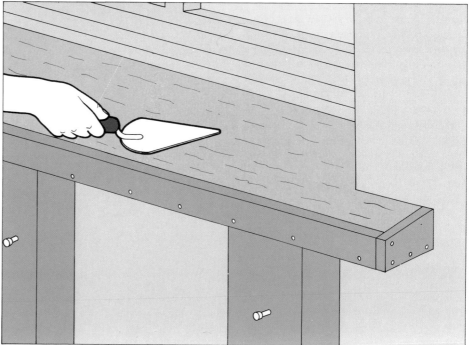

Plaster Repairs for Walls and Ceilings

Plaster is extremely durable and has been a common material in houses for centuries, both for mouldings *(pages 40–43)* and as a smooth coating for internal walls and ceilings. But it is also brittle and will deteriorate when it is damp for long periods.

Cracks and small holes in walls and ceilings can be quickly fixed with a cellulose filler, available either pre-mixed or as a powder for mixing with water. To repair deep holes no more than 100 mm in diameter, first stuff into the hole a ball of crumpled newspaper that has been soaked in water and then in plaster of a creamy consistency. Leave the newspaper to harden, then fill the remaining depression with a cellulose filler.

On brick or block walls, larger areas of damage can be repaired by first chipping away the old plaster, then applying successive coats of fresh plaster. For the base coat, modern backing plasters are available in several formulations—ensure that you use one suitable for brick or blockwork, usually known as "browning". Use a finish plaster of the same brand.

On ceilings and internal walls of lath and plaster—a common type of construction in old houses—the damaged plaster can be replaced by nailing gypsum plasterboard over the laths, then applying a finish plaster of the type specially formulated for coating plasterboard.

A "one-coat" gypsum plaster can be used to repair walls and ceilings of any construction. It fulfils the functions of both backing and finish plaster, and can be built up in layers to a total thickness of 50 mm. Some special tools are needed, but instructions are provided by the manufacturer.

The tools you will need for the operations shown on the following pages include a hand hawk, a steel laying-on trowel, a plastic or wooden float, and a special aluminium straightedge known as a featheredge (a suitable length of perfectly straight timber will do). For your worktable—or "spot board"—use a sheet of plywood sealed with knotting or button polish.

To mix plaster, sift four or five handfuls into a bucket half filled with clean, cold water, then stir vigorously until the plaster has dissolved completely. Add more plaster and stir, and repeat until the desired consistency is achieved. Finish plaster should be slightly wetter than backing plaster, but in both cases a line cut through the mix with a stick should not fill in. Avoid adding too much plaster and then having to add more water, which causes the plaster to set—or "go off"—too quickly, and shortens your working time.

Plastering is messy work, so protect flooring with polythene sheets and keep your tools clean when not in use. After completing the repair, allow four or five days before decorating the plastered area. Do not attempt to speed the drying process with heaters, as this can cause the new plaster to crack.

Patching a Masonry Wall

1 **Preparing the wall.** With a hammer and cold chisel, chip away all the damaged and loose plaster to expose the brickwork or blockwork, making the edges of the patch as straight as possible. Brush down the masonry with a stiff dry brush to remove dust. Prepare the backing plaster in a bucket, then wet your tools and the spot board and empty the plaster on to the table. Dampen the brickwork and the edges of the old plaster by flicking clean water on to it with a large paste brush or paintbrush.

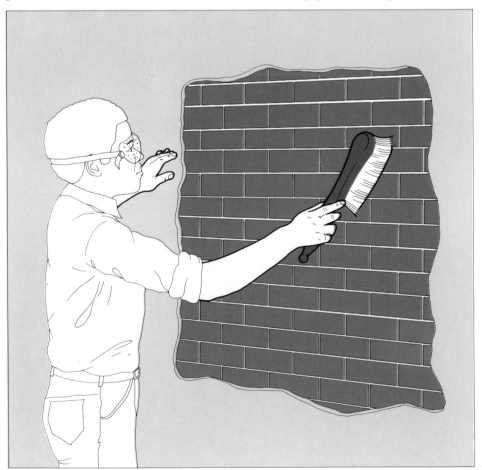

2 **Applying the backing coat.** Scrape two or three trowelfuls of plaster on to the hawk with the laying-on trowel, then load the trowel by tilting the hawk towards you and pushing the edge of the trowel into the plaster and upwards. Starting at the bottom edge of the patch, hold the trowel against the wall with its upper edge about 10 mm from the surface and sweep it upwards, forcing the plaster against the wall. Apply a 10 mm-thick coat of plaster over the entire patch, using horizontal strokes near the top and finishing by working inwards from the edges. Then immediately apply a second coat, bringing the surface of the new plaster 3 to 4 mm proud of the old. If the plaster is more than 20 mm thick, do the job in three layers.

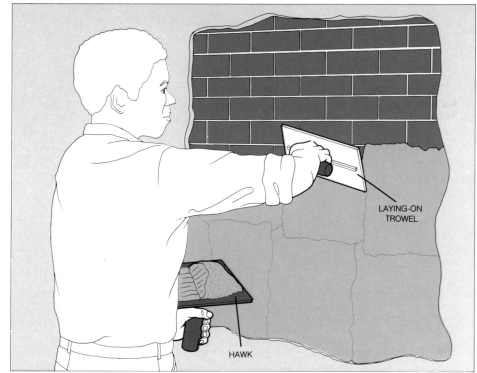

LAYING-ON TROWEL

HAWK

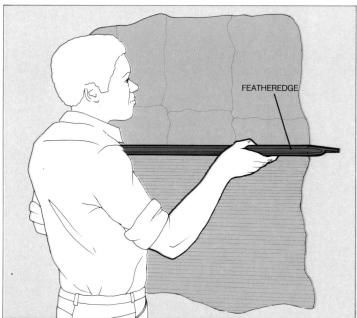

FEATHEREDGE

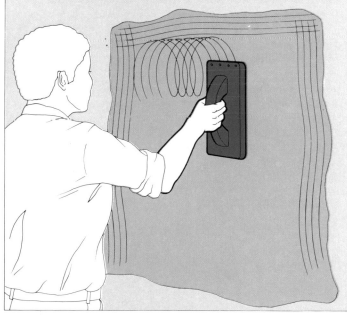

3 **Ruling off the backing coat.** With the trowel, scrape away any scraps of plaster round the edges of the patch. Hold a featheredge horizontally across the patch and, with a back-and-forth sideways motion of 25 to 50 mm, move it up the patch to remove half the excess thickness of plaster, taking care not to "tear" the new plaster. Then repeat, this time keeping the ends of the featheredge pressed against the original plaster on either side of the patch to level the new plaster flush with the old. Fill in any shallow depressions and rule off again.

4 **Making the key.** Allow time for the plaster to become firm to the touch, but not set—the manufacturer's instructions will specify the time required. Then carefully scrape back the entire patch with a cleaned and dampened trowel, shaving off about 2 mm of plaster. Use a wooden or plastic float with three or four nails punched through one end, their tips protruding 1 or 2 mm through the face, to scarify the patch; first go round the edges to make a wavy pattern, then use a circular motion to cover the patch, leaving no blank areas.

5 **Applying the finish coat.** Allow several hours for the backing coat to set, then mix a small quantity of finish plaster. Trowel a first coat about 1 mm thick on to the patch, finishing by working outwards from the edges so that the trowel runs off the patch on to the existing plaster. Wait a few minutes, then apply a second thin coat with minimal pressure. Run the trowel round the edges of the patch, overlapping only 25 mm of the trowel on to the fresh plaster *(right)*—this border will serve as a guide for the final smoothing. Wait for the plaster to become dull and firm to the touch: between 10 and 60 minutes. Using a clean trowel and wetting it frequently, smooth the entire patch level with the surrounding plaster.

A Plasterboard Patch for a Ceiling

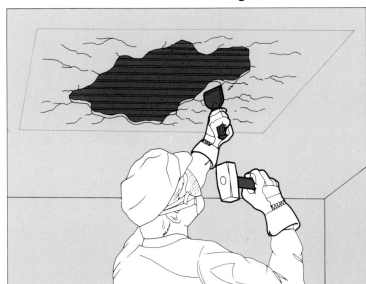

1 **Removing the damaged plaster.** With a straight-edge and trimming knife, cut lines through the plaster along the centre of the joists on either side of the damaged plaster. Join up the cut lines to complete a rectangle that extends just beyond the damaged area. Wearing goggles and a face mask, use a hammer and cold chisel to carefully chip out the plaster within the rectangle *(above)*. If loose plaster starts to sag or fall outside the marked lines, remove it and extend the rectangle. Then use an old wood chisel to scrape off about 2 mm of the old plaster round the opening, creating a stepped border about 50 mm wide.

2 **Nailing the plasterboard.** Cut a plasterboard rectangle about 5 mm smaller than the opening. Position the plasterboard over the exposed laths with the white side up and the grey side facing down into the room, then secure it with galvanized plasterboard nails driven into the joists at intervals of 150 mm

3 **Attaching the scrim.** Mix a small quantity of board-finish plaster. Brush the edges of the scraped-back plaster with clean water, but do not wet the plasterboard. Scrape a small amount of plaster on to the hawk, and with a laying-on trowel cover the join between board and old plaster with short strokes, starting from just outside the board and working inwards. Cut lengths of scrim and use the trowel to push them into the new plaster on the join *(right)*. Then trowel more plaster over the scrim with long strokes, following the sides of the patch.

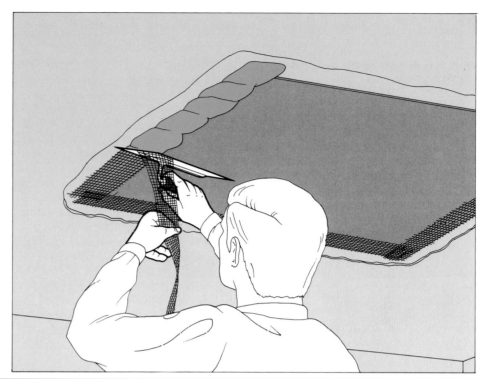

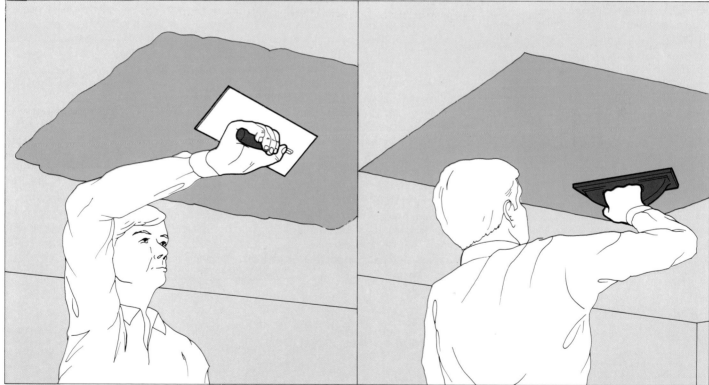

4 **Finishing the patch.** Pulling the trowel towards you in long strokes and working inwards from the edges, trowel a thin layer of plaster over the entire patch to the edges of the scraped-back plaster *(above, left)*. Immediately apply a second layer of plaster, this time using a plain plastic float pressed flat against the ceiling and making long strokes backwards and forwards *(above, right)*.

At the edges of the patch work inwards, and then back outwards again.

Rule off the patch with a featheredge *(page 109, Step 3)*, keeping the ends of the featheredge pressed against the existing plaster either side of the patch and drawing it towards you with a sideways sawing action of 25 to 50 mm. Make good any shallow depressions and rule off again. Wait

until the plaster goes dull and is firm to the touch—about 45 minutes—then mix up a fresh batch of plaster and apply a third very thin coat with the laying-on trowel. Following the same procedures as for a wall patch *(opposite, top)*, scrape back a 25 mm border round the edge of the patch, wait until the plaster goes dull, and finally smooth the surface with the trowel.

111

Floor Sags: Their Causes and Their Cures

Some structural faults in a floor, especially near staircases, baths and load-bearing walls, are obvious when an old house is first inspected. Others show up only after a heavy object such as a newly installed refrigerator or a piano has burdened the floor for a few weeks. Sags in the middle of a floor are typically caused by inadequate support from joists below the floor. Sags near an exterior wall usually indicate that the ends of the supporting joists—or the wall plates on which they rest—have rotted, or that the masonry housings for the joists are crumbling.

A timber floor located above a cellar may sag slightly or feel bouncy near the middle of a house. It can be firmed up temporarily by shoring the floor joists with a framework of beams and supports *(opposite page, above)*. To eliminate such sags permanently, however, you must slowly jack the floor back to level, using an adjustable prop or, in a space that is not high enough to accommodate a conventional prop, a bell-shaped screw jack. Both types of prop are available from tool-hire shops. Once the floor is level, replace each of the props with a 75 by 75 mm post.

Since posts will obstruct movement round a cellar, you may prefer to reinforce the joists instead. You can stiffen weak joists by nailing new boards to one or both sides. At stairways, strengthen the joints between the trimming joists with metal framing connectors.

Where a sag near an exterior wall is caused by loose housings at joist ends, you can rebuild the crumbling masonry with bricks and mortar. Rotten sections of wall plates must be cut away and replaced with new lengths of treated timber or with bricks and mortar. If the rotten section of a joist end is less than one-tenth of the full span of the joist, a pressure-treated reinforcing board can be fixed as a brace to the sawn-off end of the joist *(pages 113–114)*. Where the rot is more extensive, or where more than two adjacent joists are affected, the joists must be removed and replaced with new ones *(page 115)*.

If you encounter cables routed through holes in a joist that has to be reinforced or replaced, switch off the electricity supply and cut round the cables carefully. Pipes are usually routed through notches, and will require matching notches cut into the top edge of the new timber *(page 114, Step 2)*; never notch a joist at the bottom, as this will weaken it. If cables are not sufficiently slack to be rehoused in notches, consult a qualified electrician.

It is always easier to repair a joist from below, as shown on the following pages. Where there is no cellar to provide access to a ground floor from below, discover the cause of a sag by removing two or three floorboards near the edge of the room and inspecting the joist ends or wall plates for decay; because the joists are supported by low "sleeper walls" and have short spans, a rotten joist end can be cut away and a new joist angled into place from above without further disruption to the room. To gain access to joists in upper rooms, either remove floorboards in the room above or cut away the ceiling underneath.

To cure a large sag in the middle of a floor caused by overloading or inadequately sized joists, you must brace the floor from below with a single sturdy beam running at right angles to the joists. A steel girder known as a rolled steel joist (RSJ) is the standard solution; the RSJ is jacked up under the ailing joists—with additional props placed directly beneath each other, supporting any floors below down to ground level—and built into the wall at either end. Although an RSJ can be boxed in with battens and plasterboard, an alternative brace—more in keeping with the exposed joists of many older houses—is a timber beam *(pages 116–117)*.

A timber bracing beam may be made of structural-grade softwood, hardwood or glue-laminated timber. Because softwood timbers are unlikely to be thick enough for the purpose, glue two lengths together—or ask a timber yard to do so—with their heartwood facing outwards. Hardwood, although more expensive, is usually available in adequate lengths and thicknesses. Glue-laminated timber, a composite material manufactured in specialist workshops, provides the strongest and most compact beam of all. Consult a structural engineer or building control officer for advice on the correct dimensions, which depend both on the type of wood and the distance it must span.

The ends of the timber beam may be built into the walls in the same way as an RSJ, but to protect the timber from damp in an exterior wall, a practical alternative is to rest its end on corbels which are themselves housed in the masonry. Corbels of reinforced concrete can be cast *in situ* in a simple timber form *(page 116, Step 1)*; for more decorative supports, ask a professional mason to fashion custom-made corbels out of stone.

Shoring a Sag from the Cellar

Shoring weak joists. To shore up a timber ground floor, build a framework of posts and beams at right angles to the joists. Lay 3 metre beams of pressure-treated 75 by 75 mm timber end to end on the floor of the cellar. Cut pressure-treated 75 by 75 mm posts to the distance from the underside of the joists—measure from the lowest joist if they are irregular—to the floor, minus the thickness of the beams and the pads. Toenail three posts to each beam, one in the centre and one 500 mm in from each end. Lay 300 mm lengths of pressure-treated 150 by 50 mm timber to serve as pads under each beam; on an earth floor use 3-metre lengths of 225 by 50 mm timber.

With a helper, lift each framework, horizontal beam on top, and set it on its pads. Tap pairs of hardwood shims between the beam and joists as necessary. Check two adjacent sides of each post for plumb using a carpenter's level; tap the bottom until the post is vertical, then toenail it to the pad. Drive in the shims. Insert an extra post beneath any joint in the beams and toenail the beams together.

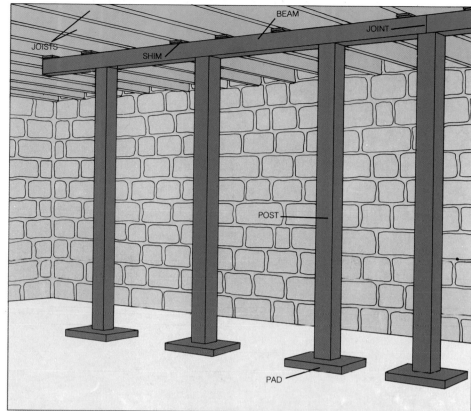

Reinforcing a Rotted Joist

1 Enlarging the joist bearing. Chop out the masonry on one side of the affected joist using a bolster and a club hammer. Chop a hole 100 mm deep and slightly larger all round than the end of the reinforcing board. Remove loose chippings and dust from the cavity.

2 **Preparing the reinforcing board.** Using a hand-saw, cut through the old joist at least 600 mm away from the rotten area. Prise down the rotten joist end with a crowbar, pull out protruding nails with pincers and coat the sawn end of the sound section with timber preservative. From pressure-treated timber of the same thickness and depth as the old joist, cut a reinforcing board at least 600 mm longer than the damaged section you have removed. Where the reinforcing board will overlap the end of the existing joist, mark positions for staggered screws every 150 mm and drill pilot holes. Notch the top of the reinforcing board to take any pipes and cables (inset).

3 **Installing the reinforcing board.** Paint the facing surfaces of the existing joist and the reinforcing board with a waterproof timber adhesive, then set the reinforcing board in place. Slot its end into the masonry cavity in the wall and pack underneath it with pieces of slate or tile to force its upper edge tight against the floorboards. Clamp the new board and old joist together and secure them with 87 mm No. 10 screws. Fill in the masonry cavity round the end of the reinforcing board with pieces of brick, then mix a small quantity of stiff mortar—5 parts sand to 1 part Portland cement—and pack it in with a pointing trowel.

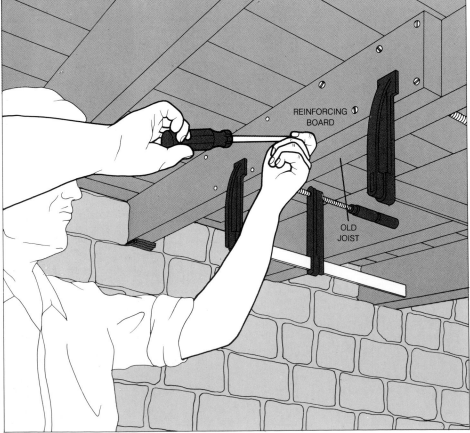

REINFORCING BOARD

OLD JOIST

Replacing a Joist

1 Removing the old joist. Using a handsaw, cut a section at least 150 mm long from the centre of the joist to be removed, and lever it out with a crowbar (*right*). At the exterior wall, chop round the end of the joist with a bolster and club hammer; at the interior supporting wall, use a cold chisel to chop away sufficient masonry under the end of the joist to enable you to pull it free of the flooring nails. Prise the two sections away from the floorboards and work free the end set in the exterior wall. Use pincers to pull down nails protruding from the floorboards.

Using the bolster and hammer, slightly enlarge the recess in the exterior wall to accept the end of the replacement joist. If both ends of the replacement are to be embedded in a wall, deepen one of the holes by at least 100 mm.

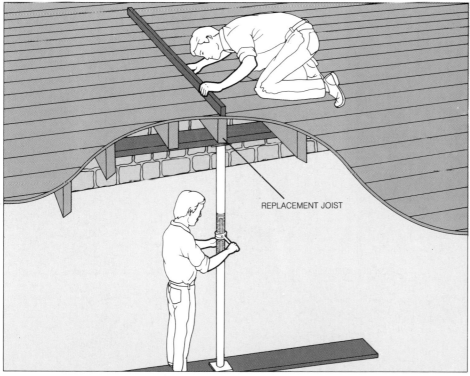

REPLACEMENT JOIST

SLATE PACKING

2 Installing and propping the new joist. With a helper, raise the new joist, slide one end over the interior wall and push the other into its housing in the exterior wall. If both ends of the joist are to be embedded in masonry, angle one end into the deeper of the two holes, then raise the other end and slide it into its housing; each end of the joist must be supported by at least 100 mm of masonry.

Place an adjustable prop directly beneath the centre of the new joist, its base plate resting on a scaffold board. Rotate the handle until the top plate is about 100 mm below the new joist, then rest a length of 100 by 75 mm timber—long enough to span two joists on either side of the adjustable prop—between the top plate and the joists. Slowly tighten the prop until the floor of the room above is completely level. To test, set a long piece of straight-edged timber in the centre of the floor, at a right angle to the boards above the prop, and get a helper to watch the effect as you tighten the prop down below.

3 Securing the joist. Wedge pieces of slate or brick under the joist ends, then pack round them with stiff mortar and allow to dry for 48 hours before removing the prop. If the floorboards are accessible from above, secure them to the new joist with flooring brads or lost-head nails two and a half times longer than the thickness of the boards. Alternatively, when nailing is not possible, drive thin shims of hardboard or plywood into any gaps between the new joist and the floorboards.

A Box Mould for Casting Corbels

Anatomy of the box mould. Made from 12 mm exterior-grade plywood, the internal dimensions of this mould are 400 by 300 mm and its height is equal to the thickness of the beam to be installed. The two short sides are held in place by battens nailed to the overlapping ends of the long sides, which are themselves supported by two sash cramps and by battens nailed to the base. Slotted into one corner of the mould is a polystyrene block cut to shape the rounded projecting face of the corbel.

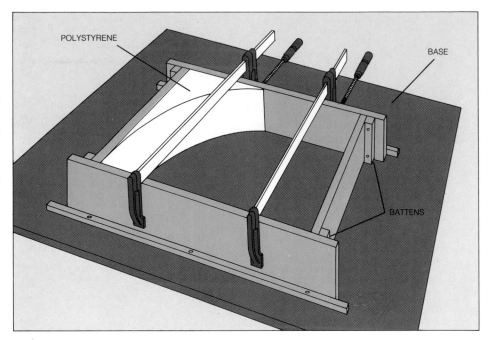

POLYSTYRENE

BASE

BATTENS

A Corbel-and-Beam Support for Sagging Joists

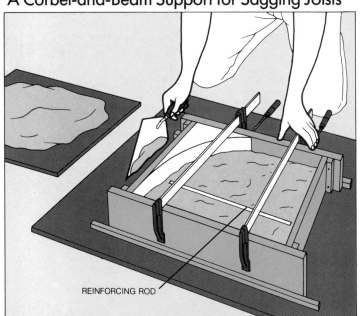

REINFORCING ROD

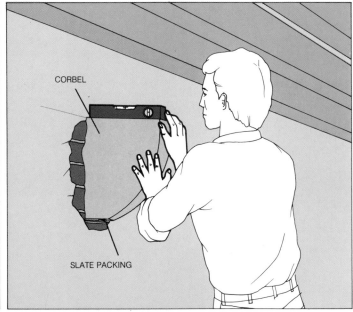

CORBEL

SLATE PACKING

1 Casting the corbels. Prepare a plywood box mould *(above)* and brush the interior surfaces with vegetable or form oil. Fill the mould one-third full with a strong concrete mix of 4 parts all-in ballast to 1 part Portland cement. Position a length of 6 mm reinforcing rod parallel to the long sides of the mould. Add another layer of concrete and a second rod above the first, then fill the mould to the top with concrete. Tamp down the concrete and gently tap the mould sides. Cover the concrete with polythene and allow it to set for 48 hours before removing the mould sides.

Cast the second corbel in the same mould. Allow each corbel to dry for a further 24 hours, then apply a bitumen-based paint to the areas that will be embedded in masonry.

2 Preparing the housings. Midway along the wall on opposite sides of the room, measure down from the nearest joist the depth of the beam to be installed and mark a horizontal line on each wall. Working down from these lines, use a club hammer and bolster to chop holes 150 mm deep and slightly longer and wider than the corbel ends.

With a helper, insert one corbel into its housing and wedge pieces of slate underneath to pack it up to the horizontal line. Check that the bearing surface of the corbel is horizontal *(above)* and that it projects at least 250 mm from the wall; if necessary, adjust the housing with the bolster and hammer. Remove the corbel from its housing and check the opposite corbel in the same way.

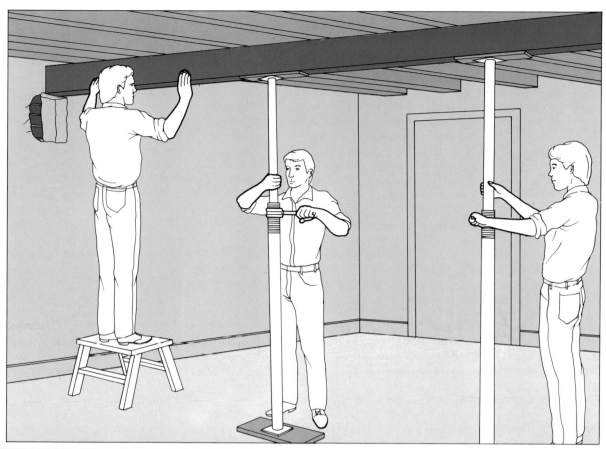

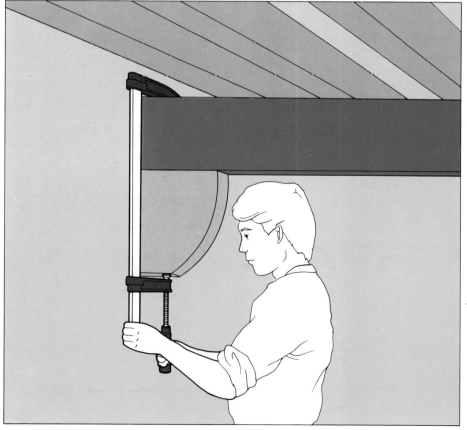

3 **Raising the beam.** Get two helpers to hold the beam in position with its ends directly in line with the corbel housings. Place two adjustable props under the beam, each a third of the way out from a wall; stand the props on 225 by 50 mm base plates and place short lengths of timber over their top plates to protect the beam. Gradually raise both props until the bottom of the beam is flush with the tops of the corbel housings.

4 **Installing the corbels.** Lay a bed of mortar on the bottom of one of the corbel housings, then spread mortar over the part of the corbel that is to be inserted into the housing. With a helper, raise the corbel into position and pack it up with pieces of slate until its top upper surface touches the underside of the beam. Clamp the corbel to the beam *(left)*, then pack mortar round the sides of and underneath the corbel. Install the second corbel in the same way. Allow the mortar to set for at least two days before removing the cramps and adjustable props.

117

Preserving Timber from Rot and Woodworm

An old house often provides shelter for a host of unwelcome visitors, including birds, rodents and insects. Of all these pests, the most destructive are the insects and fungi which feed on timber and can, unless they are checked, cause extensive structural damage.

The main culprit among the wood-boring insects is the common furniture beetle, which attacks both softwoods and hardwoods. Less common but equally voracious are the house longhorn beetle, which attacks only well-seasoned softwoods such as roofing timbers; the powder post beetle, which confines its attention to hardwoods; and the death-watch beetle, which preys almost exclusively on oak that is already partly decayed. The life cycles of these beetles vary in length but follow a similar pattern: the larvae, after hatching from the eggs of the female beetle laid in cracks and crevices in rough timber, burrow through the timber for as long as three or four years before changing into the chrysalis and then into the adult form. On emerging from the wood, the adult beetles leave behind them the telltale signs of their presence—tiny exit holes and a scattering of light-coloured bore dust.

Having found signs of infestation, carry out a thorough inspection of the house, paying particular attention to skirtings, floorboards and roof timbers *(page 13)*. Extensive areas of infestation should be treated by a specialist company; many firms offer free surveys and estimates, and in most cases the treatment is guaranteed for 30 years. If the outbreak is fairly limited, however, you can treat it yourself with a proprietary insecticidal fluid.

After probing the timber for soundness with an awl or screwdriver blade, cut out and burn the badly weakened sections. Insecticidal fluid can either be injected directly into the flight holes or applied to the surface with a brush or spray *(opposite page)*. A pressurized garden sprayer with an extension lance is especially convenient for reaching less accessible areas, such as the top of the eaves or the underside of the floorboards. Leave treated floorboards for at least four weeks before covering them with carpet, and for at least six months before attempting to lay any kind of impermeable floor covering.

Woodworm fluid is noxious, corrosive and highly inflammable. When applying the fluid, wear overalls or old clothes, heavy-duty gloves, goggles, a face mask and a head covering; if you are working in the attic, a safety helmet will prevent you from banging your head on the rafters. Open any windows in the room you are spraying and do not smoke in the working area, either during treatment or in the 48 hours following. Cover cables or water tanks with polythene sheeting; remove any insulation material from between the joists, and do not replace it before the timbers are dry. As soon as you have finished, wash contaminated clothing.

A powerful torch will usually show up any exit holes in timber more clearly than an overhead bulb. If you do need to provide additional lighting in an attic or basement, make sure that the switch is well away from the working area—sparks caused by a faulty switch could ignite the fumes given off by the fluid.

Unlike woodworm, the two types of wood-decaying fungi—wet rot and dry rot—need moisture in order to develop. An attack usually occurs where timber is in direct and continuous contact with damp masonry or brickwork—in door and window frames, for example, or in floor and skirting boards beside an exterior wall *(overleaf)*. However, whereas wet rot remains localized to the source of moisture, dry rot can spread far away from it, transferring itself not only to dry timber but to other materials such as stone, brick, mortar and plaster.

Wet rot is the more prevalent, but is also more simple to treat *(pages 120–121)*. It can be detected by testing with a pointed tool for softness in the wood; the strands—or "hyphae"—of the fungus grow in a dark, veinlike pattern, but except in advanced cases there may be no visible evidence. The fungus can be eradicated by removing the source of the damp and allowing the timber to dry out, but you will need to treat replacement sections of wood, and also all sound timber surrounding the affected area, with a preservative. Apply the preservative in the same way as woodworm fluid, using a pressurized garden sprayer, and follow the same safety precautions.

Treatment for dry rot is best left to a professional. The fungus produces thick, grey hyphae which mat together in fluffy masses, and when in an advanced stage of growth give off a distinctive mushroomy smell. If you are not sure whether wet rot or dry rot is causing the trouble, get an expert opinion. To prevent rot recurring, it is essential to remove the original source of damp. The most common causes of damp include blocked or defective gutters and downpipes *(pages 92–95)*, slipped tiles on the roof *(pages 88–91)*, leaking pipes *(pages 74–75)* and a defective DPC *(page 122)*.

Dealing with Woodworm in an Attic

1 **Cleaning the timber.** Take up any insulating material between the joists, and cover water tanks and exposed pipes and cables with polythene sheeting. Scrub all areas of infestation and surrounding timbers with a stiff brush to remove dust and dirt. Use a vacuum cleaner fitted with a nozzle to remove the debris between the joists.

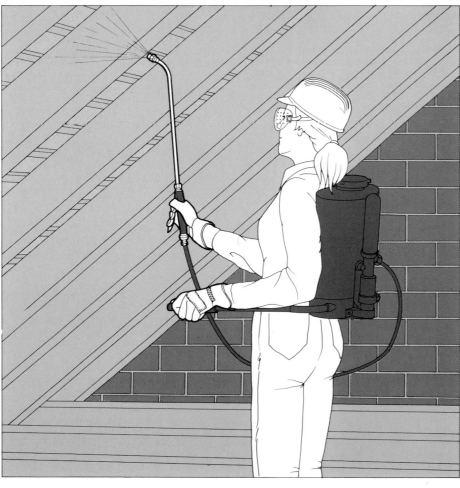

2 **Spraying the fluid.** Using a pressurized garden sprayer, apply insecticidal fluid both to the infested areas and to the surrounding timbers. Hold the nozzle close to the timber and apply the fluid liberally, paying particular attention to cracks, joints and end-grain. Leave the first coat to dry for about three weeks, then apply a second coat of fluid in the same way.

If necessary, adjust the spray pressure or change the nozzle of the sprayer after testing it on some of the infested timber. Too fine a spray will cause the fluid to vaporize, and too coarse a spray will drench the timber and cause puddles.

Tackling Wet Rot
in a Timber Floor

1 **Removing damaged skirting.** Probe with a penknife or screwdriver to identify areas of soft wood, then use a tenon saw to make vertical cuts through the skirting board at least 500 mm outside the decayed area. Insert a thin crowbar behind the rotten section and prise it away from the wall, using a timber block to protect the wall and provide leverage. To remove a long section of skirting board, prise from the middle to the ends, using timber wedges to hold the seam open.

2 **Removing damaged boards.** Starting at the source of the rot, lift every floorboard until you reach sound timber. To lift a square-edged board, insert a bolster chisel on one side about 75 mm from the end, and lever the board up; then insert the chisel on the other side and repeat. Support the raised end with a piece of timber, then lever up the rest of the board, starting at the opposite end *(above)*. To lift tongue and groove boards, split off the tongue of the first board before prising up the others *(page 53)*.

If the rot falls short of the end of a board, use a jigsaw or a padsaw to cut through the board across the centre of a joist and lever the board up with the bolster chisel. If you intend to treat the whole of the area beneath the floor, remove every sixth board beyond the rotten section, which should allow you sufficient access.

3 **Cleaning and spraying.** Probe the exposed joists to test for rot—if any are affected, they must be replaced *(page 115)*. Rub down all exposed timbers with a stiff brush and remove dust and debris from between the joists with a nozzle-type vacuum cleaner. Using a pressurized garden sprayer, treat both above and below the floor with a proprietary preservative containing a fungicide. Allow the first coat to dry, then apply a second coat. If necessary, use some of the spare boards to make a working platform over the joists.

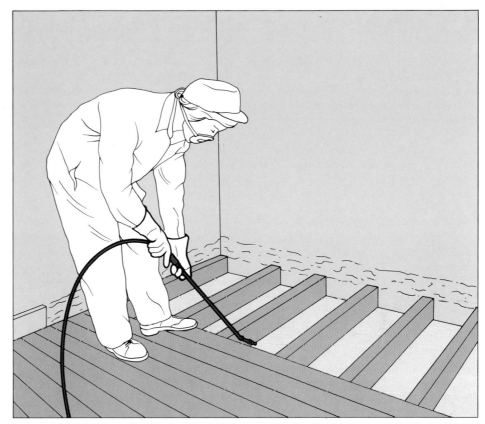

4 **Treating replacement timber.** Brush two coats of preservative on to any of the old floorboards you are using again *(right)*, and make sure that all the new timber is pressure-impregnated with preservative. If you have to cut any of the new timber, stand the sawn ends in a bucket of preservative for at least 10 minutes. When all surfaces have dried out completely, nail down the new floorboards to the joists and the new skirting boards to the wall.

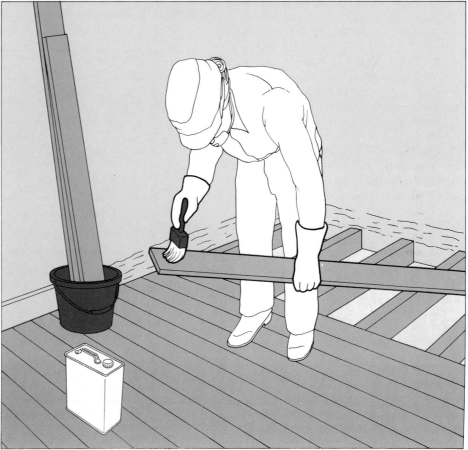

A Chemical Barrier Against Rising Damp

One of the most serious problems affecting older houses is rising damp. It not only damages paint, plaster and wallpaper, but also threatens the adjoining woodwork by creating an ideal environment for wet rot and dry rot. The damp is drawn by capillary action from the soil into the walls and is a sign either that the house lacks a damp-proof course (DPC) or that a DPC already in place is damaged or defective in some way.

To check whether or not your house has a DPC, examine the outer walls just above ground level. An extra-wide mortar course means that you have the traditional type of DPC, consisting of a layer of slate, lead or copper. A thin black line means that you have a DPC of polythene sheeting or bituminous felt. If the DPC has been bridged by earth heaped up against the wall or has been rendered over down to ground level, you can cure rising damp by clearing the earth or stripping off the rendering. If you find that your home has no DPC, however, or if the existing DPC is broken or inadequate, you must install a new barrier against rising damp.

The easiest, quickest and most effective solution is to inject the walls with a silicone or aluminium stearate water repellant. This cuts off the capillary action of the masonry, preventing the passage of moisture up from the ground. The process involves drilling a series of holes in the wall and then using a pressure injection pump to force the damp-coursing solution into the holes. Solid walls up to 225 mm thick need be drilled from one side only (*opposite page*), but solid walls which are thicker than 225 mm and cavity walls must be drilled from both sides.

A tool-hire shop should be able to provide all the equipment you need. An injection pump consists of an intake hose for drawing the damp-coursing solution into the system, and supply hoses with detachable nozzles for injecting the fluid into the drilled holes. The fluid itself, which you should be able to buy from the shop where you hire the pump, is generally available in 2.5, 5 and 25 litre drums. For a standard solid wall you will need about 1 litre of fluid for every 300 mm of length. The exact amount required, however, will depend on the type of wall and the extent of the damp, and you should ask the hire shop to give you an estimate based on the manufacturer's recommendations.

Make sure, before starting, that you have easy access to the walls round the house. Strip off any rendering to a height of 450 mm above the line of visible damp; a new waterproof section can be applied later. Inside the house, strip off plaster to the same level; later replace it with plaster containing a waterproofing solution.

Damp-coursing solution has a pungent odour and is highly inflammable. Always wear goggles and heavy-duty gloves when you are handling the solution, and do not smoke. If you apply the solution inside the house, keep the doors and windows open.

Injecting a Damp-Coursing Solution

1 Drilling the injection holes. Using a heavy-duty hammer drill, make a series of holes round the house about 150 mm above ground level. The holes should be 75 mm deep, 10 to 15 mm in diameter and 100 to 150 mm apart—the exact spacing and diameter will be specified by the manufacturers of the damp-coursing solution. Wind some insulating tape round the bit, 75 mm from the end, as a depth guide, and angle the drill slightly downwards as you work.

Where an old DPC runs round the house, drill the holes just above it. If the ground floor of the house is solid concrete, try to align the holes with the damp-proof membrane in the floor; for a suspended timber floor, ensure that the holes are below floor level.

2 Preparing the pump. Plug the pump into the mains electricity supply, attach the 75 mm injection nozzles to the supply hoses and connect the hoses to the pump outlet. Insert the pump intake hose into the drum of damp-coursing solution, then turn on the pump at low pressure and use the primer to draw fluid through the machine. Check for airlocks in the supply hoses according to the manufacturer's instructions. When the fluid is flowing smoothly, switch off the pump.

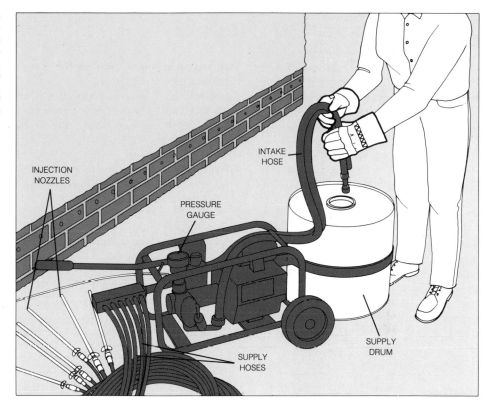

INJECTION
NOZZLES

PRESSURE
GAUGE

INTAKE
HOSE

SUPPLY
HOSES

SUPPLY
DRUM

3 Injecting the fluid. Starting at one end of a wall, insert the nozzles into consecutive holes. Turn the wing nut on each nozzle to force the barrel against the inside of the hole, thus ensuring a tight fit. Switch on the pump, open the valves on the hoses and adjust the main valve on the pump itself until the pressure gauge shows about 65 bar. Wait until the brickwork is saturated—this should take only a few seconds—then turn off the valves on the hoses, move the nozzles along to the next set of holes and repeat the process.

When you reach the end of the wall, switch off the pump and drill the holes you have just treated to a depth of 190 mm. Swap the 75 mm injection nozzles for 190 mm ones and inject the fluid as before. Immediately after use, flush the equipment through thoroughly with white spirit or paraffin to prevent the fluid from "curing" and causing damage. Allow a minimum of one week for drying out and then make good the holes in the walls, using a mortar mix of 1 part Portland cement to 3 parts fine sand.

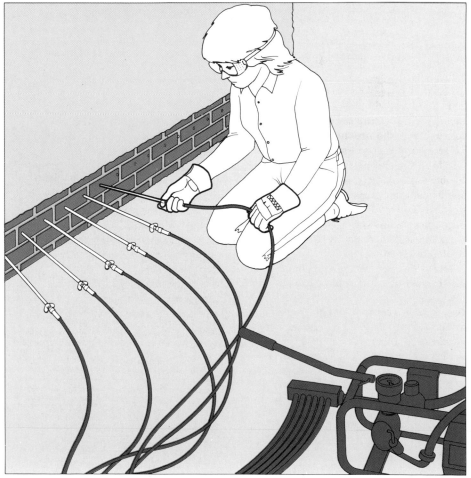

Picture Credits

The sources for the illustrations in this book are shown below. Credits for the illustrations from left to right are separated by semicolons, from top to bottom by dashes.

Cover: John Elliott. 6: John Elliott. 9–19: Drawings by Oxford Illustrators Ltd. 22: John Elliott. 24–27: Drawings by Oxford Illustrators Ltd. 29–31: Drawings by John Massey. 34: Drawings by Walter Hilmers Jr.—drawing by Oxford Illustrators Ltd. 35: Drawing by Oxford Illustrators Ltd.—drawing by Walter Hilmers Jr. 36: Drawings by Walter Hilmers Jr. 37–39: Draw-ings by Oxford Illustrators Ltd. 40–43: Drawings by Frederic F. Bigio from B-C Graphics. 44–49: Drawings by Oxford Illustrators Ltd. 50: Drawings by Ray Skibinski. 51: Drawing by Ray Skibinski—drawing by Oxford Illustrators Ltd. 52–57: Drawings by Oxford Illustrators Ltd. 58, 59: Drawings by Eduino Pereira. 60–63: Drawings by Oxford Illustrators Ltd. 64: John Elliott. 66–74: Drawings by Oxford Illustrators Ltd. 75: Drawings by John Massey. 76: Drawing by Oxford Illus-trators Ltd.—drawing by John Massey. 77, 78: Drawings by John Massey. 79: Draw-ing by John Massey—drawing by Oxford Illustrators Ltd. 80–85: Drawings by Oxford Illustrators Ltd. 86: John Elliott. 88: Drawing by Oxford Illustrators Ltd. 89: Drawings by Walter Hilmers Jr. 90: Draw-ing by Oxford Illustrators Ltd.—drawing by Walter Hilmers Jr. 91–95: Drawings by Oxford Illustrators Ltd. 96, 97: Drawings by Snowden Associates, Inc. 98–103: Drawings by Oxford Illustrators Ltd. 104: Drawings by Peter McGinn. 105: Drawing by Oxford Illustrators Ltd.—drawings by Forte, Inc. 106–123: Drawings by Oxford Illustrators Ltd.

Acknowledgements

The editors would like to thank the fol-lowing: Black & Decker, Slough, Berk-shire; British Chemical Dampcourse As-sociation, Reading, Berkshire; Paul Davis, Corby, Northamptonshire; Anna-Marie D'Cruz, London; Cathy Dickinson, White-way & Waldron, London; Tim Fraser, Sydney, Australia; Peter Hillman and Alan May, Vauxhall College, London; Elizabeth Hodgson, London; G. Jackson & Sons Ltd., London; Lopez Ltd., London; Kevin McNamara, Townsends, London; Wayne Ohlback, Bass Hill, N.S.W., Aus-tralia; Jim Phillips, Trend Cutters, Wat-ford, Hertfordshire; Yves Piron, Grenoble, France; Vicki Robinson, London; Sally Rowland, Thaxted, Essex; Penny Sea-brook, London; Colin Southwell, Southwell Stockwell Ltd., London; TRADA, High Wy-combe, Berkshire; Walcot Reclamation, Bath, Avon; Wylex, Manchester.

Index/Glossary

Included in this index are definitions of some of the typical terms used in this book. Page references in italics indicate an illustration of the subject mentioned.

Adjustable steel props, *87*, 112; using, *115, 117*
Algae, removing from masonry, 98, *99*
Alterations, inspecting, 15
Aluminium roofs, 9
Ammoniated cleaners, using, 33
Apron flashing, see Flashing
Architects, 20
Architrave: *decorative moulding round door or window frames*; see Wooden moulding
Ashlar wall, replacing stones in, 98
Attic: checking insulation in, 13; checking timbers in, *13*; checking ventilation in, 13; treating woodworm in, 118, *119*

Baluster: *vertical post in a staircase balustrade*; inspecting, *15*; repairing, *62–63*; stripping paint from, 32; tightening, 62

Bathroom: checking caulking in, *18*; checking for damp, 14, 15; checking tiles in, *18*
Beam, timber bracing, 112; casting corbels for, *116*; installing corbels for, *117*; preparing housings for, *116*; raising, *117*
Beams, timber ceiling, 44; applying preservative to, *45*; cleaning, *45*; exposing, *44*; installing plasterboard between, *45–47*; staining, *45*; testing for woodworm, 44
Beeswax, using, 33
Beetles, see Woodworm
Bleach, using on wood, 32
Blow-torch, using, *25*, 32, 33
Boiler, central-heating: checking flue of, 19; checking for gas leaks, 19; checking oil-fired, *19*; checking solid-fuel, *19*
Boiler union, 76
Box mould: anatomy of, *116*; using, *116*
Brass: cleaning, 27; preventing from tarnishing, 27
Brick walls, see Walls, masonry
Bricklayers, 20
Browning, 108

Building contractors, 20
Butane torch, using, *25*, 32, 33

Cable, electric: checking, 16; concealing in plaster, *82*; feeding inside walls, *82*; notching joists for, 112, *114*; running under floorboards, *82*
Came: *lead channel holding edges of glass panes in a stained glass window*; cutting, 28, *30*; soldering, 28, *31*
Carpenters, 20
Carpet layers, 21
Caulking gun: *tool for applying sealant from a cartridge*; using, *104*
Caulking iron: *tool used to pack caulking yarn into joints*; 74; using, *75*
Caulking yarn: *rope-like sealant impregnated with oil*; 74; using, *75*
Caustic-paste paint strippers, 32, 33; using, *34*
Ceilings: exposing beams in, *44–47*; inspecting, *14*, 15; patching with plasterboard, 108, *110–111*; plastering, *108–110*. See also Cornice, plaster
Cellars: analysing cracks in, *12*; checking

ventilation in, 12; detecting damp in, *12*; examining timbers in, *12*

Central heating system: adding circulating pump to, 70, *73*; balancing radiators in, 70; draining and refilling, 71; inspecting, 7, *19*. See also Radiator; Thermostatic radiator valve

Chemical strippers, 32, 33; using, *34*

Chimney: anatomy of, *66*; checking updraught in, 15; cleaning of, 66; extending flue of, 66; inspecting, 8, *9*, *66*; installing dovecote cap on, *68*; renewing flaunching around pot, *68*; replacing pot, *68*. See also Fireplace

Chopped strand mat, 96; using, *96–97*

Cistern, cold water: inspecting, 17

Cladding, timber: caulking joints in, *104*; filling large cracks in, 87, *105*; removing rust from, *104*; removing old paint from, 104; replacing damaged sections of, 104, *105*

Clay tiled roof, 9; replacing tiles on, *90*

Compression nuts, *72*, *73*, 77

Concrete, patching with fibreglass, *96–97*

Concrete contractors, 20

Concrete tiled roof, 9; replacing tiles on, *90*

Consumer unit: *unit housing fuses or circuit breakers for an electrical installation*; *16*; checking fuses in, 80, *81*; replacing fuses in, *81*

Convector unit: *heating unit with a fan that draws air over a heating coil*; removing dust from, *19*

Corbel: *masonry or concrete wall projection that supports a beam*; 112; casting, *116*; installing, *117*; making box mould for, *116*

Cornice, plaster: *decorative plaster moulding round the top of an internal wall*; plaster mix for, 40; removing paint from, 40; renewing "plain-run" sections, 40, *42–43*; repairing chips in, *23*, *40*; replacing small section of, 40, *41*

CPVC pipe, 74, 76

Cylinder, hot water: inspecting, *18*

Damp, 87; common causes of, 118; detecting in cellar, *12*; inspecting for, 8, *11*, 15. See also Damp-proof course

Damp and rot specialists, 20, 118

Damp-proof course, 87; checking, *11*, 122; injecting chemical, *122–123*

"Dead man": *T-shaped timber support used to hold plasterboard in position while fixing to a ceiling*; using, *46*

Death-watch beetle, 118. See also Woodworm

Decorators, professional, 21

Door, panel: adjusting strike plate of, *54*; causes of sticking in, 54; inspecting, 14, 15; planing edges of, 54, *55*; repairing hinge screw holes in, *55*; replacing split panel in, 54, *57*; shimming hinge of, *55*; strengthening joints of, 54, *56*

Dovecote cap: *concrete slab on supports set over a chimney opening*; installing, *68*

Downpipe, cast-iron, 17; inspecting, 8, *10*; recaulking joint in, 74, *75*; removing, 92; replacing section of, 76, *78–79*; replacing with plastic, *95*; unblocking, 92

Drain and sewer cleaners, 21

Drain rods, using, *79*

Drainpipe, see Downpipe, cast-iron

Drains: examining, *17*; unblocking, *79*

Driveways, inspecting, 8

Drum sander, 48; using, *50*

Dry rot, 12, 87, 118

Dry-wall screws, 44; using, *46*

Duckboard, 88

Edge sander, 48; using, *50*

Efflorescence: *powdery white stains that appear on masonry walls as dampness dries out*; as sign of damp, 8, *12*; removing, 98

Electrical circuit: adding new socket to, *84–85*; consumer unit for, *16*; earthing of, 16; inspecting, *16*, 80; installing two-way switch in, *83*; miniature circuit breakers for, *16*, 80; overloading of, 80; replacing socket in, *81*; residual current circuit breakers for, 80, *81*; rewiring fuse in, 80, *81*; routing new cable for, *82*

Electrical fittings, testing, *80*

Electricians, 21

Epoxy filler: making, 28; using, *29*

Excavation contractors, 21

Fanlight, shaping new bars for, 37

Fascia board: *board fixed to rafter ends that supports guttering*; *92*; inspecting, *10*; repairing, 92, *93*

Featheredge: *long rule with one edge tapered*; 108; using, *109*

Federation of Master Builders, 20

Felt, roofing, 9

Fibreglass: bandaging pipe with, 74, *75*; patching corners and curves with, *97*; patching flat surfaces with, *96–97*

Filler, wood: using, *36*

Fireplace: anatomy of, *66*; conducting smoke test for, *67*; inspecting, 15, *66*; installing throat restrictor in, 66; opening up, 66; reducing opening of to

prevent smoking, 66, *69*; repairing firebrick joints in, *67*. See also Chimney

Flags, see Stone tiled roof

Flashing: *weatherproof strips used to seal joints between adjacent roof sections or between roofing and a wall*; *9*, 88; repairing, 88, *91*

Flashing tape, using, *91*

Flaunching: *sloping cap of mortar on top of a chimney*; *66*; cracked, *9*; renewing, *68*

Floor layers, 21

Floorboards, see Floors, wooden

Floors, wooden, 48; causes of sagging in, 112; concealing gaps round skirting, 48; eliminating squeaks in, 48; filling cracks between boards, *49*; inspecting, 15; lifting boards in, 48, *52*, 120; plugging holes in, *49*; reinforcing joists beneath, 112, *113–114*; replacing joists beneath, 87, *115*; replacing tongue and groove boards in, 48, *52–53*; running cable under, *82*; sanding, 48, *50*; supporting with posts, 112, *113*; supporting with corbel-and-beam structure, 112, *116–117*; treating for wet rot, 118, *120–121*; treating for woodworm, 118. See also Parquet flooring

Fungus, see Dry rot; Wet rot

Furniture beetle, common, 118. See also Woodworm

Fuse: checking, 80, *81*; replacing, *81*

Fuse box, 16

Glass, cutting, 28, *30*

Glass fibre, see Fibreglass

Glaziers, 21

Glue-laminated timber, 112

Grozing pliers: *tool used for shaping and fitting glass in leaded windows*; 28; using, *31*

Gutter, cast-iron: inspecting, 8, *9*, *10*; patching with fibreglass, 96, *97*; preventing corrosion of, 92; removing, 92; replacing with plastic, *94*; unblocking, 92

Hardwood: staining, 32; stripping, 32

Hawk: *square board with handle for carrying mortar*; using, *100*, *103*, *109*

Hearth, see Fireplace

Heating, central, see Central heating system

Heating contractors, 21

Hinges: repairing screw holes caused by old, *55*; shimming, *55*

Hot-air paint stripper, 32, 33; using, *35*, 104

Immersion heater, inspecting, *18*
Inspection chamber, *17, 79*
Inspection tool kit, *7, 8*
Insulation installers, 21
Insulation mat, installing, 44, *46*
Iron railings, 24; repairing joints in, 24; securing loose post in, 24, *26–27*; stripping paint from, 24, *25*

Jack plane, using, *51, 55*
Joiners, 20
Joint filler, *100*
Jointer, bricklayer's: *tool for shaping mortar joints between bricks*; using, *100*
Joist: *horizontal timber beam that supports flooring*; checking for sag, *12*; determining direction of, 48; notching for cables, 112; reinforcing, 112, *113–114*; replacing, 87, *115*; shoring up, 112, *113*; supporting with corbel-and-beam structure, 112, *116–117*

Kitchen, inspecting, 14, 15
Knot-holes, filling, *49*
"Knotting", shellac, 32

Lacquer, removing, 32, 33
Ladder, securing, 87, 88, 92
Lath and plaster: *plaster adhering to a grid of thin timber strips, used in old walls and ceilings*; inspecting, *14*; patching with plasterboard, 108, *110–111*; removing, *44*; replastering, 108
Lavatory, inspecting, *18*
Lead roof, 9
Leaded window, see Stained-glass window, leaded
Leaks: listening for, *17*; signs of in attic, 13; stopping in pipes, *74*
Lichen, removing from masonry, 98, *99*
Linseed oil, using, 33
Locks, old, 24; cleaning, *24*; mortise, *24*; removing mortise, *25*; removing rim, *24*; rim, *24*
Lockshield: *smooth cover of a radiator return valve*; 70
Loft, see Attic
Longhorn beetle, 118. See also Woodworm

Mains-tester screwdriver, *80*
Marble mantelpiece: cleaning stains from, 29; filling cracks and chips in, 28, *29*; removing paint from, 28
Masonry walls, see Walls, masonry
MCB, see Miniature circuit breaker
Metal roof, 9
Methylated spirit, using, 32, 33
Methylene-dichloride strippers, 32, 33; using, *34*

Miniature circuit breaker (MCB), *16*, 80
Mortar: mix for rendering, 102; mix for repointing, 98, 101; removing stains from, 98
Mortise lock: *lock housed in the closing edge of a door*; anatomy of, *24*; cleaning, *24*; removing, *25*
Moulding, see Cornice, plaster; Wooden moulding
Moulding compound, cold-pour, 40; using, *41*
Moulding plaster: mixing, 40; using, *41*
"Mouse": *small weight that pulls cord or cable through an enclosed space*; using, *82*

Newel post: *structural top or bottom post of a staircase balustrade*; inspecting, *15*; reinforcing, 62, *63*
Nib: *hook-like projection under the top of a tile*; *90*
No-hub fitting: *coupling for securing replacement section of cast-iron pipe*; 76; using, *78–79*

Oil-fired boiler, inspecting, *19*
Orbital sander, using, 32, *35*
Oyster knife: *tool used to prise up sections of lead came*; using, *28*

Paint stripping: on iron railings, 24, *25*; on marble, 28; on masonry walls, 98, *99*; on plaster mouldings, 40; using chemicals, 32, 33, *35*, 104; using hot-air gun; on wood, 32, 33, *34*
Painters, professional, 21
Panelling, wooden, see Wooden moulding
Paris white, see Whiting, painter's
Parquet flooring: replacing pieces of, 48, *51*; sanding, 48, *50*
Paths, inspecting, 8
Pebble dash, repairing, 102. See also Rendering
Picture rail, see Wooden moulding
Pipes: bandaging with fibreglass, 74, *75*; cast-iron, 74; copper, 17; clogged, 17; CPVC, 74, 76; installing slip fitting to repair, *74*; joining copper to lead, 76, *77*; joining copper to steel, *65*, 76, *77*; joining plastic to steel, 76, *77*; lead, 17, 74; lifespan of, 17; listening for leaks in, *17*; rusted, 17; solvent-welding to plastic connector, *76*; steel, 17, 74. See also Downpipe, cast-iron
Plane, jack: using, *51, 55*
Plane, smoothing: using, *51, 55*
Plaster moulding, see Cornice, plaster
Plaster of Paris, see Moulding plaster
Plasterboard: attaching, 44, *45–46*;

cutting, *46*; feathering joints in, *47*; filling and taping joints in, *47*; inspecting, *14*; patching wall or ceiling with, 108, *110–111*; removing, *44*
Plastered wall, see Wall, plastered
Plasterers, 21
Plastering: applying backing coat, *109*; applying finish coat, *110*; keying backing coat, *109*; mixing plaster, 108; preparing wall for, *108*; tools required for, 108
Plumbers, 21
Plumbing, see Central heating system; Pipes
Pointing: checking, *11*; renewing, see Repointing
Polyurethane varnish, 33; removing, 33
Poultices, stain-removing, 29
Powder post beetle, 118. See also Woodworm
Pressure washer, 98; using, *99*
Propane torch, using, 74, *75*
Props, see Adjustable steel props
PTFE tape, 70; using, *71, 72*
Pump, circulating, 70; installing, 70, *73*; venting, *73*
Putty powder, 29
PVA bonding agent, using, 106, *107*

Quadrant moulding: *quarter-round timber moulding*; installing, *48*

Radiator: balancing, 70; inspecting, 19, 70; installing, 70; installing thermostatic valve on, 70, *72*; resealing valve on, *71*; signs of corrosion in, 70; valve on, 70; venting of, *71*
Rafters: *sloping timbers extending from the ridge of a roof to the eave*; inspecting, *10, 13*; repairing ends of, *93*
Railings, see Iron railings
RCCB, see Residual current circuit breaker
Rendering: *mortar coating on the outside of a wall*; inspecting, *11*; patching with fibreglass, *96–97*; patching with mortar, *102–103*; removing, *102*; repairing cracks in, 87, *102*
Repointing: *raking out and refilling deteriorated mortar joints*; 11, 98, *100*; mortar mix for, 98, 101
Residual current circuit breaker (RCCB), 80, *81*
Resin, epoxy, 96; using, *96–97*
Resin, polyester, 96. See also Resin, epoxy
Ridge tile, 9; rebedding, *88*
Rim lock: *lock mounted on the inside face of a door;* anatomy of, *24*; cleaning, *24*; removing, *24*
Ring final circuit: *wiring circuit in which*

all outlets are linked by a cable that starts and ends at the consumer unit; 84
Rolled steel joist (RSJ), 112. See also Beam, timber bracing
Roof: covering materials for, 9: fitting wooden shingles to, 90; inspecting, 7, 8, 9, 88; rebedding ridge tile on, 88; renewing timber batten in, 88; repairing flashing on, 91; replacing slates on, 89; replacing tiles on, 90. See also Attic; Chimney; Gutter
Roofers, professional, 21
Rot, see Dry rot; Wet rot
Rot specialists, 20, 118
Router: anatomy of, 37; safety precautions when using, 37; using, 37, 38, 39
RSJ, see Rolled steel joist
Rust: removing, 25; removing stains from marble, 29; removing stains from timber cladding, 104

Sander: drum, 48, 50; edge, 48, 50; orbital, 32, 35
Sash cord, 58; replacing, 59–60
Sash window, see Window
Scotia moulding: *concave timber moulding*; installing, 48
Screw jack, bell-shaped, 112
Screwdriver, mains-tester, 80
Scrim: *coarse fabric used in repairing cracks or bridging joints*; attaching, 111
Secret nailing, 48, 53
Septic tank, inspecting, 17
Shimming, 55
Shingles, wood, 9; replacing, 90
Shiplap cladding, see Cladding, timber
Shoe fitting; *fitting on the bottom end of a downpipe that channels water away from house wall*; securing, 95
Shuttering box, 106; making, 106–107
Silicone polish, using, 33
Skirting boards: checking, 15; cleaning, 32, 33; concealing gaps beneath, 48; filling dents in, 36; removing, 120; stripping paint from, 32, 33, 34–35
Slate ripper, 88; using, 89
Slate roofing, 9; replacing damaged, 88, 89
"Sleeper wall", 112
Slip fitting: *fitting for sealing a leaking pipe*; 74; installing, 74
Smoothing plane, using, 51, 55
Socket, electrical: adding to circuit, 84–85; inspecting, 16; replacing, 80, 81; running cable to, 82; testing, 16
Socket outlet tester, 16
Soffit: *underside of the edge of a roof*; 92; inspecting, 10; repairing, 92, 93
Softwood, stripping paint from, 32
Soil stack: cleaning eye in, 79; replacing

section of, 76, 78–79
Soldering: of copper connectors, 77; to repair leaded windows, 31
Solid-fuel boiler, inspecting, 19
Solvent-welding, 76
Spalling: *eroded or flaking masonry*; 11
Spindle moulder, 37. See also Router
Stained-glass window, leaded: cleaning, 28; repairing crack in, 28; repairing loose glass in, 28; repairing when bowed, 28, 31; replacing glass in, 28, 30–31
Stains, removing: from marble, 29; from masonry, 98, 99; from timber cladding, 104
Staircase: "closed-string", 62; inspecting, 15; "open-string", 62; reinforcing newel post of, 62, 63; strengthening joints of, 112. See also Baluster
Stone tiled roof, 9; replacing tiles on, 90
Stone walls, see Walls, masonry
Stonemasons, 21
Stoptap, mains, 17
Strike plate: *metal plate that receives the bolt or latch of a door lock*; adjusting, 54
Strippers, paint: chemical, 32, 33, 34; hot-air, 32, 33, 35
Stripping tank, 32, 36
Subcontractors, 20
Subsidence, checking for, 10
Sugar soap, using, 32, 33
Surveyors, 21
Swan's neck: *pipe unit joining a downpipe to a projecting gutter*; fitting, 95
Swarf: *slivers of cut metal*; removing, 26
Switch, two-way: installing, 83

Tap wrench: *tool used for cutting a screw thread in metal*; 24; using, 26
Termites, checking for, 8
Thatched roof, 9
Thermostatic radiator valve (TRV), 70; installing, 72
Tile, roof, 9; replacing, 90
Tin oxide powder, 29
Tingle: *metal strip used to secure replacement slates*; using, 89
Tongue and groove boards: cutting tongue for, 52; finding replacements for, 48; removing, 52, 120; renewing, 53; secret-nailing of, 53
Torque-wrench socket tool, using, 79
Transition fitting: copper-to-lead, 76, 77; copper-to-steel, 65, 76, 77; plastic-to-steel, 76, 77
Trees, inspecting, 8
TRV, see Thermostatic radiator valve

Union connector, 65, 76; using, 77

Valley flashing, see Flashing
Varnish: applying, 32, 33; removing, 32, 33

Walls, masonry: cleaning, 98, 99; inspecting, 8, 10, 11; mortar mixes for, 98, 101; patching with fibreglass, 96–97; replacing brick in, 101; repointing, 11, 98, 100; stripping paint from, 98, 99. See also Rendering
Walls, plastered: checking, 14; concealing cable in, 82; filling holes in, 108; patching with plaster, 108–110; patching with plasterboard, 108, 110–111; repairing cracks in, 108
Walls, retaining: checking, 8
Walls, rubblestone; replacing stone in, 98
Water, hard, 17
Water pressure, testing, 14, 18
Wax polish, using, 33
Weatherboarding, see Cladding, timber
Wet rot, 87; detecting, 7, 8, 118; treating in timber floor, 118, 120–121
Wheelhead: *knurled cover of a radiator flow valve*; 70
Whiting, painter's, 28, 29
Window: anatomy of, 58; checking, 14, 15; easing tight sash of, 59; freeing frozen sash of, 58; removing sash from, 59; replacing sash cords in, 58, 59–60; strengthening joints in, 58, 61. See also Stained-glass window, leaded; Window sill
Window sill: casting concrete, 106–107; filling cracks in stone or concrete, 106; filling hole in stone or concrete, 106; replacing rotten wood in, 106; testing for wood rot, 106
Wiring, see Electrical circuit
Wood-block flooring, see Parquet flooring
Wooden moulding: bleaching, 32; cleaning, 32, 33; finishes for, 33; painting, 32; patching dents and cracks in, 36; removing, 36; removing varnish from, 32, 33; replacing section of, 37, 38–39; sanding, 32, 35; sealing knots in, 32; staining, 32; stripping paint from 32, 33, 34–35, 36
Woodworm: inspecting timber for, 13 (in attic), 44 (in beams), 12 (in cellar), 15, (in floors), 15 (in stairs); life cycle of, 118, treating attic for, 118, 119; treating floors for, 118
Wrought-ironsmiths, 21

Yarning iron: *tool for packing caulking yarn into joints*; 74; using, 75

Zinc roof, 9

Metric Conversion Chart

Approximate equivalents—length

Millimetres to inches		Inches to millimetres	
1	$^1/_{32}$	$^1/_{32}$	1
2	$^1/_{16}$	$^1/_{16}$	2
3	$^1/_8$	$^1/_8$	3
4	$^5/_{32}$	$^3/_{16}$	5
5	$^3/_{16}$	$^1/_4$	6
6	$^1/_4$	$^5/_{16}$	8
7	$^9/_{32}$	$^3/_8$	10
8	$^5/_{16}$	$^7/_{16}$	11
9	$^{11}/_{32}$	$^1/_2$	13
10 (1cm)	$^3/_8$	$^9/_{16}$	14
11	$^7/_{16}$	$^5/_8$	16
12	$^{15}/_{32}$	$^{11}/_{16}$	17
13	$^1/_2$	$^3/_4$	19
14	$^9/_{16}$	$^{13}/_{16}$	21
15	$^{19}/_{32}$	$^7/_8$	22
16	$^5/_8$	$^{15}/_{16}$	24
17	$^{11}/_{16}$	1	25
18	$^{23}/_{32}$	2	51
19	$^3/_4$	3	76
20	$^{25}/_{32}$	4	102
25	1	5	127
30	$1^3/_{16}$	6	152
40	$1^9/_{16}$	7	178
50	$1^{31}/_{32}$	8	203
60	$2^3/_8$	9	229
70	$2^3/_4$	10	254
80	$3^5/_{32}$	11	279
90	$3^9/_{16}$	12 (1ft)	305
100	$3^{15}/_{16}$	13	330
200	$7^7/_8$	14	356
300	$11^{13}/_{16}$	15	381
400	$15^3/_4$	16	406
500	$19^{11}/_{16}$	17	432
600	$23^5/_8$	18	457
700	$27^9/_{16}$	19	483
800	$31^1/_2$	20	508
900	$35^7/_{16}$	24 (2ft)	610
1000 (1m)	$39^3/_8$		

Metres to feet/inches		Yards to metres	
		1	0.914
2	6' 7"	2	1.83
3	9' 10"	3	2.74
4	13' 1"	4	3.66
5	16' 5"	5	4.57
6	19' 8"	6	5.49
7	23' 0"	7	6.40
8	26' 3"	8	7.32
9	29' 6"	9	8.23
10	32' 10"	10	9.14
20	65' 7"	20	18.29
50	164' 0"	50	45.72
100	328' 1"	100	91.44

Conversion factors

Length

1 millimetre (mm)	= 0.0394 in
1 centimetre (cm)/10 mm	= 0.3937 in
1 metre/100 cm	= 39.37 in/3.281 ft/1.094 yd
1 kilometre (km)/1000 metres	= 1093.6 yd/0.6214 mile
1 inch (in)	= 25.4 mm/2.54 cm
1 foot (ft)/12 in	= 304.8 mm/30.48 cm/0.3048 metre
1 yard (yd)/3 ft	= 914.4 mm/91.44 cm/0.9144 metre
1 mile/1760 yd	= 1609.344 metres/1.609 km

Area

1 square centimetre (sq cm)/ 100 square millimetres (sq mm)	= 0.155 sq in
1 square metre (sq metre)/10,000 sq cm	= 10.764 sq ft/1.196 sq yd
1 are/100 sq metres	= 119.60 sq yd/0.0247 acre
1 hectare (ha)/100 ares	= 2.471 acres/0.00386 sq mile
1 square inch (sq in)	= 645.16 sq mm/6.4516 sq cm
1 square foot (sq ft)/144 sq in	= 929.03 sq cm
1 square yard (sq yd)/9 sq ft	= 8361.3 sq cm/0.8361 sq metre
1 acre/4840 sq yd	= 4046.9 sq metres/0.4047 ha
1 square mile/640 acres	= 259 ha/2.59 sq km

Volume

1 cubic centimetre (cu cm)/ 1000 cubic millimetres (cu mm)	= 0.0610 cu in
1 cubic decimetre (cu dm)/1000 cu cm	= 61.024 cu in/0.0353 cu ft
1 cubic metre/1000 cu dm	= 35.3147 cu ft/1.308 cu yd
1 cu cm	= 1 millilitre (ml)
1 cu dm	= 1 litre see **Capacity**
1 cubic inch (cu in)	= 16.3871 cu cm
1 cubic foot (cu ft)/1728 cu in	= 28,316.8 cu cm/0·0283 cu metre
1 cubic yard (cu yd)/27 cu ft	= 0.7646 cu metre

Capacity

1 litre	= 1.7598 pt/0.8799 qt/0.22 gal
1 pint (pt)	= 0.568 litre
1 quart (qt)	= 1.137 litres
1 gallon (gal)	= 4.546 litres

Weight

1 gram (g)	= 0.035 oz
1 kilogram (kg)/1000 g	= 2.20 lb/35.2 oz
1 tonne/1000 kg	= 2204.6 lb/0.9842 ton
1 ounce (oz)	= 28.35 g
1 pound (lb)	= 0.4536 kg
1 ton	= 1016 kg

Pressure

1 gram per square metre ($g/metre^2$)	= 0.0295 oz/sq yd
1 gram per square centimetre (g/cm^2)	= 0.228 oz/sq in
1 kilogram per square centimetre (kg/cm^2)	= 14.223 lb/sq in
1 kilogram per square metre ($kg/metre^2$)	= 0.205 lb/sq ft
1 pound per square foot (lb/ft^2)	= 4.882 $kg/metre^2$
1 pound per square inch (lb/in^2)	= 703.07 $kg/metre^2$
1 ounce per square yard (oz/yd^2)	= 33.91 $g/metre^2$
1 ounce per square foot (oz/ft^2)	= 305.15 $g/metre^2$

Temperature

To convert °F to °C, subtract 32, then divide by 9 and multiply by 5	
To convert °C to °F, divide by 5 and multiply by 9, then add 32	

Phototypeset by Tradespools Limited, Frome, Somerset
Printed and bound by Artes Gráficas, Toledo, SA, Spain

D. L. TO:205-1987